INTRODUCTION TO BUSINESS ARCHITECTURE

Chris Reynolds

Course Technology PTR

A part of Cengage Learning

COURSE TECHNOLOGY
CENGAGE Learning™

Australia, Brazil, Japan, Korea, Mexico, Singapore, Spain, United Kingdom, United States

COURSE TECHNOLOGY
CENGAGE Learning

Introduction to Business Architecture
Chris Reynolds

Publisher and General Manager, Course Technology PTR:
Stacy L. Hiquet

Associate Director of Marketing:
Sarah Panella

Manager of Editorial Services:
Heather Talbot

Marketing Manager:
Mark Hughes

Acquisitions Editor:
Mitzi Koontz

Project Editor:
Kim Benbow

Technical Reviewer:
Lisa Conway

Editorial Services Coordinator:
Jen Blaney

Copy Editor:
Heather Urschel

Interior Layout:
Jill Flores

Cover Designer:
Mike Tanamachi

Indexer:
Kelly Talbot

Proofreader:
Melba Hopper

For product information and technology assistance, contact us at
Cengage Learning Customer & Sales Support, 1-800-354-9706

For permission to use material from this text or product, submit all requests online at **cengage.com/permissions**.
Further permissions questions can be e-mailed to
permissionrequest@cengage.com.

Unified Modeling Language and UML are trademarks of Object Management Group, Inc. in the U.S. and other countries.

The Zachman Framework is a trademark of Zachman International, Inc.

TOGAF (The Open Group Architecture Framework) is a trademark of The Open Group in the U.S. and other countries.

All other trademarks are the property of their respective owners.

Library of Congress Control Number: 2009924521

ISBN-13: 978-1-4354-5422-4

ISBN-10: 1-4354-5422-7

Course Technology, a part of Cengage Learning
20 Channel Center Street
Boston, MA 02210
USA

Cengage Learning is a leading provider of customized learning solutions with office locations around the globe, including Singapore, the United Kingdom, Australia, Mexico, Brazil, and Japan. Locate your local office at: **international.cengage.com/region**

Cengage Learning products are represented in Canada by Nelson Education, Ltd.

For your lifelong learning solutions, visit **courseptr.com**

Visit our corporate website at **cengage.com**

Printed in the United States of America
1 2 3 4 5 6 7 11 10 09

This book is dedicated to my wife, Barbara, and our children, Geoff and Mandy. It is only because of their patience and support that I could take a tiny kernel of an idea and turn it into this book. More importantly, it is because of who they are that I've had the chance to become the person I am. They give me cause for celebration.

Acknowledgments

There are a great number of people who have directly or indirectly contributed to this book. I am grateful to each and every one of them.

Mitzi Koontz is a very brave acquisitions editor who took a chance that I could actually make this book idea a reality.

Kim Benbow is a sympathetic taskmistress of a project editor who kept me focused when I might otherwise have drifted.

Heather Urschel made many insightful and useful suggestions as copy editor, which greatly improved the readability of this book.

Lisa Conway kept me honest and accurate as my technical editor; her input was invaluable.

Jill Flores handled the artistic layout for the book and made my attempts at illustrations something worthy of print.

Each of them has directly and positively impacted the quality of this book, and for that I thank them. Any errors remaining in this work, however, are exclusively my own fault.

I would also like to thank:

- Howard Podeswa for introducing me to the world of authorship.
- My parents, Victor and Edith Reynolds, for instilling in me the belief that with dedication and perseverance, great things can be accomplished.
- My stepparents, Ron Stewart and Kathy Reynolds, who have been every bit as supportive as anyone could hope for.
- My current and past employers and clients who have all given me opportunities to learn. They have helped me by giving me the experience that led to this book.

About the Author

Chris Reynolds has spent the past 25 years observing and influencing businesses of different sizes in a vast array of industries. He has spent a significant amount of time showing employers and clients why they need to understand their business in the context of its environment as a means of understanding the change they need to undertake to become better. Over the past 15 years, Chris has spent a significant amount of time doing business analysis work and defining how business architecture and business analysis work together as disciplines. He has taught and coached others regarding this topic for the last seven years.

When not working, writing, or pondering the future of the business architecture discipline, Chris loves to spend time with his wife and kids, along with their menagerie of pets. This quality time is spent camping or sailing, or taking the kids to their various pursuits.

TABLE OF CONTENTS

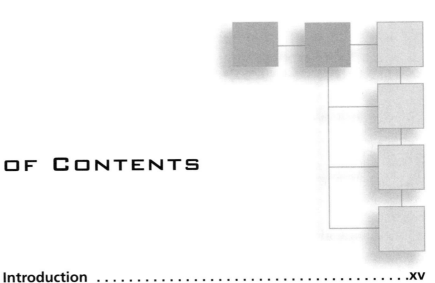

INTRODUCTION

The discipline of business architecture has been around in some form or another, largely undefined, for the better part of the past decade, and possibly longer. This book is an attempt to provide some structure and definition to this thing that people have been attempting to produce. Hopefully, readers will see a genuine need for what this book describes and look at ways they can begin to apply the discipline of business architecture in their own environments.

This book contains all the information you will need to understand to begin applying the principles of business architecture to your work environment. As you read, you will find the following:

- A framework for business architecture work
- Case studies about where aspects of business architecture have been successfully applied
- How to create your own business architecture
- Practical uses for your business architecture
- Ties between business architecture and technology systems, including IT (systems) architecture

Who This Book Is For

This book is for those who need, those who practice, and those who are interested in the topic of business architecture. Because the book is introductory in nature, it appeals to a wide audience with diverse roles and interests.

Business executives will learn about how business architecture can support them in their work. Business architects and business analysts will get practical information about ways to apply this to their work. Project managers and project portfolio managers will see how business architecture can positively impact their work. Project team members will get valuable information about how business architecture should influence the type of work they are being asked to do. IT (systems) architects will see how the work of the business architect can and should influence their work. This book is also for business management consultants looking for ways to reliably and positively impact the businesses they work with.

How This Book Is Organized

The book is divided into six parts, each covering a major theme related to business architecture.

Part 1, "What Is Business Architecture?" contains chapters related to defining the discipline of business architecture:

- **Chapter 1, "What Is Architecture?"** provides a definition and basic understanding for architecture.
- **Chapter 2, "Why You Need Business Architecture,"** provides you with an understanding of the value it affords.

Part 2, "What Is Business Architecture Comprised Of?" contains a definition of a framework for business architecture and chapters that give details of the various views that make up the framework:

- **Chapter 3, "The Goals View,"** helps you understand how to organize the goals of a business.
- **Chapter 4, "The Facades View,"** helps you organize all the ways a business interacts with the rest of the world.
- **Chapter 5, "The Communications View,"** helps you organize internal and external communication flows the business needs in order to operate successfully.
- **Chapter 6, "The Processes View,"** helps you organize the tasks that a business needs to execute.
- **Chapter 7, "The Business Entities View,"** helps you to organize all the information a business needs to understand.

Part 3, "Putting Together Your Business Architecture Model" contains chapters that describe approaches to developing a business architecture for your business:

- **Chapter 8, "The Bottom-Up Approach,"** discusses how to create a business architecture starting from the existing artifacts that your business has.

- **Chapter 9, "The Top-Down Approach,"** gives you information about how to create a business architecture without worrying about existing content.

- **Chapter 10, "When Are We Done?"** helps you understand that a business architecture is never complete, but can be sufficiently completed for envisioned future situations.

- **Chapter 11, "Representational Languages for Business Architecture,"** discusses some of the diagramming language options you have.

- **Chapter 12, "Frameworks,"** helps explain how your business architecture work integrates with enterprise architecture.

Part 4, "Understanding Your Business," contains chapters that help clarify some basic business structure types:

- **Chapter 13, "Product-Driven Business Structure,"** explains what to look for in your business architecture model when your business is product driven.

- **Chapter 14, "Service-Driven Business Structure,"** helps you understand what to look for in your business architecture model when your business is service driven.

- **Chapter 15, "Price-Driven Business Structure,"** discusses what to look for in your business architecture model when your business is price driven.

- **Chapter 16, "Business Architecture and Business Drivers,"** helps clarify which business structure model is the main driver for your business.

Part 5, "Practical Uses for Your Business Architecture," contains chapters on some fundamental work that is facilitated by having a business architecture in place:

- **Chapter 17, "Shifting Business Structure Models,"** discusses using the business architecture model as a tool when the business is considering shifting its business structure model.

- **Chapter 18, "Acquisition,"** looks at acquisition and the role of the business architecture model (whether your business is acquiring others or being acquired by another).

- **Chapter 19, "Reengineering for Efficiency,"** considers business architecture as applied to business reengineering.

- **Chapter 20, "Planning,"** talks about how the business architecture model feeds into the roadmap and planning work.

- **Chapter 21, "Project Initiation,"** discusses the relationship between the business architecture model and projects.

Part 6, "Appendixes," contains some useful reference material for creating your business architecture model:

- **Appendix A, "Typical Sections in a Business Use Case,"** provides a starting point for creating documents related to facade interactions.
- **Appendix B, "UML Cheat Sheet,"** outlines some basic symbols from the Unified Modeling Language you may want to use in creating your diagrams.
- **Appendix C, "BPMN Cheat Sheet,"** gives you some basic symbols from the Business Process Modeling Notation for use in creating diagrams.

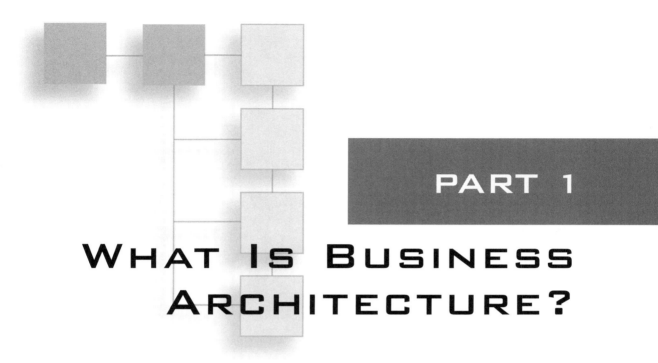

PART 1

WHAT IS BUSINESS ARCHITECTURE?

This section of the book will discuss what *architecture* is and how it relates to the topic of *business architecture*. The concept of a business architecture model will also be introduced. So, then, what is architecture?

Architecture: *1] the art or science of building, specifically the art or practice of designing and building structures and especially habitable ones; 2] formation or construction resulting from or as if from a conscious act <the architecture of the garden>.* (From Merriam-Webster online: www.merriam-webster.com/dictionary/architecture.)

The most important aspects to consider of this definition are that architecture considers something as it relates to its environmental context and that architecture looks at not only the fit with current conditions but also the fit with expected, planned future conditions.

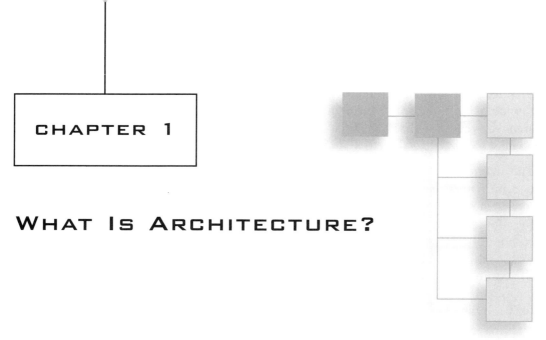

CHAPTER 1

WHAT IS ARCHITECTURE?

Architecture is a complex discipline that, as suggested by the definition in the Part 1 introduction, looks at designing and building structures in the context of the environment they will be part of.

Architecture for a Home or Building

A business is a complex thing in the same way a building is a complex thing. Imagine trying to construct a building without a set of plans or blueprints—you might succeed, but you are far more likely to end up with a mess.

Architects who design the buildings we live and work in have long understood the complexities of constructing the right building—ensuring it will be an aesthetic fit within a community, as well as meeting the needs of its owners and tenants in a practical sense. Architectural drawings, plans and elevations, as well as documented specifications, are the means by which these complexities are documented and vetted.

Architecture is useful for understanding basic needs and making sure those needs are met by the design. This would include, in the case of construction, needs of the building occupants (living, cooking, sleeping space for a home), the needs of regulatory bodies (in the form of building codes that constrain the design), and the needs of the utilities that will support the services the building will require (electrical, plumbing, gas, and so on). Various drawings are produced by the architects to reflect how the various needs will be met by the design. Floor plans will show the various spaces within the building as well as the relationships between them. Structural drawings, including plumbing and electrical plans, will show how the services will connect with the environment and be delivered to the building occupants. All drawings will show how the design is compliant with building codes.

Architects don't just draw buildings, though. They draw a building in the context of its surroundings: both current surroundings and the surroundings envisioned for the future. The
architect is concerned with the fit of what they are proposing and the environment in which
it will serve as well as the actual building itself.

The architect also knows that there are a significant number of levels of complex detail
necessary to ensure the building being designed will work properly: the structural skele-
ton must support the building and still present the facade the architect had in mind;
the plumbing and electrical systems must integrate with the services provided by the
community and serve the needs of the owner and tenants; drainage, landscaping, parking,
interior design, and so on must all aid in ensuring the building is functional and fits within
the community. The architect will call in experts from various fields to assist in the
creation of the complete set of plans and specifications that become, in essence, the *model*
for the building to be constructed.

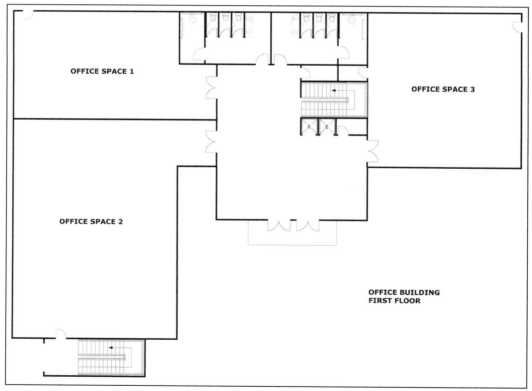

Figure 1.1
An architectural floor plan for a small office building.

Figure 1.1 shows a single view of a potential small office building. There are many other views that would be needed to fully model what this office building might look like. What about the other floors? What about the basement? What about the various sides of the building? What about the roof? Where will lighting be installed, and what about heating and cooling vents?

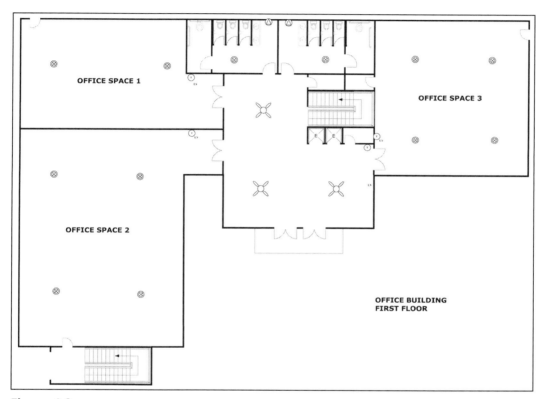

Figure 1.2
A partial HVAC plan of the office building shown in Figure 1.1.

Figure 1.2 shows the same floor for the hypothetical small office building, but with the addition of vents, fans, and thermostats—part of the heating, ventilation, and air conditioning (HVAC) view for the model. This is just one of many views that would be employed to help illustrate the building plan. It still represents the same structure as that shown in Figure 1.1, but it conveys different information in order to enrich the model of the building.

> Model: *a description or analogy used to help visualize something (as in an atom) that cannot be directly observed.* (From Merriam-Webster online: www.merriam-webster.com/dictionary/model.)

So a model isn't just that plastic toy many of us played with as kids. A model can represent anything that we want to conceptualize and understand—physically, mathematically, textually, or diagrammatically. We can use models for systems, and even businesses, just as models are used to help visualize buildings that are yet to be constructed. When it comes to buildings, architects will use diagrammatic models in the form of plans, and sometimes even physical models. With business modeling, however, diagrammatic models are the primary means of representation. After all, a business can't be observed the same way as a building can.

Architecture for Information Technology Systems

So, now that you know that a model is a representation of some complex thing to be considered, it is easy to see that models might better help us understand the information technology (IT) systems a business needs.

A *systems architecture model* is a representation of which systems do what, how they interact, and how we expect them to evolve over time within the IT environment of a business.

System architects will readily know what functionality needs to be available on a given system. They will know which systems are targeted for retirement and why. They will know which systems are currently operational and which systems will be introduced in the future. They will also understand all current and planned future interfaces and how each system fits into its environment.

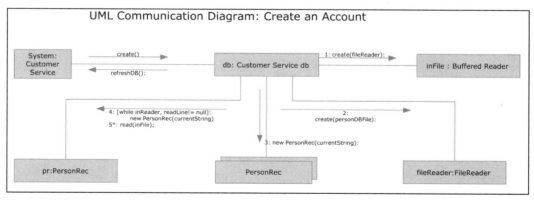

Figure 1.3
Sample UML communication diagram.

The diagram in Figure 1.3 is just one of many views that would make up a system architecture model. It shows how various system components communicate in order to create an account for a customer. As you can well imagine, this is not the only view needed to understand how to create an account. Many diagrams in many views would be needed to understand the model completely.

Figure 1.3 is drawn using the Unified Modeling Language, or UML. UML grew out of the IT world where it was first used to describe aspects of IT systems. Because businesses are also types of systems (not just strictly technology systems), many people realized that UML could be used to describe aspects of businesses just as it was being used to describe aspects if IT systems. (See Chapter 11 for more information on UML, and see Appendix B for a UML cheat sheet.)

You will find that most large organizations have a system architecture model, or a collection of models, and consider it a very important tool for planning and managing IT systems for the business. Even mid-sized and smaller businesses are seeing the value in having a system architecture model, even if it isn't as fully and formally documented as it would be in a large business. Keep in mind that a model can be built up from a collection of smaller models.

Architecture for Businesses

A *business architecture model*, then, is an extension of the concept of architecture applied to a business as a whole. In this case, the business is treated as a very elaborate system comprised of technologies, people, and processes.

More specifically, a business architecture model is a representation of what the business does, how it interacts within its environment, and how it's expected to evolve over time within the business environment it exists in.

Business architects know which business functionalities belong within which departmental areas of a business. They know which areas of the business are targeted for increased or decreased prominence within the organization as a whole. They also understand all "interfaces" with other businesses and other entities within their business environment. It is important to know that in this context, *interfaces* do not necessarily mean a technology interface (system-to-system communication), but rather any level of interaction or communication between businesses and other business-affecting entities.

Many businesses have a departmental model that includes some definition of the goals of the departments. Many businesses have at least a basic understanding of the functions their departments perform and the processes they execute. What is lacking in most cases is formality and organization around these views of the business, as well as any documentation around a planned future state for the business. This is despite the fact that most businesses try to plan for the future and that most business leaders do have a vision.

A business architecture model tries to apply enough formality and structure to the views and plans of a business to easily communicate the roadmap from today's position to where the business wants to be in the future. Where there is a business architecture, there is an opportunity to evaluate the impacts of problems or opportunities and quickly understand what changes will be needed if the business chooses to resolve the problem or pursue the opportunity. Where there is a business architecture, it becomes easy to build a portfolio of projects or initiatives that will help the business move forward in a strategic way, with each initiative bringing the business closer to the envisioned end state of the roadmap.

You will find that most businesses do not yet have a formal business architecture today despite the fact that they perform many of the activities that would, if organized properly, comprise a formal architecture. Governments and some businesses have started to develop business architecture models and are seeing benefits from the exercise.

So what should a proper business architecture model include? The answer, of course, depends to some degree on the maturity of the business and the architects, how complex the business is, and what the business wants to get from its architectural models. Every good business architecture model should give some consideration to all of the following:

- The goal hierarchy of the business.
  - The departmental makeup of the business, including definitions and responsibilities.
  - The goal statements that each department of the business will be striving to achieve. (The goals may include statements of the measures that will be used to judge successful achievement but do not have to include them.)
- The facades the business presents to various aspects of its environment.
  - How does the business look to clients, suppliers, government and regulatory bodies, and competitors?
  - What "business functionalities" does the business expose through each of these facades? These functionalities can be thought of as interactions between the business and the outside world.
- The processes—internal to the business, possibly cross-departmental—that support the facades and business interactions.
- The communications structures that the business needs.
  - Communications with external bodies.
  - Communications that are inter- and intra-departmental.
- The business entities that the business cares about.
  - The "things" that the business needs to understand, manipulate, or be aware of.
  - The relationships that exist and matter between these business entities.

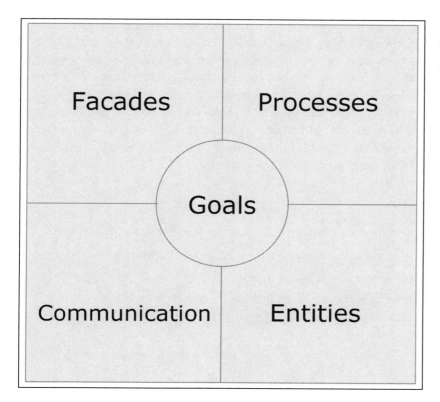

Figure 1.4
A basic framework
for business
architecture.

This book presents a specific *business architecture framework*, one that offers a holistic view of the business by way of a set of views or models that, in aggregate, describe the business (see Figure 1.4).

A proper business architecture will always model the *future state*, what business needs to look like and how it needs to operate in the future. The business architecture may also include a *current state*, which represents what the business looks like today. The current state is often performed in cases where there isn't much existing documentation, or there is a poor understanding of how things work today, in order to understand the gaps between the current state of the business and the envisioned future state. The *roadmap* that accompanies a proper business architecture is a portfolio of projects or initiatives that will ultimately transform the business from the current state to the envisioned future state.

The portfolio of projects often documents not only the list of projects but also the order of the projects and any interdependencies so that if the portfolio needs to be adjusted over time, impacts of those various decisions can be understood. Typically, foundational projects or programs of projects will be undertaken first, followed by other projects that expand on the foundational work and further enhance the business as per the roadmap.

The portfolio should contain a balance of strategic, tactical, and operational projects or initiatives. This book won't provide an exhaustive understanding of each category of a project, but it will provide a bit of context for each. *Strategic projects* are those designed exclusively with the goal of moving the business closer to its envisioned future state. *Operational projects* enable the business to better operate within the current state. *Tactical projects* are usually a hybrid in that they enable better operation in the current state while also moving the business a bit closer to its envisioned future state. As a rule of thumb, strategic projects are typically the biggest projects in a portfolio, operational projects are usually the smallest, and the tactical projects fall somewhere in the middle.

In Your Business

Here are some things to consider while thinking about architecture in your business:

- Does your business have a system architecture model or collection of these models?
- Does your business have a business architecture model?
- What are the architectural models of your business currently used for?
- Who has access to the architectural models?

Summary

Business architecture is a model that represents various views of a business, including the Goals, Facades, Processes, Communications, and Business Entities views. It shows what state a business wants to be in, as well as where a business currently is. It also outlines a list of the right projects to work on, as well as when to work on them to get to the envisioned future state.

A business architecture model can be a vital tool for most businesses, and in fact, it is increasingly proving to be so. The business architecture model can be used to capture information about a business, help determine the best way to execute the changes that a business will need to undergo to get to its desired future state, and understand how well a business is aligned with the way it is trying to do business. All of these aspects of using a business architecture model allow you to plan for and achieve growth in your business, find ways to operate more efficiently and at lower cost, and help you understand your competition and how to effectively outperform them. The business architecture model can, and should, be used to make your business better in just about every way imaginable.

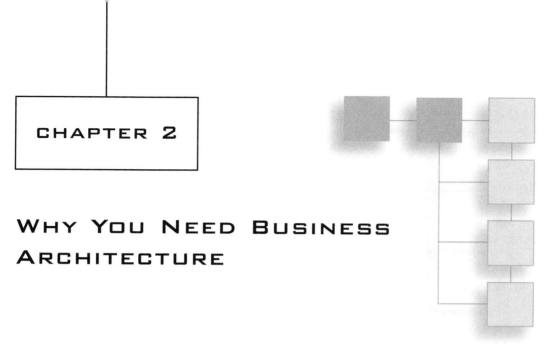

CHAPTER 2

Why You Need Business Architecture

A business is a complicated, many-faceted system of people, technologies, suppliers, customers, and governing and regulatory bodies. It is critical that a business understand itself and all its various (and often competing) aspects if it is to be successful. So how does one comprehend all the aspects and systems that make up a business? A set of plans, or *architecture*, is an easy way to reduce the complexities of a business and its environment to an easily understandable model.

A business has goals that it is trying to achieve. It will also have multiple facades containing many functionalities or interactions that it presents to the different members of its external supply chain. For example, a business will look different to retail clients versus commercial clients, different to suppliers, and different again to regulatory or governmental bodies. The business has to be internally structured in such a way that all its processes facilitate these facades and interactions, essentially arranged in ways for the business to connect with the community in which it will operate. The business needs to know what the mandatory and appropriate communications are for each of its partners and within its own structure. In addition, a business will have a list of things it needs to know about and manipulate, as well as what the various relationships are between these various things.

Consider the different ways a given building will look depending on which direction you approach it from—this is precisely how the building architecture metaphor supports the business architecture concept.

Understanding What Your Business Currently Has

Business architecture gives you a holistic model of your business. The model depicts the current state of your business as well as the future state you are striving to achieve. This holistic view helps you understand what your business currently has in the way of a model.

This understanding includes what goals the business is trying to achieve; how it interacts with all aspects of its environment, including customers, suppliers, and regulatory bodies; how the business will operate internally to support its environmental interactions; how it will communicate internally and externally; and what information it will deal with. The current state of all of these things describes the business' current fit, while the future state describes how you want it to fit. This future state gives you the opportunity, through the use of the business architecture model, to ensure a better fit between the business and its environment than it currently enjoys. The rest of this book describes how to achieve this better fit in the future state of a business architecture model.

A complete business architecture will include the following:

- A clearly articulated set of goals for the business
- A model that shows what the business looks like within its environment, including what interactions the business offers to its customers and suppliers
- A model that shows how the business needs to operate as a set of processes in order to support the interactions it exposes to the outside world
- An understanding of the mandatory and appropriate communications between the business and its environment, as well as internal communications that would be relevant and important
- An understanding of all the information, in the form of business entities, that the business cares about, as well as the inter-relationships between the business entities that the business cares about

The business architecture model is a collection of related submodels, or views, that relate to specific aspects of the business being described. Chapter 3 will describe the Goals view; Chapter 4 will describe the Facades view, including all the interactions that make up a facade; Chapter 5 talks about the Communications view; Chapter 6 is about the Processes view; and Chapter 7 is all about the Business Entities view.

This information will provide you with a good understanding of your business and where you fit into your environment. You will have both an understanding of where you are in the present and where you want to be in the future. This is important for a few reasons:

- It is easier to train new staff if you have documentation explaining how the business operates.
- Audits and proof of compliance are much easier when you can demonstrate your operational behavior to the examiners.
- You can more easily identify problems within the organization if its behavior is documented and predictable.

The problems that can be identified by a business architecture model include, but are not limited to, the following:

■ Goals that are in conflict with each other, causing the business to work at cross-purposes

■ Not having all the necessary facades, or having facades that aren't needed, causing problems of inappropriate fit with the business environment and possibly waste

■ Process inefficiencies and opportunities to increase efficiencies

■ Other view discrepancies that would lead to waste

■ Misalignment with business drivers (see Chapters 13 through 16 for more details on business drivers)

Quite possibly the most important aspect of having a business architecture model is that it enables a business to see very quickly how well all the different aspects of the business are aligned to achieve common goals. When there is misalignment, it becomes evident very quickly in the model, and the business can plan how it will deal with getting properly aligned again. This is a key aspect of understanding where you fit. Of course, the business architecture model needs to be kept current if it is to be useful over time. (See Chapter 10 for a discussion of how to ensure your model is kept current.)

Understanding How Your Business Fits with Its Environment

If a business doesn't define how it fits into its environment, it will struggle, and its likelihood of resounding success is greatly diminished. Understanding the fit of a business within its environment is a complex, multi-faceted exercise. And it is the very complexity of this exercise that makes it all the more important to undertake. A business needs to understand who its customers are, what their needs are, and how they can be reached. The business also needs to know who its suppliers are. The business needs to understand how it fits within industry and governmental regulation. The business also needs to understand its competition. Only when all of these relationships are understood can the business ensure it is shaping itself to be successful.

The Supply Chain

Every business exists as part of a supply chain. If a business is to earn money, it needs to have customers, and in most cases, satisfying customers means that the business will also need suppliers. A supply chain is the set of links from customers through the business to the suppliers.

Understanding where a business fits within its supply chain is crucial to understanding what the business will sell to customers and what it will need to purchase from suppliers in order to sell things to customers.

This fit is many faceted: it covers interaction, communication, processes, and information related to how a business is part of the supply chain. The fit should, if it is to be effective, be completely aligned with the goals of the business.

The Customer

Once the business knows what it will sell to customers, it can begin to understand who its target customers are. Will they be retail customers, or will the business primarily sell to other businesses? Will the business sell to niche clients with very specialized needs, or will it sell to the general population? Will there be a lot of preparation in understanding the needs of a specific customer before the sale is made, or will customers be purchasing things without any preparation? These and other questions about prospective customers have major implications on how the business should be set up to optimize interaction with those customers.

If the business is going to sell to retail customers, for example, it will need to be set up in such a way that retail customers can access the business. This might mean a storefront location, an Internet shopping presence, a customer service center, or more likely, a combination of all three.

If the business is selling to other businesses, it will have to be able to reach the other businesses. This will typically involve advertising and also having a strong shipping department so that one business doesn't have to physically approach the other for the sale of goods to take place. In some cases, a selling business will have some sort of storefront for direct shopping, but typically they will instead concentrate on a sales force, customer service, an Internet storefront, or some combination of these.

If a business is going to sell to niche customers with specialized needs, it will have to understand the niche and who the members of the niche are. This will typically mean a dedicated sales force as well as market researchers. There's also the question of how the niche customers will be made aware of the offering(s) of the business. There are a number of different approaches that can be taken to ensure that the right niche client is identified and engaged.

Of course, to some extent, the business needs to understand its prospective customers before it defines its product or service offerings. What sort of customers might want the product or service that the business plans to sell—what is the customer market?

The business architecture model helps define existing and future customers. It also defines what their needs are that the business will fulfill. This is captured in the customer-facing interactions in the model, as well as in the definition of certain things the business keeps information about.

The Supplier

Many businesses sell services instead of products, and so have little apparent need of suppliers, but even pure service businesses need consumable supplies. This means that, at some point, every business is going to need at least one supplier (and most likely more than one) that they will rely on.

Selecting the right supplier or set of suppliers can be more complex than it would seem at first glance. Obviously, the supplier must provide the supplies your business needs, and they should provide them at the lowest price. There's also the question of their ability to fulfill your supply needs: Can they reliably provide the supplies when needed, can they supply as much as you need, and can they provide it where you need it?

Identifying a supplier shouldn't be a one-time event. Over time new suppliers come on the market, others change their offerings, and the needs of the business change. Over time, understanding the available suppliers, and selecting the appropriate ones, should be done on a regular basis. The good news is that if your business is large enough, the suppliers will come to you; of course regardless of your business size, ensuring you find the right suppliers for your business is ultimately your responsibility.

Within Your Industry

Every industry consists of a distinct group of businesses working in a common way or providing a similar product or service. Most businesses fit within one industry, although some may fit into more than one. It is important to understand what industry your business is a part of.

Many industries have trade associations, some have purchasing cooperatives, and others have professional associations that provide governance and oversight. If a business is to succeed, it needs to understand where it fits within its industry, what aspects of the industry it can take advantage of, and what industry regulation and governance it needs to comply with.

Some industries are more dynamic than others; some aspects of industries are more dynamic than others. It is important for a business to stay informed about its industry so as to ensure that it has the best industry fit possible.

The business architecture model allows you to capture industry information. Facades and interactions can be used to capture details of how your business fits with members of the industry, suppliers, and customers. The Communications view can be used to show the flow of important industry information into and out of the business, who it comes from, and who it goes to. The Business Entities view can capture relationships between business and industry information that the business would want to keep track of.

Relative to Your Competition

If your business is going to be successful, it's going to have to attract and retain customers. Your competition, however, is going to want to attract and retain those same customers. The best way to avoid losing customers to competition is to understand who the competition is and what they offer. Only when a business' competition is identified and understood can the business hope to ensure that what they are offering will continue to attract and retain customers.

The business architecture model will allow you to capture information about your competition: who they are and what they offer that most effectively competes with your business. One of the most important bits of information you will want to capture about the competition will often be its product and/or service models. This will be done in the Business Entities view, just as your business' product and/or service offerings will be modeled.

Lead or Follow

Some businesses lead their competition and their industry in innovative offerings to their potential customers. This leadership makes it easy to attract new customers as well as take customers away from competition. There is, however, a significant cost of innovation that leading businesses need to consider. This cost comes in the form of research and development (R&D) as well as the costs associated with introducing new products and/or services to a market that does not yet know anything about them. This could mean educating consumers, developing processes without any existing examples to leverage, learning costs as your business experiences things related to the new product and/or service that are unprecedented.

If a business does not want to incur the considerable cost of innovation, it can choose to follow the industry leader and attempt to "steal away" customers from the leader, typically by offering similar products or services at lower prices or with value-added items after they figure out how to duplicate what the leader is offering via its innovation.

In some businesses, there is even a combined lead/follow approach. In this case, the business chooses to lead with some products and/or services, while following with other offerings. For example, you might see something like this in a manufacturing business, where the business offers one or two key differentiating products, which it is willing to invest in leading with, while its other products are based on following other businesses (typically because the business in question doesn't see value in leading with these other products).

It is important to realize that either of these business approaches can be a viable and correct approach for any given business. The business needs to make a conscious decision as to which approach they want to take and commit to that approach. The business architecture model gives you information about whether your business is poised to be a leader or a follower. With this information, the business can then determine if it is content with its position, or whether it wants to revamp itself to change its position.

Understanding Where You Want to Go: The Roadmap

When an architecture model is in place, a business knows where it is and where it wants to go. The gaps between the current state and the envisioned future state represent a misalignment of the business with its envisioned future state.

Identifying misalignment issues and understanding problems and opportunities for the business shape the portfolio of work that needs to be undertaken by the business. This portfolio creates a vision that is a very important aspect of the business architecture—the business architecture, fundamentally, is a vision of the future.

Many large organizations have project management offices (PMOs) charged with the responsibility of maintaining a portfolio of projects. This is fine, except that the PMO is seldom given the right information about goals and priorities to effectively manage priority of projects within the portfolio, which means that there have to be regular, time-consuming meetings among a variety of different groups: executive steering committees, lots of back-and-forth between various sponsors of projects, originators of the bright ideas that lead to projects, those who will ultimately provide the solution for the projects, and senior management. Having a business architecture model to refer to can eliminate a lot of this thrashing about, as well as save a lot of time and cost for all of the various parties involved.

The business architecture model makes it easy to see the right priorities for projects because you can very quickly see in the model what projects will support which goals. The obvious prioritization of projects in the business architecture model then lets the PMO get on with the business of slotting the projects into the schedule and managing and reporting on the progress of the projects.

While the PMO typically owns accountability for managing the portfolio of projects, it does not own accountability for the business architecture model. It is not impossible for the PMO to own the business architects and the model, but it is more typical to see the business architects aligned with the senior management of the business. Wherever the business architects report, they will have to work collaboratively with the PMO to get the portfolio of projects set and maintained.

In Your Business

Here are some things to consider about architecture in your business:

- What business architectural content does your business currently maintain?
- Does your business differentiate between a current state and a future state with any of the content it maintains?
- How does your business understand and manage its fit within its environment?
- How does your business create, maintain, and prioritize its portfolio of projects?

Summary

This chapter looked at why your business needs a business architecture model. I discussed how a business architecture model is used to understand the fit of your business in its environment, including its customers, its suppliers, its industry, and its competition. The chapter talked about the concept of leading or following in business, and how the business architecture model helped clarify which was right for your business. Finally, I discussed how the business architecture model is used as a tool for planning a portfolio of projects to help the business evolve toward the envisioned future state.

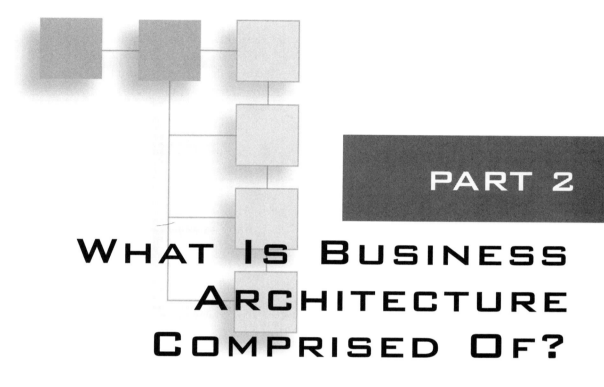

PART 2

WHAT IS BUSINESS ARCHITECTURE COMPRISED OF?

In this section of the book, we will explore the most common aspects of a business architecture model, including the views that are generally the most useful and how to construct those views. We will also look at case studies where the use of the view has been of real, tangible value to an organization. (The case studies come from practical experience in the author's consulting career; the names and exact details of the businesses involved have been changed for reasons of confidentiality.)

There are five views of a business that are part of the business architecture model as defined in this book. These are a "view into the business," if you will. Each of these views can be considered a model unto itself, but when looked at with the other views or models, you have a very holistic picture of your business. The views can include a current state that describes the way things are in the business now, and a future state (often called the *envisioned* future state, since it is based on a vision for the future) representing how the business wants to be.

Chapter 3 will look at the Goals view. It includes a discussion of what is in the view and how to construct one. Chapter 4 looks at the Facades view. It describes what facades are, how they are made up of interactions, as well as how to model facades and document interactions that comprise the view. Chapter 5 is about the Communications view—the various types of communication flows that are needed within a business and how to effectively document them as part of this view. Chapter 6 discusses the Processes view. Business processes are explained and methods of documenting them into a view. Chapter 7 discusses the Business Entities view, about what business entities are and how to effectively describe them and their interrelationships. Each of these chapters also talks about how the views interrelate to create the business architecture model.

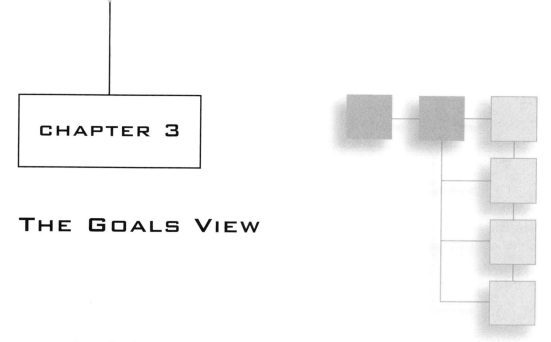

CHAPTER 3

THE GOALS VIEW

G oals are fundamental to the way humans behave, grow, and succeed in life. Our first goals were set by our parents: learning to walk, saying our first words, and going to school. As we grew up, we defined our own goals: learning to ride a bike, asking someone on a date, graduating from high school, and going to college. As we get older, we start to develop more mature goals, many of which are long-term, such as planning for retirement, buying a house, and getting married. Goals, then, are targets that we all strive for in our daily lives.

Personal Goals

You set goals for yourself as a way to focus your energy on desired outcomes. When you articulate what you want to achieve, you can ensure that the actions you take do not harm your chances of attaining that desired outcome. As you become more disciplined at working toward a goal, you actively make sure that all the things you do move you closer to that goal. When you set goals for yourself, you also learn to evaluate them to ensure that they are not in conflict. For example, it is obvious that the two goals of saving for a first home and having lots of luxury toys (fancy sound systems, yachts, cars, and so on) are in conflict. You know that you cannot achieve both of these goals at the same time, and you would not even try to do so.

Goals are not just for individuals. You set goals as part of a partnership in marriage (my wife and I will always take an evening each week just to spend time together). You set goals for your household (we will cut our energy bill by 2% this year by turning off the lights when we leave a room, shutting off TVs when we are not watching them, and so on). Again, once goals have been articulated, you can focus your energy on achieving the goals, whether you are an individual or part of a team or partnership.

Business Goals

If goals are such an integral part of our lives as individuals and as groups of human beings, can businesses also benefit from the use of goals? Absolutely! Most businesses set goals, and in many cases, the goals help. Goals for the business overall (also known as *main goals*) might be something like increase number of first-time buyers of our products this fiscal year by 2% over last fiscal year or reduce customer complaints this month by 1% over last month. As you can imagine, having goals like these could help a business grow. It could have more new customers, or fewer dissatisfied customers, once it had achieved its goals. Either of these situations would have a positive impact on just about any business.

The problems that arise with business goals tend to fall into two categories:

- Goals that are not communicated to and shared by all members of the business
- Goals set by the business that are in conflict with other goals of the business

If the management team of a business sets a goal, they need to make sure that all those working in that business understand the goal and that their work is aligned with achieving that goal. The easiest way for employees to become misaligned with business goals is when the employees do not know what the goals are. Always state the business goals in clear, simple terms. Publish the goals openly and often so that they become part of the culture of the business. Once they are part of the everyday environment, the odds of someone inadvertently doing things to jeopardize the goals will be reduced.

Just as you don't want conflicting goals in your personal life, the same applies to a business. Conflicting goals result in wasted energy and a failure to achieve either goal. The problem, of course, is that a business is more complex than a person or a single household, so it is easier for the conflict between two or more goals of a business to go undetected, especially when the business is not good at articulating goals and stating them openly to the entire business.

The business architecture model Goals view can assist a business with both of these issues. The view becomes a great communication tool by ensuring that everyone within the business understands the goals, and it facilitates the analysis of goals to ensure that conflicts are identified and eliminated (see Figure 3.1).

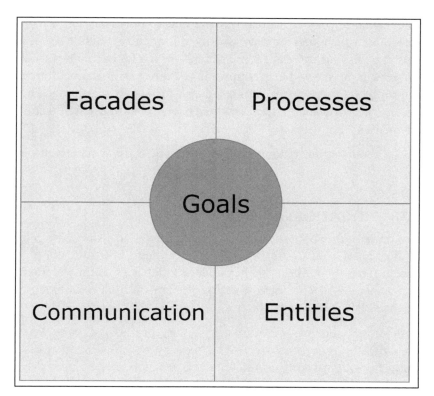

Figure 3.1
The Goals view within the business architecture framework.

The Goals view is central to the entire business architecture model. Goals will inform everything you do in all the other views of your business architecture model.

To be effective, a business cannot focus on too many main goals at one time. Generally speaking, one or two main goals are plenty for any business to try to achieve at once. Each goal should be something that, when it is achieved, will make the business better (more profitable, stronger in its industry, more capable of serving customers effectively, and so on). The business may have a number of goals that it wants to work on. In fact, may of these goals are departmental or team goals and don't apply to the entire business. In other cases, the goals aren't appropriate, but this can't be identified without the holistic Goals view. Once the goals of the business have been diagrammed in the Goals view, you have a hierarchy of goals:

- Main goals of the business as a whole.
- Departmental goals. (Depending on the size of the organization, there may be multiple levels of "departments" and corresponding levels of departmental goals.)
- Team goals.

If there are more than a few main goals that the business wants to pursue, it will need to prioritize them and determine which ones are most worthy of immediate pursuit. There is no single way to prioritize goals, but there are some general principles to follow. Ensure that the goals the business will pursue will help it move in the direction it wants in order to grow, become more profitable, and so forth. Also consider which goals are most achievable given the current state of the business. (Here is where having a Business architecture model helps to evaluate goals.)

So how does a business go about setting a main goal for itself? The mission statement can be a great start.

The Mission Statement as a Goal

A *mission statement* is a declaration about why the business exists, what its primary purpose is. Business schools spend a great deal of time teaching students how to develop an effective mission statement. They do this because they understand that a mission statement essentially defines the primary goal of a business. A well-written mission statement focuses an entire business on achieving a common goal.

When a business has a mission statement, you've got a good start for the Goals view. When a business doesn't have a mission statement, there's a bit more work to do. In either case, the Goals view isn't complete with just a mission statement. The Goals view needs to delve deeper if it is to be an effective tool. The Goals view needs to be a complete structure of related goals overlaid onto the organizational elements (departments, teams, etc.) of the business that will be accountable for achieving the goals.

Structure of the Goals View

A Goals view resembles an organizational chart (*org chart*), and it lists each department within a business (organization) as well as its unique goals. There is no standard modeling language specific to mapping goals. Experience shows that using a standard org chart to diagram the goals and their relationships is sufficient for the communication and analysis of goals that any business might want to achieve.

Each department should, much like the business as a whole, have one or two goals that it wants to achieve. When a department achieves a goal, the department becomes better (stronger, more efficient, more profitable) and, if the departmental goal is aligned with the overall goal of the business, it will also move the business closer to its overall goal. Sometimes departments are so large or complex that it makes sense to split the department up into smaller groups, each of which has its own goal or goals. Again, these goals, when achieved, strengthen the group, while also moving the department and the overall business closer to its goals. Departmental goals may be set by the business executive or by the department head. The more successful approach is usually to have the department head set the goals that they will be accountable for achieving, as long as the business executives and the business architect evaluate and agree to those goals.

Most businesses are of such a size that a single diagram will suffice to document the entire Goals view. When this is not the case, it is reasonable to have a main diagram with the highest-level goals followed by sub-diagrams that delve deeper into specific goals within a specific area of the business. If you need to split a Goals view into more than one diagram, make sure that the sub-diagrams are each focused on a single logical topic and that they reference the higher-level goal they decompose from.

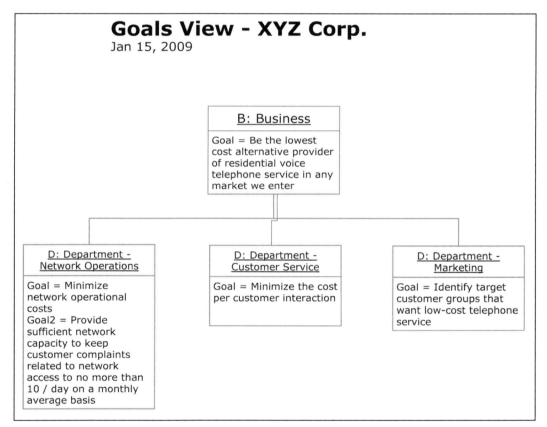

Figure 3.2
A simple Goals view diagram for a fictitious telecom business.

When the process of diagramming goals becomes an integral part of the articulation and approval of business goals, it is simple and straightforward to keep your Goals view current.

Analysis of the Goals View

The Goals view shows all the goals in relationship to each other and how the department goals all support the main goals of the business. This makes it easy to find any goals that are out of alignment with other goals, either with other departments or with the business as a whole. Referring to Figure 3.2, imagine that the Customer Service department decides its goal should be to provide customer satisfaction no matter what the cost. Without a Goals view diagram, this change of goals and the resultant conflict might go unnoticed; it wouldn't be easy to see that the Customer Service department was spending significant money on customer satisfaction while the main goal is to be cost conscious. Different departments within the business would be working at cross purposes and thus would not be moving the business any closer to its overall goal. As an example, the network department is trying to minimize network cost, yet providing customer satisfaction no matter what the cost might cause significant network cost. With the Goals view diagram, however, it is impossible not to notice that the Customer Service department would have a goal out of alignment with other departmental business goals. If updating the Goals view diagram were part of the goal articulation and approval process, the Customer Service department's new goal of providing customer satisfaction no matter what would never be approved without a discussion as to how it fits with the other goals of the business.

There may be times when the Goals view diagrams suggest that the business isn't organized appropriately. You may see that the only reason for a department to exist is to execute a goal that is fundamentally in opposition to the rest of the organization. The Goals view diagram can be a very useful tool in identifying organizational change opportunities.

The Goals view is also very important for ensuring that all the contents of the other views of the business architecture model are aligned. This is why the Goals view is shown as central to the business architecture model in the framework diagram. The goals of the business will

- Inform how the business wants to fit in with the world around it (Facades view).
- Shape the communications of the business (Communications view).
- Guide the processes the business needs to put in place in order to be effective (Processes view).
- Help in understanding the entities that will matter to the business (Business Entities view).

While there is no formal modeling language or syntax for creating Goals view diagrams, there are some modeling options that work effectively. A standard org chart layout can be effective. The drawback to this approach is that the amount of text needed to document goals can make the org chart far too wide to be managed in most software tools. Another effective approach to diagramming goals is to use the Unified Modeling Language (UML), specifically the object model diagram. The business as a whole and each department within the business are treated as objects. The goals are listed as attributes of the various objects. Standard UML relationships are used to show linkage between the departments and the business as a whole. The UML object model diagram was used to create Figure 3.2. (See Chapter 11 for a detailed discussion of UML, and see Appendix B for a UML cheat sheet.)

In the Goals view, language choice isn't what is important. What is important is that the Goals view and its diagrams become an integral part of defining, articulating, and approving business goals. The Goals view also needs to be kept current. (See Chapter 20 for a discussion on planning and the business architecture model, including how to renew the Goals view.)

SMART Goals

You've explored the need for goals that are aligned, and you've explored the language options available for diagramming goals (organizational charts and UML object diagrams) so that they can easily be analyzed. You still need to consider what, fundamentally, makes a goal useful, good, or effective. One useful evaluator is the SMART framework. SMART stands for Specific, Measurable, Attainable, Realizable, and Time-bounded. Each of these categories of the SMART framework will help you ensure that goals documented for a business are all useful, good, and effective. The SMART framework is useful for goals, but also for other concepts, like requirements and needs (though these are concepts outside of the business architecture model).

Useful, good, or effective goals are those that will help guide the business. They will provide realistic direction as to how to organize and operate the business for the future.

Specific Goals

Goals need to be specific if they are to be useful. *Specific* means that the goal is clearly stated, is unambiguous, and can be easily understood by those who must work to achieve it. A goal is specific when employees do not have to ask for any clarifications when they read it. Specificity is of vital importance in goals analysis because ambiguity in goals will mean that comparison will be difficult or impossible.

Measurable Goals

A goal is considered *measurable* if a way can be devised to record differences before and after the goal is implemented. You want to ensure that any defined goals can be measured so that you can determine whether they have, in fact, helped the business. If it can't be measured, the value of implementing the goal will be called into question.

Attainable Goals

An *attainable* goal is one that you can reasonably expect is possible to implement. An attainable goal violates no constraints outside of the business (laws of physics, laws within the jurisdiction the business operates in, and so on). If a goal isn't attainable, there is no point in making it a goal of the business—it simply cannot be fulfilled.

Realizable Goals

A *realizable* goal is fundamentally similar to the concept of attainable goals, but with a different set of constraints to be tested against. Realizable goals are ones that violate no constraints internal to the business (the goal is within financial reach, the workforce has the skills to execute it, and so on). If there is no way the business can expect to realize the goal, there is no point in making it a goal of the business—again, it simply will not be fulfilled.

Time-Bounded Goals

Time-bounded goals are those that have specific target start and completion dates. There is no point in setting goals that are indefinite and may never be completed. If the goal has no defined start and end points, the business may never get around to beginning or completing its execution. Either way, the goal will not be reached.

All goals need to adhere to the SMART principles if they are to be effective. Because you have already seen the importance of goals in your business architecture model, you can easily see how important it is to ensure that the goals the business sets are all SMART goals.

Goals Case Study—XYZ Telco

XYZ Telco was a start-up telecom that was providing broadband phone and data service over a fixed wireless connection to the telecom backbone. This fixed wireless "last mile" connection was a key differentiator for the business, but it meant that the business needed not only cellular-like broadcast locations, but also receiver equipment at any physical location in which they had a customer. Both the broadcast locations and receiver locations required real estate agreements with landlords before any physical work could be done.

The Situation

The Sales and Marketing department at XYZ Telco had a goal of signing at least three customers in a building before requesting that a receiver unit be provisioned because they knew that fewer customers meant that the company would lose money on the provisioning. The salespeople ensured that first customers in a building knew this restriction and that their agreement was provisional until such time as three or more customers were signed up.

The Real Estate group within XYZ Telco had a goal of entering into leasing agreements with landlords as soon as a candidate building was identified so that there would be no hold-ups within their department once a provisioning order came in. The problem was that the Real Estate group wasn't aware of the break-even issue and the need to have three customers signed up before beginning the provisioning process.

The Point

The Sales and Marketing group had set a goal that made sense for the business as they understood it. The Real Estate group had also set a goal that made sense for the business as they understood it. Both groups were working for the same business, supposedly supporting the same goal of building sustainable growth in their customer base.

This was a start-up business, so it took a while for reports from the various groups to come together and for someone to notice that there were a large number of leases for buildings where there was only one customer, or worse, no customer at all.

Had there been a Goals view diagram and sufficient discussion around SMART goals before the groups were sent off to do their work, the discrepancy between the goals of Sales and Marketing and those of the Real Estate group would have been caught. At that point, there could have been meaningful conversation about which group was better aligned with the overall goal of the business and which group needed to adjust its goal.

Ultimately, the discussion about goal alignment did occur, and it was determined that, even if it meant there might be some delays in securing leasing agreements once the customers were signed up, it made most sense to adjust the Real Estate group's goal to one of securing a leasing agreement for a building as quickly and economically as possible after the building had sufficient customers to make it viable.

In Your Business

Here are some things to consider when thinking about goals in your business:

- Does your business have a mission statement or main goal?
- Do the departments of your business have goals, and do they relate them to the main goals of the business?
- Does your business revise goals on an ongoing basis?
- Does your business use goals as a means of shaping itself?

Summary

This chapter was all about introducing the Goals view of the business architecture model. This chapter covered the following:

- What a goal is
- The purpose of having goals
- What a Goals view diagram is
- How to construct and model a Goals view

Also discussed was a case study illustrating where a Goals view diagram would have helped a business.

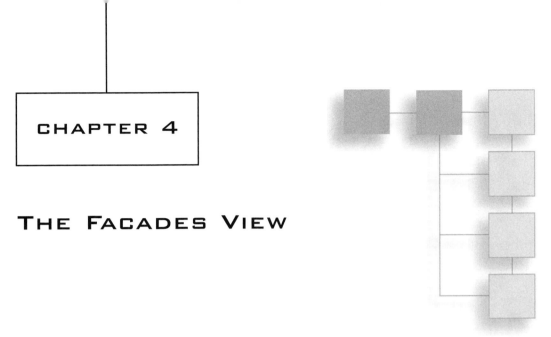

CHAPTER 4

THE FACADES VIEW

As you remember from the earlier discussion of architecture for buildings, any given building can have multiple facades, each of which may be described differently.

> Facade: *Any face of a building given special architectural treatment.* (From Merriam-Webster online: www.merriam-webster.com/dictionary/facade.)

The facade, then, describes how you want to present yourself to viewers who approach you from various perspectives. Just as your home looks different from the street than it does from the backyard or to your next-door neighbors, your business is going to look different to your customers, your suppliers, and the regulatory bodies that govern you. Facades are only about how your business will look to others outside of it. Other views will show the inner workings of the business (for example, the Goals view shows the organizational structure, and the Processes view shows the internal operations).

Facades of the business architecture framework are the focus of this chapter (see Figure 4.1). While you focus on facades, you need to make sure that you never completely lose sight of the other aspects of the overall business architecture model—the goals, communications, processes, and business entities—and the framework helps to remind you of this. The framework diagram (Figure 3.1 in Chapter 3) illustrated how the views all relate to each other and how the Goals view is central to the entire business architecture model—it is the central influence on the entire framework.

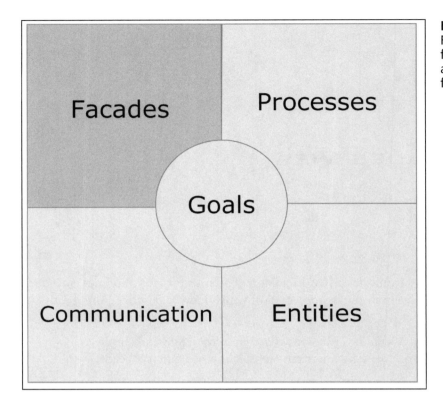

Figure 4.1
Facades highlighted
from the business
architecture
framework.

The value of a business facade is the way in which it describes how the business will interact with those who approach the business from their unique perspective. You describe how the business will interact with customers in the customer facade and define interaction with suppliers in the suppliers facade, each of which, along with any other facades you need, are part of the business Facades view.

UML

So, how do you describe all of these interactions that make up a business facade? You could do it with lists of the interaction types that the business will support. This sort of list is not recommended, as it would be difficult to capture all of the important information about the interactions that are readily available diagrammatically. The Unified Modeling Language (UML) offers us the diagrammatic alternative. (See Chapter 11 for more information on UML, and see Appendix B for a UML cheat sheet.) UML provides a *use case* as a unit of functional interaction that provides a meaningful goal to the actor who is interacting with your business. The UML use case represents an interaction with a system, including the way the interaction is intended to go (happy path or primary flow), and all the other ways the interaction could go (alternate flows). (See Appendix A for a description of the typical sections in a business use-case document.) The *actor* is a person, organization, or other system that has some interaction with your business.

UML and the concept of the use case comes from the IT industry where it was initially used as a means of describing technology systems (software). The use case itself can be "stereo-typed" to become a *business use case*; essentially, this means it is an interaction that treats the business as a system. The "stereotype" concept in UML takes a generic UML element, like a use case or an actor, and gives it a more specific meaning, or a specific context (like turning a use case into a business use case, where it implies that the use case treats the entire business as a "system"). So by creating one or more UML use-case diagrams with business use cases and business actors, you can build up a representation of each facade of the business. You will know who interacts with your business and what *business functionality* they can invoke when they interact with the business.

This book will give a brief overview of business use-case modeling. For more information, seek out books dedicated to the topic. An excellent one is *UML for the IT Business Analyst* (Course Technology PTR, 2009) or *The Business Analyst's Handbook* (Course Technology PTR, 2009) both by Howard Podeswa.

The Business Actor

In UML, an *actor* is any person, organization, machine, or third-party system that inter-acts with the system you are modeling. In the case of business actors and use cases, the systems previously mentioned would be businesses. UML is very careful to suggest that the actor represents a role, not a specific person or job title (which would be an entity). The role is very carefully defined to ensure that there is no ambiguity and no implications of specific entities.

You will also see a definition of the business actors as business entities in the Business Entities view of the business architecture model. This is because your business will want to store information about each of these business actors, as well as relationships between business actor information and other information. (See Chapter 7 for more details on the Business Entities view.)

UML also allows for a process called *stereotyping*, whereby a generic symbol is given a more specialized meaning. This stereotyping concept is used in your Facades view to turn a generic actor into a business actor, an actor at the level of business functionality that is interacting with an entire business as a system. It is important to stereotype the actor in your Facades view diagrams because, even though a business actor is an actor, you want to remind your readers (and yourself, for that matter) that you are focused on the business as a system and not just documenting an IT system (as per UML's original purpose) but something higher level.

Typical business actors include customers, prospective customers (also known as *prospects*), outside sales agents, shippers, goods suppliers, tax auditors, and so on. Obviously, specific businesses will have their own set of business actors, some of which will be like those listed here, and others will be quite unique to their business. As an example, some industry-specific business actors might be a radio frequency license supplier for a radio station or a dry-dock manager for a maritime shipping business (see Figure 4.2).

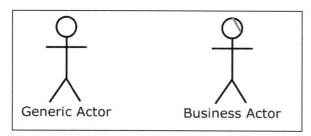

Figure 4.2
Actor iconic symbols in UML.

The actor symbol in UML is the familiar "stick man" or "stick person." The business actor symbol is very much like the standard actor symbol, but it has a diagonal slash across the head of the symbol (a concerning distinction to many). You want to use the business actor symbol in the diagrams you create for your facades because you want to remind readers that you are talking about interaction at the business level. The business actor will also be an important concept in your Business Entities view.

The Business Use Case

The *business use case* is the basic unit of functionality that you will make available to any business actor interacting with your business. A *unit of functionality* is any meaningful inter-action between the business actor and your business for the purpose of achieving a goal of the actor. Typical business use cases include functional interactions like placing an order or signing up for service.

The business use case is a stereotype of the more generic use-case symbol in UML. The business use-case stereotype is needed, though, to remind the reader that you are talking about interaction with the business and not with an IT system (which as you'll recall was the original intent of the use case within UML). All attributes and behaviors of the generic use case are carried over to the business use case, with the exception of the level of inter-action. The level of interaction of an unstereotyped use case is with an IT system or piece of software; the level of interaction of the business use case is with the business as a whole. This means that with the business use case, the unit of functionality is a business interaction that may encompass manual steps and/or steps on one or more IT systems to support a goal of the actor (customer, supplier, and so on).

The use-case symbol in UML is a simple ellipse or oval (see Figure 4.3). The business use-case symbol is much like the standard use-case symbol, except that it has a diagonal slash across the upper-right side of the ellipse.

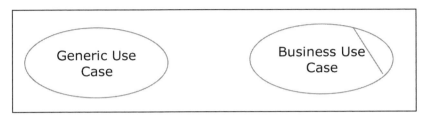

Figure 4.3
Use case iconic symbols in UML.

The business use case is more than just an ellipse on a diagram, though. It represents a document that contains a set of flows of interaction: the *basic flow* (the way the interaction goes when everything goes the way you want it to and gets the actor to the goal) and *alternate flows* (all the other possible ways the interaction flow can deviate from the way you want it to go).

It is beyond the scope of this book to teach you how to write use-case documents, but you will need to understand the basics if you are going to employ business use cases as an important component of the Facades view in your business architecture model. (Please see Appendix A for a more complete description of the sections in a typical business use-case document.)

The business use case also plays an important role in organizing the processes of a business, as you will see in Chapter 6, "The Processes View."

The Business Use-Case Diagram

The *business use-case diagram* is the way in which you show how business use cases are related to business actors and to each other. A business use-case diagram is the basic element with which you build the Facades view of your business architecture model.

The business use-case diagram is a UML construct, and the UML conventions for symbols and syntax. The diagram symbols include the business actor and the business use case, as well as packages, notes, and relationships. *Packages* are a UML element for the logical organization of big models into consumable "chunks" of content; think of them like a file folder. *Notes* are used to annotate one or more elements of a diagram or the diagram as a whole. *Relationships* are arrow-like symbols that denote how business actors and business use cases interrelate within the context of the diagram. Each of these elements is very useful when trying to show the functionality a business is trying to expose through a facade.

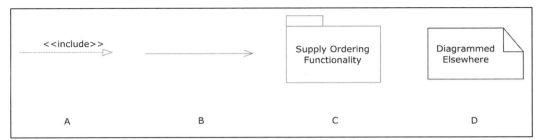

Figure 4.4
Other symbols for business use-case diagrams.

Figure 4.4 illustrates additional symbols used in business use-case diagrams:

- The <<*include*>> relationship symbol (A in Figure 4.4) is a link between two business use cases showing that the functionality being pointed to is considered part of the functionality of the business use case that is doing the pointing. The <<include>> relationship is very useful when factoring out common behavior that will be used by more than one business use case, or when one business use case is so complicated that it will be easier to understand if it is split up into "sub-functionalities."

- The arrow (B in Figure 4.4) illustrates the *Communicates* relationship between business actors and business use cases. When the Communicates relationship points from a business actor to a business use case, it means that the business actor initiates the functional interaction that the business use case represents. When the Communicates relationship points from the business use case to a business actor, it means that the actor in some way supports the functional interaction that the business use case represents. The Communicates relationship, in the context of a business use-case diagram, *never* indicates the flow of activities or the flow between functionalities (other UML diagrams are used for this sort of representation).

- The box labeled C in Figure 4.4 represents a package as it would be shown on a diagram. The package represents a logical subset of the model that is "packaged" to reduce complexity and increase understanding.

- The note symbol (D in Figure 4.4) can apply to the entire diagram or it can be "anchored" to one or more elements with a dashed line that has no arrowhead. When one or more anchor lines are applied to a note, the note only has meaning in the context of the elements of the diagram that it is anchored to.

In the sample business use-case diagram shown in Figure 4.5, you can see examples of all the most common diagram elements being employed. Although it is a very simple diagram, it is very rich in information. You can see that there is a business actor called the Customer. This Customer is allowed to interact with your business using three functionalities: the Customer can apply for an account, the Customer can charge a purchase, and the Customer can pay a bill. The diagram also tells you that both the Apply for an Account and Pay a Bill functionalities include the Look Up Account functionality as part of the way they provide interaction with a Customer. You also can see in the diagram that there is another package of information about your business called Supply Ordering Functionality, which you are told is diagrammed elsewhere in your Facades view.

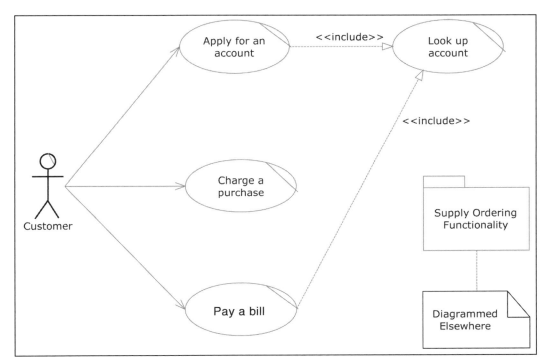

Figure 4.5
Sample business use-case diagram.

One thing that you cannot determine just from this business use-case diagram is any order or flow between business use cases. For instance, there is nothing on this diagram to indicate whether a customer has to set up an account with your business before they can charge a purchase. This sort of flow between business use cases is sometimes dealt with in process flow diagrams (see Chapter 6 for information about processes and the Processes view), and sometimes in the preconditions specified in a business use-case document (as previously mentioned; see also Appendix A for a description of the precondition section of a business use-case document).

Structuring the Facades View

Any system as complex as a business is typically going to have more than one facade, and within any single facade, there will be one or more diagrams to capture the complexities of the functionality that is being exposed through the specific facade being described.

The package is the UML element that is used to provide structure and break down the overall Facades view into logical groupings that are easier to comprehend. The package can be thought of as analogous to a file folder. It can hold a number of different things that have some sort of a logical connection that the modeler wants to emphasize. Packages can contain diagrams, actors, business use cases, relationships, notes, and even other packages. (UML has a number of other elements, not germane to this discussion, that can also be contained in packages.)

To be effective, the highest-level packages of the Facades view should each represent a specific facade of the business. Within each of these facade-level packages, you can then have any number of other packages that represent logical groupings of the functionality related to the facade. There is no single right way to split the facade into packages; it is simply a question of grouping things into subsets that make sense not only to those who are creating the model, but also to those who must read and make use of the model ("consume" the model). Make sure that you avoid using so many layers of sub-packages that it becomes impossible to understand what belongs in which packages and where to find them in the model hierarchy. Find the balance between too many layers of packages and too few to achieve an optimal structure for yourself and especially for your audience.

Tying It All Back to the Facades View

While a simple business use-case diagram can be a rich source of information, it is hard to imagine that most businesses could represent all of their business functionality on a single diagram without it becoming too complicated to readily comprehend. The Facades view of a business architecture model would typically be packaged into separate package-per-business facades. Within each facade package, there can be one or more layers of sub-packages used to further logically organize the functional interactions of a facade.

Typical facade-level packages would be ones like Customer Facade, Supplier Facade, and so on. Within the Customer Facade package, you might want to organize functional interaction into packages like Account Functionality, Order Functionality, Financial Functionality, and the like. The kinds of business use cases that might show up in the Account Functionality package might include things like Set Up Account, Maintain Account, Close Account, and so on. You might use one or more business use-case diagrams to show all the interrelationships between these business use cases and the business actors that would be involved in the interactions.

The Facades view of the business architecture model, then, is simply a collection of related business use-case diagrams and elements, as well as the business use-case documents that detail what the various functional interactions would behave like.

One of the ways the Facades view is very useful is that it helps to ensure that all the functionalities the business exposes to business actors align with the goals the business has set for itself. By looking at each goal in turn, a business architect can then analyze each business use case and determine whether it supports the business goal or not. Business use cases that do not support the business should be evaluated to determine whether the functionality they represent should continue to be offered by the business.

Facades Case Study—Alpha Wholesale Restaurant Supply

Alpha Wholesale Restaurant Supply was a well-established business that had been operating for more than 100 years, supplying consumable products for many restaurants that were mainly within the downtown area of a single city. They also supplied consumable products to a handful of restaurants outside of the city center. Alpha Wholesale Restaurant Supply also supplied a few very specific types of paper consumable products to hotels/motels that were not just in the city but also across the country in which they operated.

Alpha Wholesale Restaurant Supply had historically been a reasonably successful enterprise, but for the past several years they had been suffering a slow but steady decline in profits. They had no problems getting supplies and fulfilling orders in a just-in-time (JIT) manner, and they were running a fairly efficient operation. Although they operated in a largely competition-free environment, much of the functionality that Alpha Wholesale Restaurant Supply offered was related to extraordinary customer service. Their entire operation was located in a warehouse about a half-hour drive from their customer base, where warehousing costs were low. They had delivery equipment that was getting older and would soon need to be replaced if they were to continue operating the same way.

Alpha Wholesale Restaurant Supply was very supportive of their employees, and wanted to make sure that any business transformation did not displace anyone or put them into roles that they would not be able to embrace or succeed in.

The Situation

Alpha Wholesale insisted that their customer base would only continue ordering if they got free delivery service. They would only order if sales reps collected orders from them personally. These functionalities were very expensive for the business to offer, but they felt that these functionalities were the cornerstone of their success. It was interesting that Alpha Wholesale considered this to be part of their success because it was determined, after some analysis, to be the primary cause of their business' decline in profitability.

By retooling the Place Order and Take Possession of Order business use cases within the Customer Facade package of Alpha Wholesale's business architecture model, they were able to reshape the way customers interacted with them. The Place Order business use case now put the onus on the customer to contact the business with an order. While sales reps would continue to occasionally visit customers and would happily take orders while they were there, the primary role of the sales rep became one of business development, introducing Alpha Wholesale to new potential customers and introducing new products to both new and existing customers.

The Take Possession of Order business use case also put the onus on the customer to get the goods from Alpha Wholesale, rather than the onus being on the business to get the order to the customer. Alpha created a pick-up center, complete with a showroom, where customers could drop in, see what new products Alpha Wholesale was offering, and get their latest supply orders quickly and efficiently. Alpha Wholesale was then able to revamp their delivery offering and charge a premium for it, but also to increase the value of the delivery.

The Point

Alpha Wholesale was offering their customers all the right functionality. Where they were failing was in the way they wanted the functional interactions to flow. Because Alpha Wholesale believed that they needed to provide a slew of free value-added services to keep orders coming in, they shaped their functional interactions in a certain way. Once they saw that they might not need to offer these interactions in the same way—that the flows could be made to operate more profitably without sacrificing orders—they were able to get the business on a more profitable footing.

In Your Business

Here are some things to consider when thinking about facades and interactions in your business:

- Does your business know all the facades it needs in order to interact with all the parties involved with it, and are those facades documented somewhere?
- Does your business have a list of all the interactions it offers to interested parties, and does your business know who all these interested parties are?
- Does your business have a document of all the ways an interaction could play out (the way they want the interaction to go and all the other ways it might go, as well as how to handle those other ways)?
- Does your business tie its facades and interactions back to its goals?

Summary

This chapter introduced the Facades view of the business architecture model. This chapter covered the following:

- UML—the main language for documenting the Facades view
- The main components of the Facades view diagram
- How to structure a Facades view into packages and diagrams
- How to use the Facades view to see whether your business interactions are aligned with the Goals view
- A case study that illustrated how the Facades view helped a business resolve complicated customer service and profitability issues

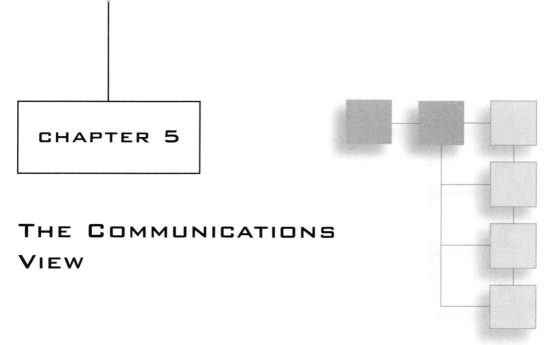

CHAPTER 5

THE COMMUNICATIONS VIEW

Communication is a simple concept, but doing it effectively is far from simple. The key to effective communication lies in understanding who should be included in communication and what communication they need to be part of. Communication is not just sending a new product pamphlet to potential customers; it can also be understanding which departments need to be made aware of a service outage, who is supposed to receive a new service order, and so on. The flow of information is what the Communications view is all about.

Communication can be internal to a business. Internal communication can be anything from ensuring everyone knows the business mission and goals to understanding how an order gets communicated to all the right areas inside a business to ensure the order gets fulfilled for the customer.

Communication can also involve third parties outside the business, including understanding what third parties need to be part of the communication and what role those third parties play in the communication.

The business architecture framework (shown in Figure 5.1) highlights the current topic, but it also shows the current topic in the larger context of an entire business. The framework is all about helping you to remember that larger context and how it will affect what you are currently concentrating on.

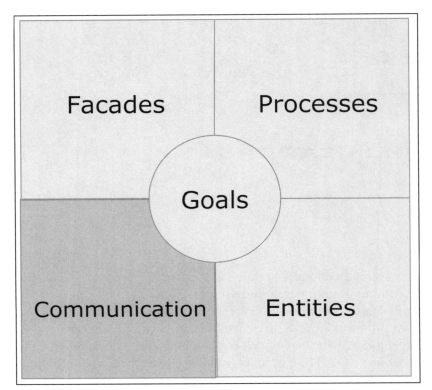

Figure 5.1
Business
architecture
framework
highlighting the
Communications
view.

Regardless of whether the communication is internal to the business or the communication includes third parties, what is important to the business architecture framework—and the Communications view specifically—is the flow of information that ensures communication occurs effectively and efficiently. As with the Facades view, UML communication diagrams are the preferred method for creating the Communications view of the business architecture model, largely because they are so well suited to descriptions of how the information flows between business entities. A business entity is a person or group that matters in the context of the business. The people/groups I'm talking about here include teams or departments within businesses, order takers, service technicians, and so on. Entities can also be third parties outside of the business in the flow of communication. See Chapter 7, "The Business Entities View," for more information on business entities.

There are, of course, other ways to show the flow of information that occurs in a business. One of the better known formats is the *data flow diagram*, which has been around for more than 30 years. The data flow diagram (DFD) can be useful when creating these types of diagrams, but it suffers from two potential disadvantages: 1) the symbols in the DFD language are not as information-rich as is necessary to show some of the more complex business communications; and 2) the DFD symbols have been used and misused enough over the years that their meaning is not very strictly enforced, which leads to significant opportunity for incorrect interpretation of the diagrams. Even if we stick to UML, we could potentially represent the flow of information as business object flows within activity diagrams (see Chapter 6, "The Processes View," for more on activity diagrams).

The communication element (the work order, the sales brochure, and so on) would be the *business object*, which would either flow from process steps or feed into process steps. The advantage to showing the information flows in the context of activity diagrams is that you can convey how the information movement is triggered by steps in a process. One disadvantage, though, is that the types of information flow that can be effectively diagrammed this way tend to be limited by the syntax of UML activity diagrams. The other disadvantage of trying to show information flow in an activity diagram is that the flow of information tends to get lost in the flow of activities. In order to avoid these disadvantages, the preferred method of representing the Communications view is a set of UML communications diagrams. You will not be able to show where communications flow into or out of specific process steps in these diagrams. However, you can, where it is needed, augment the Communications view with references to specific process diagrams in the Processes view where you can show the communication element flowing relative to process steps. In this case, you would note on the communication diagram which process diagram(s) the reader should also consider in order to get a complete understanding of the communication being documented.

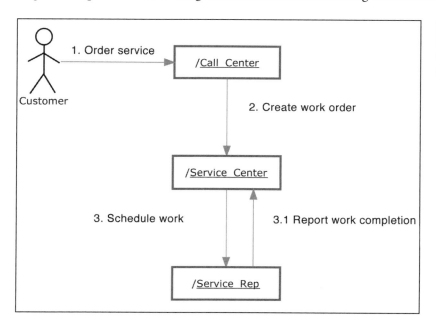

Figure 5.2
Sample communication diagram.

Figure 5.2 shows a simple UML communication diagram depicting the flow of information necessary to provision a service for a customer. This is a communication diagram in the context of the business environment because it includes an entity outside of the business (the customer). The diagram illustrates very effectively who issues the communication and who receives it, as well as how the communication flows from start to finish. Notice that each arrow represents a unique communication that, when strung together, completes a communication of value to the business (in this case ensuring that a customer receives a service they ordered). Some communications may be *unidirectional* (information is passed only one way without significant response expected), while others may be *bi-directional* (significant information is passed in both directions). In the case of bi-directional communication, the numbering of the communication messages reflects that they are related (notice 3 and 3.1 in Figure 5.2).

We may have to generate or act on information passed during these communications. By diagramming information in the Communications view, we have the chance to see how we interact in the communication chain both now and in the future.

Inside the Business

Many communications are internal to a business and are important to the function of the organization, but they don't require communication with any third party. One example of a communication inside the business would be to ensure that the Finance department is notified when the Operations department decides to write off a delinquent account. In this case, the communication is entirely internal to the business (see Figure 5.3).

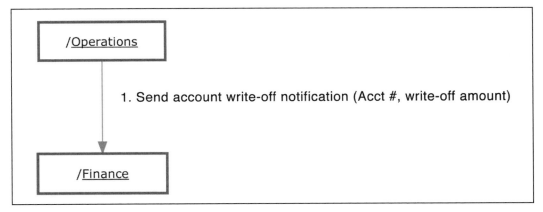

Figure 5.3
Account write-off communication diagram.

In Figure 5.3, there are only two business entities and a single communication, yet the diagram conveys a lot of information. It not only describes the communication that occurs, it also shows what information (as business entities) gets communicated, in this case the account number (Acct #) and the write-off amount. This information is vital to understanding the nature of the communication.

Communications in the Business Environment

When we talk about communications in the context of the business *environment*, we mean communications that cross the boundary of our business and involve entities beyond, as well as entities within, our business. We do not bother with trying to model communications that are entirely outside the boundary because we simply aren't aware of the existence of these types of communications. We diagram the communications that involve our business and third parties because we need to understand how these communications may impact how our business will have to function.

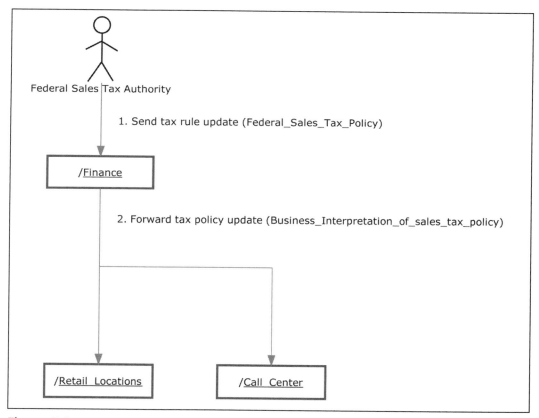

Figure 5.4
Communication diagram including third parties.

Notice that, in Figure 5.4, the Federal Sales Tax Authority, a third party outside the business, sends information to its primary point of contact within the business, the Finance department. After Finance has understood and interpreted the Federal Sales Tax Policy update, they send their interpretation of how the business needs to respond at both retail locations of the business and the call center. Neither the Federal Sales Tax Authority nor the Finance department expects any return message as a result of this communication.

Communications Case Study—Omega Enterprises

Omega Enterprises is a roofing materials company that manufactures and supplies customized materials for large-scale commercial roofing projects for both new construction and re-roofing of existing buildings. Omega consists of a head office and multiple manufacturing sites that produce the materials for jobs in their geographical area across the country.

Omega Enterprises identified two distinct sets of communications that were vital to their continued operational success. The first was the communication cycle that included telling the estimators that there was a job to price, and which ended when the price was communicated back to one or more roofers that bid on doing the roofing work. The second cycle involved a roofer placing an order for materials with Omega Enterprises because they had successfully landed the job. This second cycle included communicating with the appropriate manufacturing plant to create the materials, the correct logistics company to haul the material at the correct time, and finally communicating to the head office to generate an invoice for the materials.

The Situation

There were two gaps found in the two key sets of communications of Omega Enterprises. Each of the two gaps, after they were discovered, was shown to significantly impact the profits of the business.

The first gap was the result of not having a feedback loop from the shippers to the estimators. When the estimators created a price for a job, it always included the cost to ship the materials from the manufacturing plant to the job site where the roofing work would be done. Estimators would sometimes get quotes from logistics companies to determine how much it would cost to ship the load, but usually they used past experience about what they'd been told was the shipping price for a similar load to a similar destination on a previous estimate. Regardless of where the shipping price came from, that price would be added into the overall price estimate for the job. Often there would be a span of a few months from the time the job was estimated to the point in time when it was shipped. Regardless of how long it took to get from being a job that was estimated to one that was shipped, there were often significant discrepancies between the logistics quote used for estimating and the actual cost to ship the materials. Sometimes the actual prices would be lower, but more often the actual prices would be higher. There was, however, no communication link between the plant and the estimators to help the estimators know that they would need to adjust their shipping numbers for future work.

The second gap resulted from a fundamental change in the way materials were manufactured. Initially, Omega Enterprises created roofing materials by sawing raw stock into a usable product. One of the outcomes of this manufacturing process was that they generated a significant amount of waste material. By doing some analysis on their manufacturing technique, it was determined that laminating two pieces of raw material in a certain way would give them two finished pieces with very little waste once the cutting was finished. The key to this was what was referred to as a lamination schedule, which let the estimators know how many pieces of each thickness of raw material would be required for all the finished pieces needed on the job. This same lamination schedule would then guide the manufacturing plant in their production of the order. The gap was that the lamination schedule wasn't making it from the estimation file to the work order file. This meant that when the Omega Enterprises plant got the order, they often had to recalculate what the lamination schedule should be. There was time lost in doing these calculations, as well as errors being introduced if the plant didn't find as efficient a lamination schedule as the estimators had. Clearly Omega Enterprises had communications issues that they didn't even recognize.

The Point

Omega Enterprises was a fairly small business, employing approximately 50–100 people at the time when these communication issues cropped up. Because of their size, they had never even considered modeling their communications within the organization. Everyone "just knew" how the communications worked. Unfortunately, everyone had different understandings of how it all worked, so vital information was falling between the cracks and costing the business time and money.

The shipping cost communication gap was discovered by accident one day when an estimator was unexpectedly copied on an invoice for a job they had priced. The estimator, being curious and luckily having a spare few minutes in their day, went back and looked at the original estimate and noticed a significant discrepancy between the price they'd estimated for shipping and the amount on the invoice. Rather than bury this information, which might have made them think their boss would be upset with them, they had a discussion with management about the issue, and the result was a change to the communication structure of the organization to put a feedback loop from shipping to estimating in place. Since the time that the feedback loop was enacted, the gap in shipping estimates to actual costs has been reduced considerably.

The lamination schedule communication breakdown was also discovered by accident. An estimator had to speak to a plant manager on an unrelated matter and happened to ask if the plant manager was able to understand a particularly complicated lamination schedule that the estimator thought had just been sent to the plant. The plant manager explained that they never received any lamination schedules and they had to create their own, which they didn't enjoy doing. After a little investigation, it was found that the admin who converted estimate files to work order files didn't know about the need for lamination schedules, and so had never included it.

In both cases, if there had been a Communications view in place, it would have been much easier to identify gaps and help everyone involved in the communication to see what their role would be. As a result of these incidents, Omega roofing has begun to model its communications in order to avoid the same sort of costly mistakes in the future.

In Your Business

Here are some things to consider when thinking about communications in your business:

- Do you have any lists of communications your business has with third parties (customers, suppliers, and so on)?
- Do you have any documentation on who is involved in any of these communications?
- Do you have any documentation about communications within the business?

Summary

This chapter introduced the Communications view of the business architecture model. This chapter covered the following:

- The concept of communication, internal and external
- Options for creating Communications view diagrams
- How communications may also be documented as part of processes
- A case where the Communications view helped a real business

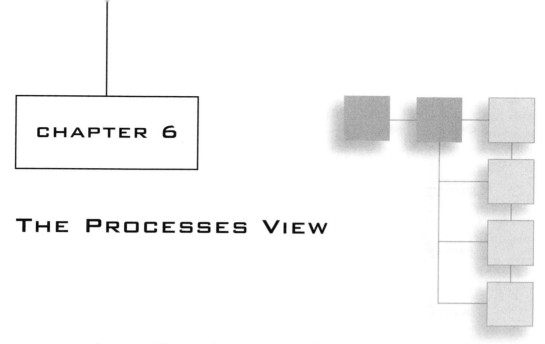

CHAPTER 6

THE PROCESSES VIEW

A *process* is a repeatable way of executing a number of tasks that achieves a certain goal. When speaking of *business processes*, the reference is to processes that are internal to the business, processes that employees of the business will execute.

Processes are probably the best understood aspect of the business architecture model. Most businesses talk about the processes they execute. Many businesses even talk about the process improvement initiatives they launch. There are whole disciplines, like Lean Six Sigma, built around process optimization. Even with all of this awareness and knowledge, though, most businesses have processes in place that do not support their business, and in some cases they have processes in place that are actually detrimental to the business.

How many times have you heard the statement "that's the way we've always done it" from a business representative? Have you ever followed up with more detailed questions about why the business would want to do things that way? When you do ask those questions, you often find that nobody in the business really understands what, if any, justification exists for doing things the way "we've always done them." Sometimes it's hard to tell if there was ever justification for doing things the way they are done; it's easy to understand that some business processes grew organically without any consideration for what the business really needed. In other cases, it's quite obvious that the process was consciously put in place at one time, but although the business has evolved, the process has not been updated to stay current with business needs. Even when the process put in place was documented, often it was created in isolation without enough understanding of how it was impacting other departments, teams, or areas of the business.

Often business processes are not actually documented, or the documentation is not referenced on a regular basis. The documentation, if it exists, is often filed away somewhere and nobody in the business knows exactly where it is any more. The process gets passed on orally from one employee to the next, often with subtle changes or errors reminiscent of the messages that are passed when children play the "telephone" game. The original process made sense, but by the time peers have trained peers through several iterations, what is actually being executed is not what was originally intended. If we still believe that a process is a repeatable way to execute a number of tasks to achieve a goal of the business, we should be very concerned about whether what is being executed is the process we intended, and whether it will still achieve our goal. Without the correct controls in place to document, communicate, measure, and control your business processes, there is a good chance that your business goals will not be met.

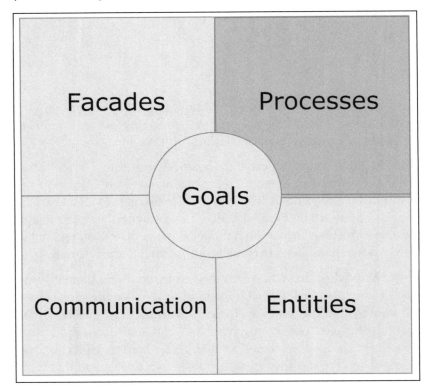

Figure 6.1
The business architecture framework highlighting processes.

Going back to your business architecture model framework (shown in Figure 6.1), you now want to concentrate on processes, while once again remembering that processes are just a part of a larger context. Processes considered without the larger context of the business architecture framework are always in danger of not being aligned with the other aspects.

The Process view of the business architecture model goes a long way in helping you to ensure that you have the correct processes, that they are well documented, and that they are available for communication to all those who need to understand or execute the processes contained in the Process view.

Contents of the Processes View

If you're going to put the effort into engineering and documenting good processes, you should also ensure that you create the right processes for your business. The best way to do this is to align your processes with other elements of the business architecture model in order to make sure that you are still properly supporting your business goals, your business facades, and your communications.

In the Facades view, you ensured that your business interactions were aligned with your business goals. Now, in the Processes view, you want to ensure that your processes are aligned with the interactions you have in your facades. You will utilize a concept from UML to do this: the *business use-case realization.*

A *realization* is a set of things to be done internal to your "system" to support the behavior that you can observe at the boundary or interface point. This is a fancy way of saying that a realization is the stuff you'll do inside your business (the system) to support how it will interact with others on the outside.

If you'll recall from Chapter 4, the business use case is the unit of business functionality (the interaction) that is exposed to allow all those who interact with your business to achieve their goals. If you then create processes designed specifically to support these business use cases, you have, in fact, defined business use-case realizations. This is a very useful concept because it supports the need to have your business processes align with the way you want others to interact with your business. You have to ensure that the processes actually support the interactions others will have with your business, and this is the easiest way to do it.

It is important to understand that a business use-case realization can consist of more than just process diagrams. Sequence diagrams, state diagrams, business entity class diagrams (all are different types of UML diagrams), among others, can assist in a complete understanding of the realization of a business use case. Some of these other diagrams will be covered elsewhere in this book as part of the business architecture model, while others, less advantageous in describing a business architecture model, will be left to the reader to pursue elsewhere.

In Figure 6.2, the business use-case realization is shown on a standard business use-case diagram. The realization is an ellipse that looks almost identical to the symbol for the business use case; the only difference is that the ellipse of the realization is drawn with a dashed line. The relationship between the business use case and its realization is shown by a dashed arrow with a closed, hollow arrowhead pointed from the business use case to the realization. A stereotyping label, <<Realizes>>, accompanies this arrow to denote explicitly the type of relationship being depicted. Remember from the earlier discussion of UML that stereotyping is a way of giving a generic UML symbol a more specific contextual meaning. In this case, the general arrow here indicates dependency, which is being stereotyped to show a "realizes" type of dependency.

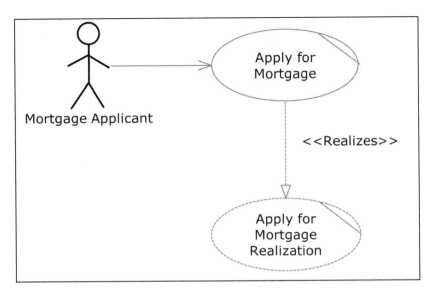

Figure 6.2
A business use-case diagram showing a realization.

Of course, this ellipse on a diagram isn't all the process documentation you need; it is merely a symbol that reminds you to align the process or processes you will document with the business use case that they support. There are a number of effective ways to diagram processes; this book will cover basic techniques from some of the more recent approaches and languages for process modeling, but it will not cover all the ways a business could document its processes.

The most basic way to document processes is with a text document that states the steps that must be taken to execute the process. This approach may work, especially for small, simplistic business processes, but it becomes incomprehensible as soon as the process becomes longer than a few tasks or has to accommodate any sort of exception handling. The inability of text to work effectively for documenting processes led to a number of visual, diagrammatic approaches to representing process tasks and all the permutations and combinations that accompany most business processes. Two of the most recent entries in the process diagramming language world are UML activity diagrams and business process modeling notation (BPMN).

UML, with its concept of stereotyping, allows users to customize the basic activity diagram (originally meant to reflect activities at an IT system level) to represent the tasks of most business processes very effectively. The flexibility of the language, combined with the fact that technology folks are pretty comfortable reading it, makes it a very effective way to represent business processes, especially when the expectation is that technology will support some or all of the tasks of the process. UML activity diagrams also look enough like more traditional process diagrams that most business people can read them without too much coaching or training.

BPMN is a newer entry to the world of modeling and has taken advantage of the weaknesses of other languages (including UML) to ensure that it was syntactically rich enough to describe almost any business process situation possible. BPMN is the only modeling language able to show how processes can be invoked or controlled by time triggers or messages. BPMN also supports pools of resources, where each pool can contain distinct "swim lanes" to differentiate roles within the resource pool. A *swim lane* is a visual tool for collecting all the steps of a single actor into one area of a diagram. This allows you to show who is responsible for the execution of specific steps within a process. The concept of a pool is unique to the BPMN. A *pool* is a collection of related swim lanes, where a step in one swim lane can trigger the next step in another swim lane. Examples of pools might be Head Office (which might contain swim lanes for Marketing, Customer Service Representatives and Technology Manger) or Regional Sales Office (which might contain swim lanes for Sales Agent and Sales Assistant). Keep in mind that if you bother to include pools in your process diagrams (and a case can be made for using them), a step within one pool cannot directly trigger a process step in another pool but rather must send a message between the pools to do the triggering.

BPMN is arguably the richest diagrammatic language for communicating processes, but it can only be used for processes. UML provides diagrams for several different kinds of views and models within and beyond the business architecture model.

Process: UML Activity Diagram

The UML activity diagram shown in Figure 6.3 is comprised of just a few simple symbols, but it contains significant information:

- The solid dot is the triggering event or start of the process.
- Each oval with the diagonal slash on the upper-right side represents an activity that is part of the overall business process.
- The thick black lines represent points of synchronization (either a fork or a join) where things must either start or end in parallel.
- The diamond represents a decision point in the process flow.
- The words [Mortgage Approved] in the square brackets are a guard condition, which is a condition that must evaluate to true in order to transit to the next activity.
- The black dots surrounded by a circle represent an end to the process. Note that while there can only be one start to an activity diagram, there can be as many ends as needed to accurately reflect the process.
- The arrows show flow from one activity to the next.
- Each actor involved in the process (both external to the business and internal) has its own swim lane where all activities related to the actor will be shown.

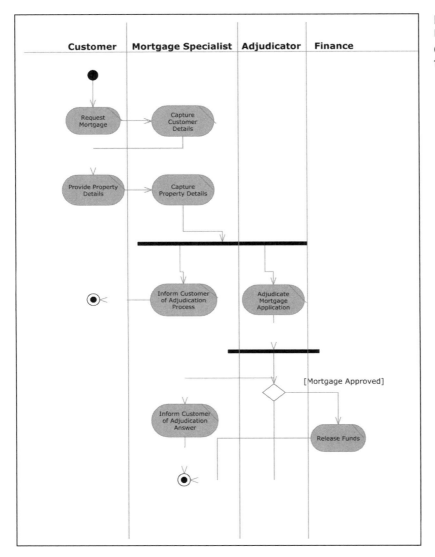

Figure 6.3
UML activity
diagram for Apply
for Mortgage.

Within this one simple business process activity diagram, you can see that there are four actors, each of whom is responsible for activities that must be executed in order to effectively provide customers with a mortgage. The customer requests the mortgage and provides all the necessary information. The mortgage specialist is responsible for initially capturing all the customer details and forwarding them to the adjudicator, while at the same time explaining the adjudication process to the customer. After the adjudicator determines whether or not to loan the money to the customer, they have the mortgage specialist explain their decision to the customer, and if appropriate, they have Finance release funds to the customer. After all of these events occur, the business process ends. The four actors are denoted by a textual name at the top of each swim lane column in the activity diagram. These same actors would have shown up as stick person elements on the business use-case diagram, but the activity diagram shows them only as textual names.

One of the difficulties of using UML to diagram business processes is the inability to indicate timing delays. In this example, there should be no expectation that adjudication will happen in real time, but UML activity diagrams can't show that the adjudication activity will potentially take considerable time and that the customer should not be expected to wait at the mortgage company office for an answer.

Please note that in the business process activity diagrams, we do not have any specific references to technology solutions. We could, in fact, implement this entire business process without using any information technology at all (though it would not be fun working for this mortgage company if they ever got busy). In the case where you explicitly want to show the participation of IT systems in the process, you can add them as one or more swim lanes (one per system) to show which steps of the process are automated by the system(s).

Process: BPMN Diagram

Once again, in Figure 6.4 you can see that with a few simple symbols a complex set of process information has been conveyed. Fundamentally, this diagram is not all that different from the UML activity diagram depicting the same process. Instead of vertical swim lanes, you now have horizontal swim lanes for the actors who participate in the process. Each swim lane contains activities that the actor related to the swim lane is responsible for, but now the activities are rectangles with rounded corners (instead of the ovals in UML).

Keep in mind that the actor concept comes from UML but is applied here for the sake of consistency. Again, the actor does not show up as a stick person; rather it is shown as a label at the beginning of the swimlane. The process initiation looks very similar, but the end points are slightly different in the two languages. The end point in BPMN is an empty circle with a thick border and has no inner dot (as the UML end did). It is acceptable to have more than one end point on a BPMN process diagram, as it is in UML, but in this example, it was easier to have everything end at the same point. This was a stylistic choice, one of many that must be made by those who produce diagrams for business architecture models.

The bigger differences in the way the process is documented in BPMN versus UML are related to parallel behavior and to timing. This is where the BPMN is a richer language than UML. The first significant difference relates to parallel behavior. Note that in UML, you have the synchronization bar, while in BPMN you show parallelism with a diamond containing a plus sign. In BPMN, the diamond is used in a number of different contexts, the differences being denoted by the symbol the diamond contains (empty for decisions, containing a plus sign for parallelism, containing an asterisk to show multiple choice, and so on).

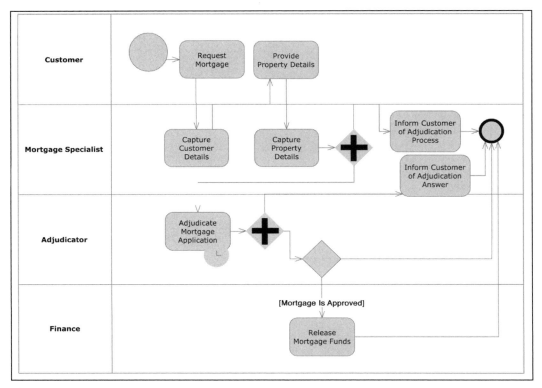

Figure 6.4
BPMN diagram for Apply for Mortgage.

The second significant difference relates to the ability to show time delays within the process. Recall that with the UML version of the Apply for Mortgage process, there was no way to indicate that there would be a delay in adjudicating the application and that the customer should not expect an immediate answer. With BPMN, you can modify a basic activity by embellishing it with a clock symbol to show that there will be a delay in that activity. You can even use the timer as a way of starting a pseudo-step in the process to show that time passes between real steps. Greater detail on modeling with BPMN is beyond the scope of this book. You may want to seek out books or Internet resources specific to this topic.

Another extremely important concept within BPMN is the notion of the *sub-process.* As processes grow and become more complex, which is a reality in business, it becomes very difficult to represent all the permutations and combinations of a given process in a single diagram. This is where sub-processes can be used to collapse complexity on parent diagrams and expand subsets of the complexity on secondary child diagrams. This allows the modeler to capture all aspects of the process, while at the same time making it easy to be consumed by those who need to read the model.

There are other concepts, such as pools of swim lanes, that are also very valuable in representing the complexities of real business processes. The pool allows the modeler to logically group subsets of the swim lanes of a process in ways that help to convey the way business really works. Pools group swim lanes that genuinely work together, while work across pools only happens via messaging.

Both the UML activity diagram and the BPMN diagram are acceptable for creating high-quality Processes view diagrams. It really is up to the business architect to determine which is the more appropriate choice for their environment. The advantages of using the UML activity diagram are that it

- Is the same language (UML) as the other views of your business architecture model.
- Will be readily understood by most IT professionals and is simple enough that business people adapt to it quickly.
- Can represent almost all processes a business typically needs to document.

The advantages of the BPMN diagram are that it

- Has the flexibility to capture virtually all business processes.
- Has a slightly more familiar syntax for business people, while still being easy for IT professionals to read.

Communication and Process

In Chapter 5 you were told that there are times when it is important to be able to express exactly where within a process a communication either gets generated, modified, or consumed. Both UML activity diagrams and BPMN diagrams allow for the capture of this sort of information by means of a concept called an *object flow*. While an object can be something other than a communication in UML (where IT systems get involved), for the purposes of this discussion, an object is a communication in the process flow.

Figure 6.5 shows the same process as that in Figure 6.4, except that now you can see an object, the mortgage application form, flowing along with the steps that actually deal with it. Notice how you can see that the two process steps, Capture Customer Details and Capture Property Details, create the Mortgage App communication business object. The Mortgage App is then consumed in the Adjudicate Mortgage Application process step.

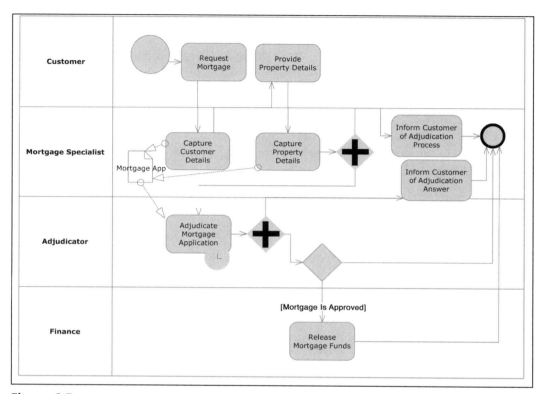

Figure 6.5
A BPMN process flow for Apply for Mortgage with an object flow.

Processes View Structure

Because we are using business use-case diagrams to show the alignment between business use cases and their realizations, the business use-case structure, then, can provide the highest layer of organization for the Processes view, just as the business use-case structure also provides organization for the Facades view. Simply by leveraging the package structure used for the Facades view, you can organize all of your business use-case realizations where the related business use cases are defined. This gives you an overall structure for the Processes view.

The business use-case realization is the unit used to organize all related processes that support a distinct business functionality. Although there can be more than one business process necessary to support a single business functionality, wherever possible, it is good modeling practice to create a single business process that is sophisticated enough to support a business functionality in its entirety. In addition, as previously noted, there may be a need for more than one diagram to fully document a single process. The UML concept of a realization, as previously mentioned, can contain more than just processes, but for the purposes of this discussion, the organization of business processes is what we will concentrate on.

Any single business process can get very complex. To provide clarity and ease of consumption of these inherently complex processes, you can use the concept of a sub-process to collapse related parts of a larger process into a single "task" that is, in fact, several tasks in their own right. The sub-process, then, is another structure that you can use to further organize your realization within the Processes view. While UML does not have a specific symbol for sub-processes, an activity can be placed on a diagram with a note attached to help readers understand that the activity represents an entire sub-process that would be detailed on a separate diagram.

BPMN, on the other hand, does provide for the concept of sub-processes. Any time that more than one diagram is used to capture the complexities of a single business process, it is important to keep the diagrams logically stored together within the Processes view of the business architecture model. This will tie logically back to the Facades view structure by way of the business use-case realizations that were mentioned earlier in this chapter.

Current State versus Future State

When creating a business architecture model, the ultimate artifacts you will produce are the *future state* processes. These processes will look the way you want them when you achieve your goal(s) and you reach your projected future state. The problem in many cases, though, is that nobody in the business understands the current state well enough to describe it without first documenting it.

The current state set of processes acts as your baseline, your documentation of how things are supposed to be operating today. Sometimes, there are variations in the way processes work in the current state, in which case you may have to indicate variations on the current state. An example of this might be that in some regions, the sales process is different than that in other regions due to local legal constraints and the like. These types of variations in the process are legitimate and must be properly identified and documented.

In other cases, there will be variations just because people have been allowed to execute their work based on their best understanding of how things are "pretty much" supposed to work. But the work gets more difficult and less accurate when it's never done the same way twice. "I'm used to doing it this way" is a standard excuse, and you can never get two or more people to agree on how it should be done. These types of variations in process are not legitimate, and they will need to be eliminated if the business is to operate effectively.

In either of the preceding scenarios, modeling the current state processes will be required as a first step in understanding the change required to get to the envisioned future state. The *future state* is a vision of how the business needs to operate in the future. There can only be one definitive future state, though as a business architect, you may go through several iterations of potential future (might-be) states before landing on the one that everyone agrees is best. This might-be work is typically done at a fairly high level, and it should precede any project work to change or update the business and underlying IT systems.

Sometimes the future state differs so dramatically from the current state that the business decides it cannot bridge the gap in a single step. In this case, there may be one or more sets of interim *milestone states*, sets of processes that will represent the way the business wants to change on its way to the ultimate future state. These interim states represent one aspect of the roadmap for transforming the business to what the business architecture ultimately envisions. (See Chapter 20 for more details about planning and the roadmap between the current and the future states.)

Processes Case Study—Gamma Telco

Gamma Telco was a start-up telecommunications company that was going to provide a number of traditional and advanced telecom services over a broadband link to commercial clients. Like any telecommunications company, they were going to have to provision services, maintain services, and bill for them. The provisioning and maintenance of services would, depending on circumstances, include new network connections, new hardware on the premises of the client and/or at the switching center, and software changes. From a revenue perspective, it would be vital to ensure that any changes to a client's service would be reflected immediately in their billing profile. Being a national service provider, Gamma Telco anticipated a sizeable client base and a significant volume of ongoing provisioning changes as their clients' needs changed.

Gamma Telco was built by a number of experts with significant telecommunications experience. The thinking was that, because there were so many experts heading up the various departments within the company, it would be easy to set up processes that would work effectively. They had experts in marketing, sales, billing, provisioning, network management, customer service, and pretty much every other aspect of a telecommunications company that would be needed.

The Situation

Each department of Gamma Telco was headed up by a professional with years of telecommunication experience pertinent to the department they were running. Very early in the life of the company, each department put effort into defining the processes the department would follow in order to execute its mandated duties. The vast collective experience of the department heads and their staff was utilized in the creation of the processes; often the processes were a direct reflection of what these professionals had done during prior periods of employment with other telecommunications companies.

Despite all the effort put into creating and documenting processes, it soon became apparent that customers were not getting what they ordered in a timely fashion, their service requests did not result in a positive client experience, and bills often didn't reflect the actual services the clients were provisioned for. Obviously, Gamma Telco was not happy with the situation and wanted to understand what was going wrong.

Upon investigation by an employee of the company who had process and business architecture experience (but was not formally a business architect at that time), it became clear that each process focused only on the department that created it, with major assumptions about interactions with other departments and the clients. Nobody had discussions to ensure that departmental interface assumptions had been validated. In fact, because not all staff had come from the same prior employers, the processes they brought with them didn't connect well, and in some cases actively worked against each other. Trying to bring different legacies together without conversations about how they would interlink was problematic to say the least.

The person with the business architecture experience called a series of meetings to walk through true "end-to-end" current state business processes to ensure that all the departmental interface points were identified, understood, and worked in the best interests of the client and the company. Within a few months of ensuring the company understood its business processes from end to end, it saw a great increase in speed of provisioning of new and changed services, and audits of its bills showed significant increase in accuracy.

The Point

The people who were primarily responsible for creating the processes were all very experienced in the telecommunications industry. Everyone invested significant time and effort to create and document processes for their department. Everyone was interested in the success of Gamma Telco. Two main things went wrong on the process front.

The first problem was that the processes put in place didn't take into account the interfaces that would be needed between departments. Because they didn't understand how the touch points or interfaces between departments would work, there was no way for the departments to work collaboratively to ensure that the end-to-end process would work. Far too many assumptions were made about how things would work "on the other side of the fence" (a term they often used to describe any department other than their own), and nobody was checking to validate those assumptions. In fact, these interface points were quite often the only problems with the processes. A new order would come in at the call center and all customer record information would be set up correctly, but the second the information was thrown "over the fence" to provisioning, problems would occur. The call center made certain service level agreements to the client at the time the order was placed, but the client service representative (CSR) taking the order didn't know what the provisioning group could realistically deliver, which lead to client disappointment in far too many cases. Another issue was that the billing folks expected the provisioning folks to trigger billing for a service once it was made available to a client, but the provisioning department thought that the billing trigger was coming from the CSR.

The second problem was that the processes put in place didn't specifically focus on enhancing a positive client experience. Often, the various departments focused on what they perceived was the "right thing to do," but what they were doing was not good for the client. They would fail to keep clients updated on the progress of their orders when provisioning was more than just "flipping a switch." Processes often interfered with speedy resolution of client issues by instead focusing on things like reporting details of network issues so that future trending could eventually be analyzed. It was important to do that kind of analysis, but not at the expense of getting the client back up and running as quickly as possible.

Both of these issues stemmed, ultimately, from not having a holistic set of documented business processes. When Gamma Telco went through the exercise of trying to stitch all its departmental processes together in a cross-departmental meeting with someone that had a business architecture background, it became obvious where the problems were, and it also became fairly straightforward to have the conversations to fix the interface point issues. It was slightly tougher to see some of the client service related issues, but as they were identified, it became easy to see how they could also be resolved. If Gamma Telco had started out by building a business Processes view for their business architecture model, they would have minimized the pain that they and their clients went through in the early days of their operations.

In Your Business

Here are some things to consider when thinking about processes in your business:

- Do you have any existing process documents that represent your current state, at least in part?

- Is your business used to doing process modeling as part of its projects (ones that change the business, the technology, or both)?

- If your business has existing processes documented, do they follow the process documents in practice? (Are they doing what they said they'd do?)

- If your business has existing processes documented, do those processes accurately reflect interaction across departments?

Summary

This chapter outlined the Processes view of the business architecture model and covered the following topics:

- Processes and the Processes view
- UML activity diagrams and BPMN diagrams for documenting processes
- Structuring a Processes view
- The concept of current state and future state diagrams
- A case where the Processes view helped a real business

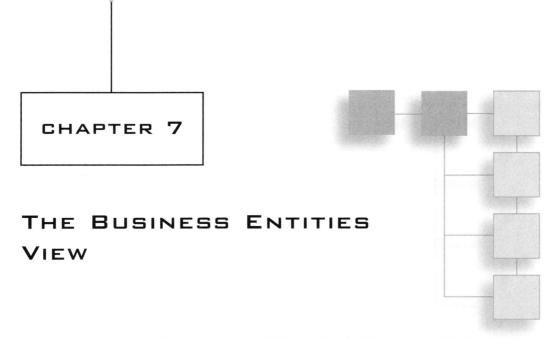

CHAPTER 7

THE BUSINESS ENTITIES VIEW

Businesses manipulate many types of information in the process of their operations. As businesses become more focused on using information, it becomes more important to understand what information they will be manipulating. Business entities are the information "things" that get manipulated, stored, and acted upon by the business. Consider the following definition:

> Entity: *Something that has a real existence; thing: corporeal entities.* (From Merriam-Webster Online: www.merriam-webster.com/dictionary/entity.)

Businesses need to manipulate things all the time. Understanding the definition of the things, as well as the relationships between them, is the core of the Business Entities view of the business architecture model. Once again we return to the business architecture framework, this time focusing on entities (see Figure 7.1). Again, remember that entities are just one aspect of a larger context.

Business entities can be thought of as logical bits of information. As an example, you can think of a client or an account as business entities. One way to discern the business entities that matter is to listen for the nouns used when talking about your business. Every noun is potentially a business entity, and by evaluating the noun, you can determine whether it really represents a logical bit of information that the business cares about. The determination is made by asking yourself if someone within the business needs to know, store, or manipulate the thing that the noun represents. If the answer is yes, then you have a business entity; if it's no, then you don't. This is sometimes referred to as a *noun challenge* process.

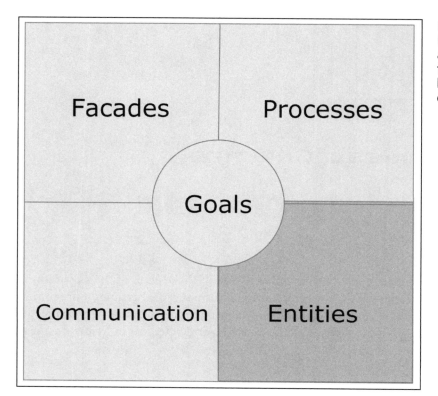

Figure 7.1
Business
architecture
framework
highlighting
entities.

The best way to model the business entities you care about, as well as the relationships between those entities, is to use the UML *class diagram* and stereotype each class as a business entity. I've talked about stereotyping in UML before—it is the concept that a very generic symbol (a class) takes on a more specific meaning (a business entity), while still retaining the basic characteristics of the general symbol. The concept of a class comes from the object-oriented approach to IT systems modeling. In the object-oriented approach, everything is an object, and similar objects are collected together in classes (e.g., Chris Reynolds is an object of the class Author because I, Chris Reynolds, wrote this book). *Classes*, then, it is useful as a means of identifying things in common, like authors, or clients, or work orders. Each of these classes will have common attributes, common things related to being a member of the class that will be tracked for each object member of the class. There is a lot more to the definition of a class that object-oriented IT professionals would care about, but it's all beyond what you need to know in order to effectively use the concept of classes for the Business Entities view of a business architecture model.

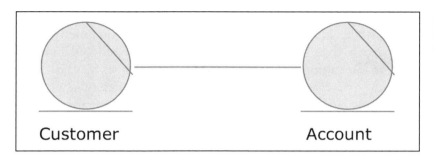

Figure 7.2
Basic business
entities diagram.

The very small diagram in Figure 7.2 is already an information-rich artifact. The basic symbol of a circle with a diagonal slash and a horizontal line underneath indicates a business entity; the name of the business entity is displayed below the horizontal line. Stereotyping it as a business entity reminds you and your readers that they are looking at a business entities diagram and not an entities diagram for a specific IT system (which is what the symbols are used for without the stereotypes). The line between the two business entities (with number ranges noted at each end; see Figure 7.3) indicates that there is an important relationship between them (shown as the Customer and Account business entities in this example).

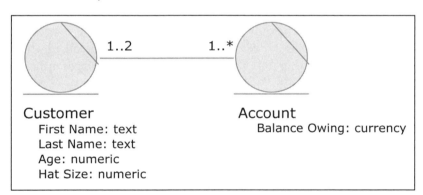

Figure 7.3
Basic business
entities diagram
with attributes.

In Figure 7.3, the cardinality (1..*) tells the reader that a customer must have at least one account, but that there is no upper limit on the number of accounts they can have; the cardinality (1..2) tells you that an account must be related to at least one, but no more than two, customers. *Cardinality* is another concept from the object-oriented class diagram; it simply allows you to constrain the number of objects of a certain class that can be related to a single object of the other class.

Each business entity has other information about it that the business is going to be concerned about. Consider the Customer business entity. Any business is going to need to know more than that it simply has customers. It needs to know things like the customer name and the customer address. There may be other things about the customer it may need to know. These related bits of information are called *attributes* of the business entity; each attribute represents one bit of information about a business entity that the business needs to track. Keep in mind that there will be attributes of business entities that pretty much every business is going to want to track (customer name, address, and so on), but there will also be attributes that are unique to your business. Some of these attributes may be related to the way the business wants to operate; others will be considered key differentiators. What is important is that the business understands what attributes of each business entity it wants to track. The basic UML Communicates relationship is the default relationship when none of the other relationships discussed apply.

Figure 7.3 shows the same business entities and relationships as those shown in Figure 7.2, but Figure 7.3 includes attribute information. The attributes are logical bits of information related to each of the business entities in the diagram. The diagram tells you that the information related to the customer is First Name, Last Name, Age, and Hat Size. (Presumably the business has an interest in tracking all of this information for each of its customers.) The diagram also tells you that for each account, the business wants to track a piece of information called Balance Owing. For each of these attributes, the diagram also gives you an idea about the basic type of information to expect: text, numeric, or currency. Other basic types you could expect include date/time and derived(). All of these types are optional, but they can be useful in helping others understand what each of the attributes means. The types should be fairly self-explanatory. The only one that needs defining is derived()—it simply means this attribute is calculated or derived from some other information, in which case the equation or algorithm for deriving the value should be shown in the parentheses.

It is not necessary to show attributes for every business entity on every diagram, but it is necessary to define all the attributes for all the business entities somewhere. Showing the basic types for each of the attributes is optional, but it can be very useful to others who will use your diagrams to build things like databases that will store the information.

Business Entity Relationships

Business entities can also be related to each other in different ways. Your business may determine that it will only allow a customer to have one billing address, but it will allow up to five mailing addresses. Your business may say that each loan you issue must have a minimum of one borrower and no more than three borrowers. These are known as *cardinality rule relationships*. Cardinalities are not necessarily bi-directional; while a loan may be attached to between one and three borrowers, any one borrower may be related to any number of loans, a minimum of zero loans, and no maximum.

There are other important types of relationships that may be of interest in documenting business entities. The first is the *generalization relationship*, which says that one type of business entity is a more general case of another type of business entity. For example, a loan is a more general case of both a mortgage and a personal line of credit. The reason that we care about this type of business entity relationship is because a mortgage and a personal line of credit would have some attributes in common. By storing those attributes with the generalized Loan business entity, you can share those attributes with all the business entities that specialize from the loan. This sharing is called *inheritance* in the world of object-oriented design and likewise in UML. The generalization relationship also allows you to categorize related business entities.

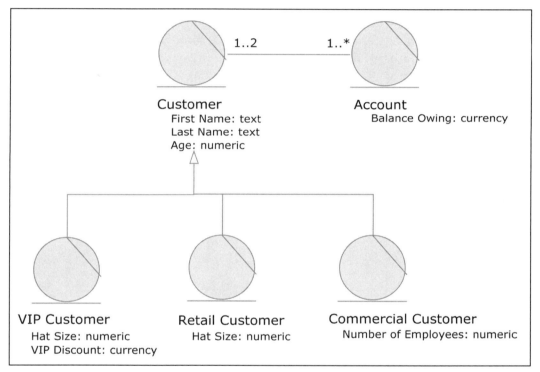

Figure 7.4
Generalization relationships.

Figure 7.4 shows that the business has further refined its definition of a customer. In fact, the business has declared that it wants to deal with three distinct categories of customers: VIP Customer, Retail Customer, and Commercial Customer. You indicate this generalization relationship with a closed, hollow arrow that points to the more general business entity and originates from each of the more specific business entities. The diagram shows that all customers, regardless of category, have the attributes of First Name, Last Name, and Age. Notice that Hat Size has been moved out from the definition of customer to the more specific Customers categories, where it makes the most sense. You would expect that hat size wouldn't make sense for a Commercial customer, since presumably there's more than one person working there. (Whose hat size would we record?) The same might also be said for the Age attribute, but a counter-argument could be made that the age in this context is the age of the business itself. For the purposes of this discussion, assume the age means how long it has been in business.

It is important to note that there is no cardinality with the generalization relationship. Generalization is all about stipulating that a business entity is a category or specialized type of another business entity.

Aggregation is another relationship that is important to understand as you add detail to your business entities. Aggregation is how you show that some business entities are actually comprised of other business entities. For example, just as a car is an aggregation of car parts, a bank statement is an aggregation of account transactions. The bank statement is a business entity, but so is each account transaction on the statement. In this case, you would say that the Statement business entity has an aggregation relationship with the Account Transaction business entity.

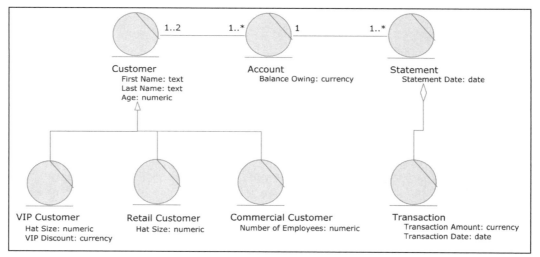

Figure 7.5
Business entities with aggregation.

Continuing the earlier example, the diagram in Figure 7.5 shows that an Account business entity can have one or more Statement business entities related to it, and that a statement can apply to one and only one account. More importantly, there is now an aggregation relationship between those statements and a Transaction business entity. The aggregation relationship is indicated with a line that has a hollow diamond at the end of the relationship, which points to the business entity that contains, or is an "aggregation of," instances of the other business entity. In Figure 7.5, the aggregation relationship means that a statement is mostly made up of transactions, but also contains some other information of interest.

Party Models

At its most basic level, most businesses in the same industry are interested in the same business entities. Even across industry boundaries, often the same core business entities are of interest to any given business. One of the key outcomes of this observation is the *party model*—a business entities model framework that can be used as a starting point for any Business Entities view. A party model typically lists the common business entities and their relationships, but it does not describe all the attributes of each business entity or all the business entities that a specific business might add to the model as informational differentiators or as a competitive edge.

The name "party model" comes from the notion that the model doesn't worry about the specifics of who your business will interact with; instead the model focuses on the idea that your business will interact with *parties*, which are simply other entities that will have an interest in interacting with your business.

Most large consulting organizations, general business consulting as well as those that specialize in business architecture consulting, offer party models for sale. The party models are sold typically for a specific industry (sometimes known as a *vertical*). The consulting companies will typically also offer, along with the sale of the basic party model, consulting services to help tailor the model to better represent your specific business. Party model information can also be found online. If you consider obtaining a party model, also consider how you will customize the model to make it specific to your business environment.

A party model can give you a real jump-start in creating a Business Entities view. It helps people get over "blank page syndrome" by starting with something on the page that your subject matter experts (SMEs) can discuss and critique, rather than staring at a blank page struggling to figure out where to start.

While party models can be a great way to jump-start an initiative to create the Business Entities view of your business architecture model, you need to realize that the party model will not be enough on its own. The party model will need to be customized to more accurately reflect your specific business. You may need to spend considerable time adjusting the party model just to get it to reflect your current state Business Entities view before you can even consider what your future state Business Entities view might look like. In some cases, if your business operates in a fairly unique manner, the effort required to adapt a party model might be greater than the effort to create a Business Entities view from scratch. Weigh the pros and cons of each before committing to a single approach.

Business Entities Case Study—Delta Telecom Billing

Delta Telecom Billing was a service provider that generated and mailed out bills for telecommunications service companies. They would generate these bills on behalf of telecommunications service companies that did not want to handle their billing in-house.

Bills could be generated on any frequency cycle needed (monthly, bi-monthly, quarterly, semi-annually, annually). The accounts for a telecommunications company could be split up into different cycle dates so that not every account got their bills on the same date. This splitting was done to distribute workload and smooth cash flow over the course of the billing period.

The Situation

In order to set up billing on behalf of a telecommunications company, Delta Telecom Billing had to understand the business entities that were important to the generation of a bill for the specific telecommunications company. Some bills would be for commercial customers with very complicated departmental structures, while others would be very straightforward retail bills. In any case, Delta Telecom Billing had to understand relationships like the account-to-customer relationship, the transaction-to-account relationship, the tax-to-transaction relationship, and many others as well. Most telecommunication service companies wanted the ability to attach more than one telephone to an account and track transactions at the telephone level. Many of the more advanced telecommunications service companies also needed to attach other services to an account and track some combination of transactions and service fees for each of them.

Beyond just understanding the business entities and their relationships, it was important to understand the attributes of each business entity that would be important to the telecommunications service company. Often telecommunication service companies would consider some of the attributes they captured as key differentiators between themselves and their competition.

Not only was it important to understand the relationships between these various business entities, it was also important to understand the cardinality rules around each of these relationships so that Delta Telecom Billing could set up its billing engine appropriately for each telecommunications service company that they were working for.

Delta Telecom Billing maintained a physical data model of its basic billing engine configuration as well as physical data models of unique differences for each telecommunications service company that used Delta's billing engine. A *physical data model* is a description of the database table structure of a system. It discusses the fields of the table, the index keys, and table relationships. What the physical data model does not do easily is describe the logical level business entities and their relationships. This meant that Delta Telecom

Billing often had trouble eliciting business entity information from its customers—Delta would be too focused on the physical layer without first understanding the logical level. As a result, the data in the billing engine was usually very highly optimized for access, but often didn't include all the information that was needed.

Delta wanted to start selling to more advanced telecommunications service companies, ones that were selling very advanced services to their customers. In order to do this, Delta Telecom Billing needed to understand very well what the service structures looked like and how they related to the customers that purchased them. The only way to get this understanding was to create a Business Entities view that showed what a typical telecommunications company's services would look like, and then analyze what it would take to evolve its own billing engine to support the advanced service billing.

The Point

Though they had never previously worked with a Business Entities view model, Delta Telecom Billing had survived largely by operating in an environment where things were simplistic enough to be understood without the aid of a model.

Once Delta decided to get to a more advanced billing model, they had to start developing a Business Entities view that would help them understand the new complexities that they would have to deal with. They brought in business architecture expertise to model their Business Entities view, which gave them a much better understanding of their service structure offerings.

The added benefit of Delta Telecom Billing having a Business Entities view was that it allowed them to have more meaningful communications with all their customers about their needs, and it allowed them to evolve their billing engine to support future customers' needs.

In Your Business

Here are some things to consider when thinking about business entities in your business:

- Is your business used to creating data models for its IT systems?
- Does your business have some sort of logical model of the information it needs, along with the relationships between types of information?
- Does your business have a model of its products and/or services, or models of the offerings of its competitors?

Summary

This chapter examined the Business Entities view of the business architecture model, including the following concepts, terms, and ideas:

- The concept of a business entity
- Diagramming business entities with UML
- Business entity relationships and cardinality
- The party model as a starting point for a Business Entities view
- A case where the Business Entities view helped a real business

PUTTING TOGETHER YOUR BUSINESS ARCHITECTURE MODEL

As you learned in Part 2, there's a lot to do to put together a full-fledged business architecture, so where do you begin, and how do you know when you're finished? The chapters in Part 3 talk about how to build a business architecture model in a practical way, without spending a fortune and without having to halt all business activity while you do it

There are two fundamental approaches to creating a business architecture model: bottom up and top down. Chapter 8 is all about how to approach the modeling from the bottom up—essentially starting from what you've already got in your business and building upon it. Chapter 9 looks at the top-down approach—more of a start-from-scratch approach. Chapter 10 addresses the question of how you know when the model is done. Chapter 11 addresses the various diagramming language options available to business architects and gives pros and cons when there is more than one option available. And finally, Chapter 12 discusses the framework for how business architecture fits into the larger picture of enterprise architecture.

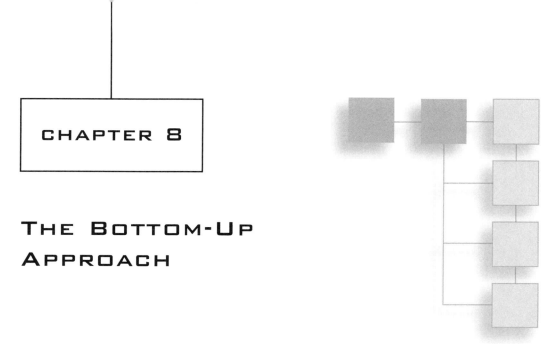

CHAPTER 8

THE BOTTOM-UP APPROACH

You've already seen how the business architecture framework can help you understand all the components you have to deal with and how they should function together to create the overall business architecture model (see Figure 8.1). The business architecture framework reminds you that you are going to need to document five views in order to have a full understanding of your business. The framework also helps you think about what aspects of your business you have the most existing documented understanding of in terms of choosing the best approach to create your business architecture model.

You should organize your existing business information into the five types of views that the business architecture framework suggests. Based on what you learned in Part 2 of this book, you'll easily see how much content you have relative to how much content you will need in each of the five views, as well as be able to make judgments about how much work you have to do to complete each of the views.

This framework also reminds you that the Goals view is central to all business architecture modeling, and as such, it should be worked on before any of the other views. After completing work on the Goals view, you should tackle the Facades view. After that, you can approach the remaining views based on the immediate needs of your business and your modeling work, as well as how much effort is needed to get the work done. (You may want to tackle the most complete views first in order to get them out of the way so that you can focus on the significant work in the last of the views.)

The bottom-up approach advocates starting from what is already known and working your way up to a consolidated business architecture model. This means you are starting from the bottom (what you already know) and working up (to a complete set of views). This allows you to build on existing content, which may significantly shorten the time it will take to get to a complete model. The bottom-up approach also allows you to work with content

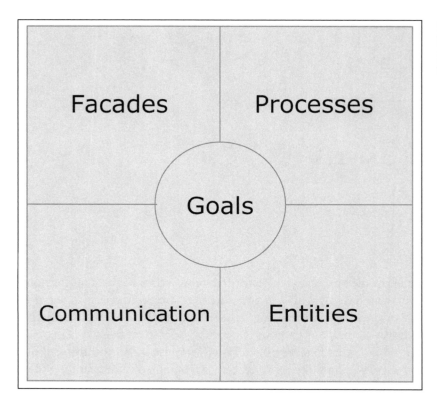

Figure 8.1
The business architecture framework.

that is already documented and understood by the business, meaning that you won't have to spend as much time trying to elicit the information from the business or trying to teach people what it is you are trying to achieve by interviewing them.

Starting the Work

When putting together a business architecture model from the bottom up, you start with what you already know, and then fill in the gaps to get the complete picture. Most businesses already have some degree of documentation. Ask your business executives for documentation related to goals and/or the mission statement. Ask departments about process documentation they may have (procedure manuals, process diagrams, training manuals, guides, and so on). Ask if anyone has documentation about the interactions the business provides to third parties. If you have no documentation to start with, you are better off using the top-down approach to creating a business architecture model. (See Chapter 9 for details.)

Document What You Know

Most businesses will have some sort of documented mission statement, which can act as the starting point for the Goals view. Once you have the mission statement, along with any other stated goals of the business or its various departments, you can begin to assemble these into a first cut of the view. After you draft this version, you can use it as a tool to discuss the holes in the Goals view and find out what you need to complete it.

The Goals view is the place to start regardless of whether you are modeling from the bottom up or from the top down. The Goals view is so central to getting the rest of the business architecture model correct that it should always be started early in the modeling effort.

When you begin to document goals, you are not trying to either elicit or validate them; you will do the elicitation and validation work later. Right now you are starting from the bottom up, so you just document what you've got. Put what you know about your businesses goals into a Goals view diagram and leave it at that.

The next area of the business architecture model to focus on is typically the current state Processes view. Typically, this view is worked on early in your bottom-up efforts because most businesses have at least some process documentation in place. Keep in mind that your business' processes may be in many formats; part of documenting them will be converting them into a standard language and format. This standard language might be whatever your business has already been using to document processes, or this may be the point at which you choose to move to one of the advanced languages described in Chapter 6. (The choice is often driven by how much content you already have in a given standard language.) Again, your initial focus is on pulling together what documents already exist. Later you'll fill in the gaps, validate content, and all the other important activities related to your model.

After you document what your business already has available on the Goals and Processes views, you need to look for whatever else you can find that will help develop the remaining views of your business architecture model—facades, communications, and business entities. Most businesses will not have information that will directly fit into your remaining views, but that doesn't mean there isn't anything of value to you.

When starting your Facades view, look for product or service catalogues. These can give you some insights into what functionality the business exposes to its customers. You can then infer some of the related functionalities the business exposes to third parties. Remember that you're not trying to finalize the Facades view yet; you're just trying to document what you already know or can easily infer about the business.

When trying to document your Communications view, you should look for any formal communications your business issues to the outside world. You should also look for any standard communications internal to the business, such as forms, work orders, reports, and so on. These sorts of communication elements won't tell you much about how they are created or how they flow, but when you know of their existence, you're well on your way to understanding the communications you will eventually have to detail in your Communications view for your business architecture model.

When it comes to your Business Entities view, you probably have a decent amount of raw information; you will simply have to do some amalgamation work. The wealth of raw information you can draw on generally comes from the IT systems of the business. If you are lucky, the IT systems will have a reasonable amount of documentation, including a logical data model. The logical data model for a system is essentially the Business Entities model specific to what a single system or application implements. The logical data model should show the entities a system stores or manipulates, along with some of the basic relationships between those entities. The real work is all about reconciliation in order to get a common view of all systems and information repositories across the business.

When you don't even have as much as a logical data model to start with, you can go to the systems and applications themselves for some clues about business entities. You can look at the fields of information the various systems and applications capture and look at how those fields are logically grouped, and then define some basic business entities from them. Of course, this will only be a best guess at your business entities, and you won't yet know much about the relationships between entities, but you are working from the bottom up. You shouldn't expect to know very much yet. You will have a better understanding later.

So you've gathered up and documented what information was readily available in your business. What happens next depends somewhat on how the arrival at an established business architecture model will be funded. If significant time and resources will be dedicated to delivering a business architecture model, then you can just go ahead and work on the deliverables that will make up the model. In most businesses, however, the time and resources needed to deliver a business architecture model like this book describes cannot be spared. When you can't justify a project just to build your model, you instead must build it as a by-product of other project work you are doing.

Filling In the Gaps

When you build your business architecture model as a by-product of other project work, it is important to have a clear vision for the model as well as an understanding of the gaps between your current content and the vision for the model. This way, when a project changes a process or adds a new service or customer type, you will be poised to capture that content and slot it into your model. Projects will now have to create their artifacts in a way that is consistent with how you need the business architecture model content to be represented. Services will have to be documented as business use cases, business entities will have to be modeled visually using UML class diagrams, and all other view content will also have to be done as per the relevant view documentation standards suitable to your model and agreed to by the business.

As projects create content and finish it, it is important that someone in a business architect role be ready to accept the content, validate it against modeling standards, and then integrate it into the overall current state part of the business architecture model. The work of integrating the content may include questioning how this new process or business entity will work with other, already existing content. As a business matures, it makes sure these questions are addressed early in a project, but in the early days of creating a business architecture model, the questions often aren't asked until after the fact. When this happens and processes aren't fully aligned in advance, project change requests may have to be raised to fix the misalignment. The sooner this happens in the project lifecycle, the less expensive it is to fix.

Using project content will only get the business so far down the path of creating a business architecture model. In fact, the business will get no further than a current state model using this approach. While it's not ideal, this is not completely a bad thing. By leveraging project content, you've already done three things for the business. First, you've built a current state model of the business at minimal incremental cost. Second, you've taught the business how to continue to use project content to keep the current state model fresh, or evergreen, by constantly contributing to it the artifacts produced in projects. Third, you've taught many employees how to read the content that will now become part of your business architecture model. Keep in mind, however, that you are not done yet. You only have a current state understanding of the business.

Next you must determine when you have enough current state content to start building the rest of the model. The question of what constitutes enough is not straightforward and will vary from business to business. The best way to determine what will be enough for your business is to discuss the question with your management team in advance. They can help you set appropriate criteria for determining what is enough content. Remember that you aren't asking when the business architecture model will be done; you are simply asking how to determine when projects have given you enough that waiting for more content from them will provide little incremental benefit. While you are establishing these criteria, keep in mind that you will get very little content from projects to help populate the Goals or Communications view, and unless you provide some guidance and influence, you typically won't get much for the Facades or Business Entities view either. If nothing else, at least make sure you are getting content for your Processes view from the projects already under way.

The only reason you really care about the point where you have as much as you can expect from projects is so that you can plan when you'll begin to finish the business architecture model based on what you've started with in the way of existing content and content from projects.

Completing the Business Architecture Model

When you begin the task of completing the model, there are a number of steps you will need to take:

- Finish the current state of the Facades, Communications, Processes, and Business Entities views. You will not work on the Goals view yet (unless there actually was some current state Goals view content available, which is rare) because the current state goals aren't as important in the bottom-up approach.
- Establish a future state Goals view.
- Establish a future state Facades view.
- Establish future state Communications, Processes, and Business Entities views.
- Create a roadmap for evolving the business to the envisioned future state.
- Establish a continuous improvement program to keep the model evergreen.

Finishing Up the Current State

At some point, you and your business are going to say it's time to finish the current state aspect of the model. When this point is reached, you need to understand the gap between where you are and your *best understanding* of the entire business. Best understanding is used because it is almost impossible to fully understand the business without having a model of it, and you don't have the model yet. The point is to get to a stable version of the current state model of your business in very short order because the business will continue to evolve as you work, and you need to develop a snapshot picture of the business before it evolves too far ahead of your model. The value of this best understanding of the model is so that you can plan what work remains in finishing your current state business architecture model.

Finishing the current state model involves first validating what you have already documented. Spend time with representatives of the business and ensure that what you've captured is correct. Start with the Goals view, and then work on the other views in whatever way makes the most sense to you and your business experts. (Typically, they will be most comfortable talking about business processes.) While you are in the process of doing this, your business experts will often find they can fill in the remaining missing details; encourage this participation, as it will fill the gaps remaining on the current state model.

As soon as you get validation of the content you previously documented, you need to get to work writing the rest of the content. Again, start with the Goals view, and then work on the other views in the order best suited to you and your business experts. The easiest way to get this work done accurately and in a timely fashion is to set up a little "skunk-works" type of initiative. Get together with a few dedicated business experts and spend the vast majority of your time doing this work. Finishing the current state model cannot be a part-time exercise for you or the experts providing input to the content. If anyone considers this as anything less than a regular business project requiring diligent focus and dedication, then you will not end up with high-quality content.

Establishing a Future State Goals View

It's time now to concentrate on the future state for the business. This is the real point of business architecture: understanding how you want the business to look and fit within its environment in the future.

You start the future state by having a short but frank discussion with senior management about how the goals of the business currently line up and how they should look in the future. Start by asking if the overall goal of the business needs to be updated. You want to make sure the business has an overall goal (main goal) that will provide it with focus for the next three to five years. After the main goal has been discussed, take a good look at the subordinate goals. Do any of the subordinate goals need to be updated to support the new main goal? Do any of the subordinate goals need to be adjusted to make sure there are no goal conflicts? Does senior management support all the goals and their implications? The implications come in the form of modifying the business in order to meet the goals—sometimes this can be a costly modification and can be more effort (and more expensive) than the business envisioned.

It is vital that the goals are finalized before any other aspect of the future state business architecture model is defined. If you do not have a firm grasp on a coordinated set of future goals for the business, the rest of the exercise will suffer. Without goals, the Facades view may not make sense, and the Communications, Processes, and Business Entities views may all be lacking in accuracy and completeness.

Establishing a Future State Facades View

A business' goals will largely be met by having the correct interactions with the outside world, with their customers and other third parties interested in the business. You work on the Facades view right after you finish the future state Goals view because it is so important for shaping the business functionality to support the future state goals.

The best place to start is with the most frequently used customer-related functionalities; you should model these as you want them to be in the future. After you cover the most frequently accessed customer functionalities, move on to the less frequently accessed ones, along with the functionalities that support third parties. Analyze each functionality's fit with goals as you work.

For each of the functionalities, ask yourself if it supports at least one of the goals of the business. If it does not, then you need to have a frank discussion with management about whether the goal is correct (presumably it is, but it is worth checking) or whether the functionality needs to be adjusted to support the goal. When you finish this analysis, you should have a future state Facades view that fully supports the future state goals of the business with no misalignments.

Establishing Future State Communications, Processes, and Business Entities Views

After you have all your future state goals sorted out and understand all the future state business functionalities that will comprise your facades, you can begin to fill in your future state Communications, Processes, and Business Entities views.

Your communications should all support either business functionalities in the Facades view or processes in the Processes view. There should be no communications that are not aligned with one or more of these other components of your business architecture model. If you have communications that don't align, you need to determine whether they need to exist in the future or not. If they do need to exist, you may need to adjust your functionalities or processes as appropriate.

Each of your future state processes should support one or more business functionalities. If you have processes that do not support at least one business functionality, you need to have a discussion about why the process should exist. If you have a business functionality that isn't supported by at least one process, you need to develop a process to support it. Each functionality must be supported, and you want to make sure there are no processes that don't support at least one functionality.

Analyze each business functionality, process, and communication to find all the business entities that the business will need to understand. Use the "noun challenge" technique to discover the entities. Once they've all been discovered, speak to your business experts about two things: validating that each one truly is an entity the business cares about, and establishing the relationships between the entity you are reviewing and all the other entities in the model. You want to make sure that every business entity you have in your model is manipulated in at least one process, functionality, or communication. There should be no entities in your model that aren't used by the business, and every entity that your business manipulates should be included in your model.

Creating Your Roadmap

Congratulations! You now have a current state and a future state business architecture model. Presumably, you do not have current and future states that are the same, and you expect the business to be different in the future. The gap between the current and future states represents the change your business needs to undergo to evolve into the future state defined in the model. How you plan to fill the gap between the current and future states is defined by your roadmap.

There exist any number of approaches that could possibly be taken to fill the gap between a given current and future state for a business. There's the all-in-one approach, and there are a number of different incremental approaches that might be suitable. The all-in-one approach should only be undertaken when there is a very small gap to fill. A small gap would be one where there is no gap in goals, only one or two minor adjustments to a business functionality, or only minor changes to one or two processes, communications, or business entity definitions. If you are going to follow an all-in-one approach, launch a project that has as its stated mandate to evolve the business from the current state to the future state envisioned in the business architecture model. As the project is evolving the business, make sure you are also putting into place a continuous improvement plan (see the next section for details).

The more typical case is that there is a significant gap between current state and the future state envisioned for the business. When this is the case, it is extremely risky and inadvisable to attempt to evolve the business in a single step. The business will need to evolve over the course of several projects that will bring incremental value to the business while also moving it closer to the envisioned future state. The real questions, of course, are "how do you parcel out the work?" and "in what order should the work be executed?" There is no single, simple answer to these questions, but there are some guidelines that you can use as you determine what is appropriate for your project.

The first guiding principle for the roadmap plan is that each project on the roadmap should provide some observable value to the business. This means that with the execution of each new project, the business should be able to, in some way, see that it is "better" than it was before. The business should have at least one improved functionality, one improved communication (either internal or external), better handling of at least one business entity, or at least one improved process. Further, the business' management should be able to see with each project that the business has moved closer to fulfilling its stated goals.

The second guiding principle is that some work has to come before other work. You can't build the roof of a house successfully if you don't already have the walls in place (except, of course, in the case of modular home construction). It is important to plan your roadmap so that the foundational projects are completed before the projects that will rely on the existence of these foundational things. An example of this sort of planning would be to make sure that implementing a business process workflow engine would be implemented before any work to implement the automation of individual business processes. If you performed the automation of the individual business processes first, most of that work would likely be thrown away once the engine was put in place. This would be expensive, cause a significant amount of rework, and probably cause your sponsors to question your ability to plan an effective roadmap. Typical things to look for when trying to plan what should come first would be as follows:

- Internal enablers for external offerings.
- Organizational change preceding procedural change.
- Technology and operational support infrastructure should precede things that will rely on that infrastructure.

The third guiding principle is that not every project will be able to deliver significant change that will advance the business along the roadmap you've defined. Sometimes the business will need to get work done outside of your planned projects. This will be a fact of life if you have a three- to five-year roadmap. What is important is that you be part of any discussions about the nature of those other projects and that you influence them to not inadvertently do things that will soon have to be undone or redone as part of planned work on your roadmap.

The fourth guiding principle is that "immediate need" for change will occasionally crop up and your roadmap will need to adapt. The business cannot stand still for three to five years while you evolve it into the envisioned future state. The business will have to react to market pressures, to client needs, and to opportunities and problems. Much like your influence on the changes needed in the third guiding principle, you will want to be part of discussions about how the business will meet these challenges. The discussion that has to happen here is a little more fundamental, though; you may need to discuss whether the envisioned future state is still valid, and if not, what the new future state will need to look like. This will include updating the business architecture model and roadmap to get you from where you are at the time of the discussion to the new future state. Keep in mind that the problem or opportunity that initiated the discussion will have to be a priority in your revised roadmap; it is what started the discussion about how the business architecture model needed to shift in the first place.

Establishing a Continuous Improvement Program

Imagine for a moment that you execute your roadmap without any interruptions or modifications. Would you expect that your business is now perfect and will never need to evolve further? Factor in the fact that, as previously discussed, the needs of the business will change due to external pressures. It's highly unlikely that the business would not need to continue to evolve after it reaches the envisioned future state and will, instead, likely need to evolve on a regular basis.

You need to reinforce the expectation with your business executives that business architecture is not a point-in-time exercise, but a key component in the continuous evolution of the business going forward. Once the executives understand this, you need to put in place a plan to ensure you can continuously improve your model and roadmap. This plan should include the following:

- Being part of all discussions about the strategic direction of the business.
- Driving the portfolio of project work the business will undertake.
- Ensuring that the team from every project the business undertakes provides the business architecture model with updates from the work products they generate.

Being Part of Strategic Discussions

In the early days of establishing business architecture as a discipline within a business, it is hard to convince the executives that the business architect should be at the table for strategic discussions. After all, these discussions will be about the future of the business, the very heart and soul of the operation. The fewer people privy to this information, the safer the confidential content that information represents. The reality, however, is that the business architect plays a vital role in shaping the strategic vision of the business and must be a part of these discussions. Without the business architect at the table asking the tough questions about the implications of decisions on all the views of the model, the business will be no better off than if it had never started the business architecture work in the first place.

As a business architect, you need to be an active participant in the strategic discussions the business undertakes. You need to be central to the discussion, asking how proposals fit with the goals of the business as well as how they fit into the other views of the business architecture model. Bring your model to the table and be ready to use it as a framework for discussion and for asking the tough questions about bright ideas. It's important for the executives of the business to see that you, as the business architect, are a significant contributor to making sound strategic decisions.

Driving the Project Portfolio

The gaps between the current state of the business and the future state described in the business architecture model represent the change that the business must undergo. Businesses undergo change typically through projects, so your gap represents some number of projects. It is up to you to logically group bits of the change together so as to provide business value while also closing the gap. This set of projects should make up your portfolio of project work.

Often other work will crop up that is not part of the planned portfolio. This is a fact of life when it comes to business; rather than fight it, it should be embraced and made part of the business architecture process. Whatever the intake process your business puts into place, ensure that evaluating the bright ideas that the intakes represent against the business architecture model is part of the standard operating procedures. Every bright idea that is implemented should strategically align with the business architecture model. If a bright idea does not match with the business architecture model, the business has two options: either the bright idea should be scrapped, or the business architecture model needs to be adjusted because the bright idea is worth pursuing and the model needs to coincide with the altered future state that this bright idea implies.

Feeding the Model with Project Artifacts

You've already discovered that projects create artifacts that resemble content important to the business architecture model. If you influence projects right from the start, you can ensure that they create artifacts in a way that will feed straight into your model. They will model facades the same way you do. They will model processes and communications the same way you do. They will model business entities the same way as you do. If you get really good at this, you can actually have a model that is modular enough that they can update parts of it as work of their project.

Regardless of whether projects are updating the business architecture model directly or if they are creating artifacts that will be incorporated into the business architecture model, the important thing to ensure is that no project is allowed to operate without contributing to the model. As soon as a project fails to update the business architecture model, the model current state is out of synch with reality and work needs to be done to bring it back in line with reality. If this isn't managed by ensuring every project updates the current state of the model, you will never be certain that your current state is accurate.

Pros and Cons of the Bottom-Up Approach

The bottom-up approach to creating a business architecture model is very practical in that very little new cost is required to create the current state model. In addition, a small team can create the model with little disruption to the regular operation of the business. The current state can often be created almost entirely with existing content that the business already has in some form or other.

The bottom-up approach does still require dedicated effort to pull together the future state view of the business; the model is not "free." The time it takes to cobble the current state aspect of the model from existing artifacts can take longer than the business is able to afford; in fact, it may take so long that you can never get a complete vision of the current state before it begins to shift. The modeling work may be at risk of never being complete if it takes too long to get the current state completed; sponsors will see little return on investment during this period and may begin to wonder if the exercise is even worth completing. When working from the bottom up, you will have a harder time socializing the concept of business architecture with the business because they have not seen it being built and they have not been a direct part of creating the content.

The bottom-up approach is the approach that most business architects will have to work with because they will most likely not be able to get funding and resources to do the model in a top-down way. This does not automatically spell disaster, but it does mean that the business architects must be aware of the pitfalls of the bottom-up approach if they are going to achieve a successful result for their business.

In Your Business

Here are some things to consider when thinking about the bottom-up approach to modeling in your business:

- Does your business have any documentation that you could leverage to begin a bottom-up approach to building a business architecture model?
- Do your existing business projects produce artifacts that you could leverage for your business architecture model?
- How does your business manage its portfolio of projects now?

Summary

This chapter has covered how you can begin to create a business architecture model using existing content from your business and from projects that are underway. There has been discussion of the following:

- When a bottom-up approach is appropriate
- Where to start on the current state and how to get content for it
- How to complete the current state model once you've exhausted your supply of existing content
- How to get to a future state model
- The concept of a roadmap for evolving the business from its current state to the envisioned future state, in an all-in-one project or with multiple projects

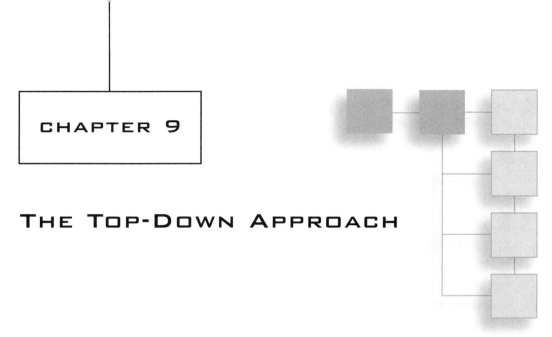

CHAPTER 9

THE TOP-DOWN APPROACH

Regardless of whether you are developing a brand new business or looking at ways to optimize an existing business that has lots of documentation in various forms, the top-down approach is a faster and more straightforward approach to creating a business architecture model than the bottom-up approach.

The top-down approach is inherently more structured than the bottom-up approach. With the top-down approach, you don't spend as much time searching out existing content and trying to shape a model around it. Instead, you define the shape of the model and create new content or retrofit existing content into the model. The structure drives the content and the plan for completion of the model. This is significantly different from the bottom-up approach, in which the available content drives the plan and shapes the model.

This type of work can be done as a result of project or initiative work, but it is often simpler to create the business architecture model as a separate initiative when working from the top down.

How to Start

Regardless of how you intend to build your business architecture model—whether on the back of other initiatives or as an initiative on its own—you will begin by determining the structure you want for your model. This structure is all about how you will organize information and what language or languages (text, UML diagramming, BPMN diagramming, or others) you will use to represent its content. When you work from the bottom up, you let the model take shape somewhat organically based on the existing documentation you have and the projects or initiatives that contribute to it; they control what content comes in at what time and in what format. With the top-down approach, you have much tighter control over what content will come in at what point in time, how it will be structured, and how it will fit the model.

The other structural consideration you need to decide early on is whether you will bother with an As Is state aspect of your business architecture model or if you will simply settle on a To Be model and not worry about the current state for now. You can take this approach when modeling from the top down if you believe that your current state is understood well enough that you will be able to do a gap analysis between the future state and your understanding of the current state. Obviously, there is risk in adopting this approach, but the risk is tempered by getting to a stable, useful model more quickly. In the end, it is up to you and your business management team to decide. Be aware, however, that you are not committed once the decision is made. You can always revisit the decision while you are modeling and discovering new things. You should actually plan to revisit the decision a couple of times during your modeling initiative, particularly around the time of key milestones for your deliverables.

You need to start with the main goal or goals of the business. You can start with the mission statement of the business, if one exists, but you will have to validate it right away if the mission statement is representative of the main goals the business intends to attain over the next three to five years.

After the main goals are documented and validated by the business management, you can begin to decompose the main goals into sub-goals. Be careful not to tie the sub-goals to specific existing business departments; tie them instead to logical functional groupings. You don't want to tie your sub-goals to specific business departments yet because one of the potential outcomes of creating a business architecture model is discovering a need to restructure your business. If your goals are too closely tied to an existing business departmental structure, you may not be able to readily see the need for restructuring when it arises.

Get management to commit to the main goals in your Goals view. Commitment means that they agree the goals are correct and that they will sponsor and support the changes necessary to achieve these goals. At this same time, you can get the management to validate that the sub-goals look appropriate, but don't ask them to commit to the sub-goals yet. You'll ask management to commit to the sub-goals later, when the entire business architecture model is closer to completion.

The Approach to Top-Down Work

After you have a draft of your Goals view, including the main goals that were committed to by management, you need to fill in the rest of the business architecture model. You do this pretty much in the order the various views were presented in Part 2 of this book. That is, you will generally proceed with the views in the following order:

- Facades
- Processes

- Communications
- Business Entities

You will work on your model primarily in this order, but there is room for some flexibility and iterative modeling. You want to foster flexibility in order to capture relevant information in the appropriate view, regardless of which view you happen to be focusing on. If a vital communication is discovered as a result of a facade element you are documenting, capture at least the basic information about the communication in the appropriate view, and then get back to the work you were doing on the facade. *Iterative modeling* means that you might take a pass at drafting the most essential aspects of your entire business architecture model, and then through validation and discussion with subject matter experts, you "iterate" through the model again, refining content and adding additional content as needed. You may need several iterations before the model is considered stable or correct. The value in taking the iterative approach to modeling is that it gains you more feedback early in the process, when fixing errors is less costly.

Facades

Right after you draft your goals, you should start working on your Facades view. You work on the Facades view early in the top-down approach because it represents the way you want the business to interact with the outside world, and those interactions, aligned with the Goals view, will shape the other views.

So then the question is, "With all the facades your business has, where do you start?" There is no single right answer. There is, however, a "most likely" starting place when working top down. Start by looking at the interactions you will need to offer to satisfy the goals of your business. Look at the products or services that the business will offer and understand what interactions with the customer will be necessary to sell and support those products and/or services.

Start with the creation of a business use-case model. For each interaction, add a business use case that represents that interaction from the perspective of the customer achieving a goal by interacting with the business. Examples of a customer goal-oriented interaction might be things like the following:

- Purchase a clothing item
- Add a new telephone service
- Cancel magazine subscription

In each of these cases, the customer gets something of value, but you, as the business, control how the customers will achieve their desired goal. As you are adding these business use cases to the model, ensure that the interaction is aligned with at least one of the goals of the business. If the interaction is not aligned with at least one goal, you need to have a conversation with the business executives to understand if you've discovered a new goal of the business, or if you have an interaction that the business shouldn't be performing in the future. This is where the business architecture model helps to shape the business and ensure you are only doing the things that you intend to in the future.

As you add business use cases to the Facades view, connect them to the primary actors that get value from the interaction and the supporting actors that will participate in the interaction. When you look at customer-facing interactions, you might suspect that most of the interactions would have the customer as the primary actor. You should, though, think about whether there are different categories of customers, and if the interactions would look different with specific categories. Consider, for instance, the idea of VIP customers versus regular customers: would VIPs be able to order products differently, or would credit checks be waived for existing customers while credit checks would be mandatory for regular customers? Would there be differences in interactions between online and face-to-face customers? These are the sorts of questions you need to ask yourself and your subject matter experts as you model the Facades view of your business architecture model.

You will still need to document the interactions with suppliers, regulatory bodies, and anyone else that your business will interact with. You should have similar discussions with your subject matter experts about different categories of suppliers as you did with different types of customers. Will there be significantly different interactions online versus face to face? Will there be different interactions with preferred suppliers versus normal suppliers? What else will be important in the interactions your business will have with the rest of the world? Remember, you have the ability to control the way the interactions will work in many cases, and you should take advantage of this to make the interactions flow in a way that's most beneficial to you. This won't be true of every interaction. (You seldom get to dictate how you will report taxes to the government, for example.) Where it is true, take advantage and model the interaction to your benefit.

When it comes to interactions with governments or regulatory bodies, you will have little opportunity to evaluate whether or not the interaction aligns with your business goals. You either comply with the government and regulatory bodies, or you are out of business. Therefore, you should have a business goal of remaining compliant, and all your interactions should align with this goal. Suppliers will give you more leeway in your interactions with them; after all, you are their customer. You can, and should, take the time to ensure that every interaction you define with a supplier is aligned with at least one goal of your business. If you have supplier interactions that don't align with at least one business goal, have a conversation about whether you have an interaction that shouldn't exist or you are missing a goal.

After the business use-case model is drawn, document the business use cases. Each business use case should be its own document. You will use these documents to detail how the interactions will proceed when everything goes as planned and the primary actor achieves their goal. These are called *primary flows*—there is only one primary flow per business use case, and they are vital to the document. You will also use these same documents to detail all the ways that an interaction might go other than the way you planned (in some cases the actor will still get to their goal, in other cases they won't), and how you, as the business, want to handle the failure of the interaction. These are called alternate flows, and there can be many of them for any single business use case. Make sure that as you document the details of the primary and alternate flows within the business use case, they still support the goals of the business.

Processes

When creating a business architecture model from the top down, after you document your Facades view, you start on your Processes view. It is vital that each process support an interaction, and therefore at least one goal of the business. This is why you need to pursue the Processes view only after stable drafts of the Goals view and the Facades view are in place.

When creating processes, you want to ensure that they actually support an interaction within the Facades view. It is amazing the number of times that you can discover processes within a business that were needed at some point in the past but add no current value to the business, yet still are followed "because that's the way we've always done it." This sort of productivity waste is rampant in many organizations, and weeding it out is a quick way to show a positive return on investment (ROI) for your business architecture initiative. (The ROI often comes in the form of reducing operating costs by eliminating unnecessary work.)

When creating process documentation in a top-down approach, you can consider existing behavior, but don't get drawn into "that's just the way we do it/that's the way we've always done it" scenarios. Top down is all about getting the content of your model right without wasting a significant amount of time on existing behavior.

Start by taking an interaction from your Facades view and reviewing it. What you are looking for are all the things the business must do internally to support the interaction. Essentially, you need to look for all the business process steps that will be required to make the interaction happen, not just for the happy path, but also for each of the alternates that make up the interaction. Do not worry about which departments will enact the steps, just make sure you document all the steps. You can assign the steps to roles, just not departments. You want to avoid departmental assignments at this point, because, again, you are looking for opportunities to restructure the business to better support the future state you are documenting. Make sure all the steps are documented, including both those that will be automated and those that should be manual. Make sure that every aspect of the interaction is supported.

Repeat documenting processes for each of the interactions in the Facades view. Document each process to cover all aspects of the interaction it supports. As you draft a process, compare it to the goals of the business to ensure you are prescribing steps that are aligned with the goals of the business. If the process effectively supports one or more interactions, there should be few gaps in the alignment between processes and goals; you need to make sure that you eliminate any remaining gaps.

Communications

Communications are important to any business, but it is just as important to ensure that the right communications occur at the right time and go to the right parties. The easiest way to make sure that this happens is to analyze your processes to discover what needs to be communicated to whom and when it needs to be communicated.

Start by looking at a process and evaluating where information needs to flow from the business to some external actor (somewhere in the rest of the world). Each of these points of information flow represents a potential for communication. Watch how the information flows through the process and document the flow using the communication diagram. Don't worry too much about existing communication flows; the top-down approach focuses mostly on the way things should work in the future state, not on how they work today.

Continue analyzing processes and documenting communication flows. With each communication, look at what information will need to flow and how it will be presented to the consumer of the information. In some cases, the communication will be a form or letter; in other cases, it might make more sense to forward information electronically using more advanced technologies. This is how you will build up your Communications view.

Business Entities

When working top down, business entities are typically one of the last things you document in your business architecture model. Business entities are the things the business needs to manipulate in the course of doing business, and so they are best discovered by looking at a well-documented model. Don't spend too much time worrying about existing documentation on business entities. If you've got existing documentation, you can consider it, but spend most of your time discovering and documenting the business entities you don't know about, not what the business does know about already.

Start by looking at the interactions in your Facades view. Read the documentation for the flows and capture in your business entity model all the nouns that show up. Each noun is a good candidate for being a business entity, a thing the business will want to know about, record, and manipulate. While you are looking at the interactions, also capture the actors involved. Each actor is very likely to be represented as a business entity in your model.

As you establish each business entity, understand and document the relationships it has with other business entities you've already documented. It is important for you to understand the relationships between business entities—the relationships are a representation of business rules that govern the operation of your business. Many of these relationships will be important to understand: they will shape how the business manipulates, validates, and stores data; they will govern how others will interact with the business; they will control product and/or service access. You don't have a view in your business architecture model dedicated just to business rules, but they are an important part of defining how your business will run, and so they need to be considered, especially in the context of your business entities.

After you analyze all the interactions for business entities, it's time to check the Processes and Communications views to see if there are any additional business entities that you need to include in your model. You'll use the same noun challenge technique to find all the nouns that are likely to be information that your business will care about. Make sure that you are not capturing the same business entity twice; you only need to define it once in your model. It's okay to show a business entity on more than one diagram within a model, but it can only be defined once. If you have more than one definition, you start to run into confusion over exactly what is meant when you speak of the business entity in question.

After you analyze all the views to find all the business entities that the business will care about, you can go through the business entity model you created to find ways to refine it. You will want to look at similar entities to see if you have an opportunity to use generalization to help define common aspects. You'll want to see whether aggregation can be used to describe how some things are really comprised of other things. Aggregation is an important relationship to capture because it represents another kind of business rule for the behavior of your business. The rules around how some things are built of other things are important to understand as part of the way information can be manipulated by your business. Generalization does not represent a type of business rule, but is very useful to avoid defining information more than once. Generalization allows you to capture common details about several different entities once, avoiding any concerns of keeping those details synchronized in several locations. (See Chapter 7 for information about both aggregation and generalization relationships.)

Pros and Cons of the Top-Down Approach

The primary advantage of the top-down approach is that you do not have to wait for projects or initiatives to provide you with the content that you will include in your model; you will create the vast majority of the model yourself. You are not as tied to the way things are done today in the business when working top down; often you focus simply on the future state. Focusing on just the future state often means that there is less cost to creating the content than if you had to create the same content going bottom up.

The single greatest disadvantage to building a business architecture model from the top down is that you will have to fund the effort to create all the content. This means that you will have to sell the business executives on the value of spending the money to create the model, whereas if you were going bottom up, you might be able to build a significant part of the model on the back of other initiatives, spending no money specifically on your model. You will also have to be careful that, since you are not typically focusing on the current state and not leveraging existing documentation, you don't get too disconnected from the realities of how the business needs to operate while you create your "ivory tower" model. (Some people will view it this way if they are not involved in the work.)

While you should be able to produce a business architecture model faster working top down than you will working bottom up, you will be more disconnected from the work of the business while working top down—so you need to make sure you deliver some usable content quickly if the business executives are going to see value in your work and continue to fund it. Remember that nothing sells like success, and this is especially important when you are working in what could be seen as isolation during a top-down modeling exercise.

In Your Business

Here are some things to consider when thinking about the top-down approach to business architecture modeling:

- Can you convince your business executives to pursue a business architecture modeling exercise?
- Will you have access to the right resources to gather the information needed to document your business architecture?
- Can you envision some quick wins that you could deliver as you create your business architecture model?

Summary

This chapter was all about creating a business architecture model using the top-down approach. This approach is used when there is little existing content to leverage within the business and/or when getting to a model quickly is important. This chapter discussed the following topics:

- When the top-down approach is most likely appropriate
- Starting with goals
- Dealing with the remaining views (Facades, Communications, Processes, and Business Entities)
- The pros and cons of the top-down approach

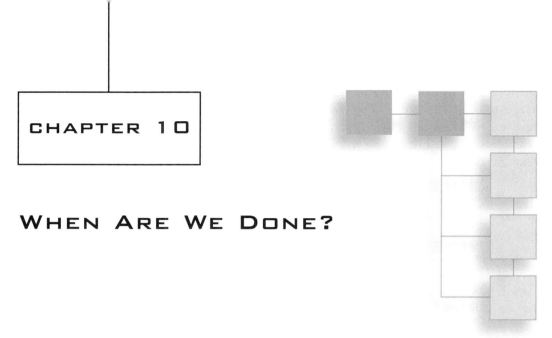

CHAPTER 10

WHEN ARE WE DONE?

So far, this book has discussed what comprises a business architecture model and has demonstrated two approaches to creating one. One critical point has been overlooked so far, though: When are we done? Is there even such a thing as "done" with this kind of work? What would "done" look like?

As long as the business continues to exist, the business architecture modeling work should continue; it is never really finished. However, you can and should set interim points at which you will be finished with a "latest iteration" of the model. In this chapter, the concept of completeness is examined, both in the context of the initial establishment of the model and in the context of future updates to the model.

Initial Business Architecture Work

The business architecture model has to be initiated at some point; it can't exist without having been created first. But it is only by setting criteria for what "done" will look like for your initial business architecture work that you will be able to avoid the nagging question: Are we there yet? It will inevitably be raised, either by yourself or by the business executives.

You must be clear about what you're trying to achieve with the initial business architecture work and make sure that what you deliver in each view of the model supports what you are trying to achieve. You may just be trying to understand your customer base and their needs; you may be looking for operational efficiencies within one area of your business; you may be looking for a complete understanding of your business' current state. Each of these options would require a different initial business modeling effort, and each case may allow you to plan for a smaller, tactical approach to putting your initial business architecture model in place.

Does the entire business need to be fully modeled in order for the business architecture model to be useful? Can you live with a subset of the model to start with, as long as you have a plan for working toward a more complete model over time? When talking about initial business architecture work, regardless of approach, it is important to understand what, at a bare minimum, will be sufficient content to be a *useful* initial model. You will need to think about all aspects of the model—all the views—collectively and in isolation. You need to think about, for example, what would be enough Goals view information to help you understand the goals of the organization, and also what would be enough Goals view information to help guide the work you will be doing in the other four views.

"Done" should not just be about creating documents and diagrams. It should be about serving a more profound, greater purpose. A more fundamental reason to be doing this work is to sort out a portfolio of projects and a roadmap for the projects that will satisfy that fundamental reason for doing the initial business architecture work in the first place.

Initial Goals View

The Goals view is probably the most problematic view when it comes to figuring out what is sufficient for an initial subset of work. The Goals view is typically small, relative to the work in other views, but it is vital in shaping the other views. Because of this, the best thing to do—regardless of the approach you choose—is to complete the Goals view in its entirety as part of any initial business architecture model. Anything other than the entire Goals view is difficult to plan and execute, especially if you are trying to make that subset of the Goals view truly useful. After all, the business needs to align these goals—if they aren't complete, it will be impossible to know if the alignment work that you do is going to be effective once the complete set of goals are in place.

If you are not going to complete the entire Goals view as part of your initial work, you need to ensure that the goals work you do perform will support the business and the work you will do in other views as part of the initial business architecture model. The best way to ensure this is to think about the overall reason for *why* you are doing the initial business architecture work. What are you trying to achieve? Are you trying to understand your customer base? Are you trying to look for organizational efficiencies in specific parts of the business?

You will need to document the overall (main) goal or goals of the business first, regardless of what else you are going to do in the Goals view, whether it is the full view or only a useful subset. After you have the main goal or goals of the business documented, you can then document the remaining goals necessary for your initial business architecture work. You can do this following either the bottom-up or the top-down approach (which you learned about in Chapters 8 and 9). It is very important to remember to get management buy-in to the goals that you document, especially when you are doing initial work. This is the first time you'll be doing this type of work for the business, and keeping them involved, especially in the goals and the value of the Goals view, will help them see what you are accomplishing, see what the value to the business is, and ensure you are getting the right cooperation and content from them in a timely fashion.

Your Goals view is complete when you have documented the goals that you stated you would have in place as part of your initial work.

Initial Facades View

The Facades view is generally easier to split up into a logical subset to deliver as part of the initial business architecture model. It is easy to focus on just the interactions that would be related to customers, for example, or to another specific area of the business. You also need to focus on whether you will be doing just current state, just future state, or both current and future state modeling. Again, you need to know this so that you will understand (and be able to communicate to others) what "done" will look like in your initial Facades view work.

The first thing you should do, before trying to settle on any interactions to document, is to try to understand what the various facades of the business are and create model packages for each facade. Then, within the package or packages you will work on first, create sub-packages to logically break up the facade into more manageable chunks. At this point you don't need to get the package structure perfect, you may find later that you need to further break up a package, you may need to amalgamate a couple of packages into one larger one, and so on. This is fine, don't worry too much about getting the final package structure perfect at the start; just make sure it is good enough that it will trigger thought about what you need to fill the packages with. What is important at this point is to provide a structure that makes logical sense to you and to your business partners. This may mean packaging by department, by customer type, by geographic region, or some other way. As long as you and the readers of your model can easily navigate through the structure you've created, you've got a good enough structure for now.

When you have your first cut at a package structure, you can begin to fill in the packages that represent what you want for your initial business architecture model. Regardless of the approach you take and regardless of how much of the Facades view you will initially do, you must ensure that the facades content you create aligns with the goals you documented. Each interaction that you document needs to align with one or more goals. This is, after all, no different than if you were building the entire model at once.

You will also need to know if you are going to diagram the entire Facades view, and not just the packages that are to be fully documented in the initial work, or will you only diagram what you document. Remember that you are using business use cases as the mechanism for creating the Facades view and that a business use case must consist of both the diagram and the document in order to be considered complete. You will be "done" when you have documented what you set out to document in the Facades view, including the appropriate diagramming.

As long as your Facades view isn't overwhelmingly large, you may want to go ahead and create business use-case diagrams for everything, even if you only intend to document a subset of it in your initial work. With the entire Facades view diagrammed, you have a visual map and index of the interactions that the business provides and that you will eventually need to document. The exercise of diagramming all the interactions at once may even force you to rethink your planning about which interactions to document first. You may discover some areas of the business that need even more business architectural attention than the ones you'd planned to address immediately. When your business is very large, the exercise of diagramming it all first might be more time-consuming than you can afford. Your sponsor may get tired of waiting for an ROI while you draw pictures. You will have to find the appropriate balance in your environment between diagramming it all first, and diagramming just what you will document.

Initial Processes, Communications, and Business Entities Views

After the initial Goals and Facades view work is complete (in whatever sense of "done" you previously defined), it becomes a straightforward exercise to sort out what initial work should be done on the Processes, Communications, and Business Entities views. The business processes that will be documented are those that support the interactions that you documented and diagrammed as part of your Facades view work. The communications that you will document are those that will support the interactions and business processes that you already created as part of the initial work. The business entities that you will document are those that represent the things that will be of interest to the business in the interactions, business processes, and communications you create in your initial business architecture modeling work.

A determination of whether you will need current state, future state, or both types of models as part of your initial work is necessary as you tackle these three views. You must figure out if you will need current state understanding of business processes, either for understanding of how the business processes should look in the future, for what the Communications view As Is model should contain, or for what the As Is state business entity model should contain. You also need to understand if you are going to need any of these current state versions in order to understand the gap between current state and the future state you are trying to achieve. This gap represents the portfolio of work that the business should be undertaking, so it is pretty critical to understand this gap thoroughly.

It is inadvisable to try to commit to only some part of a given business process or communication being documented as part of the initial business architecture modeling work. Understanding only part of a process never provides enough clarity to understand the gap between current and future states. The same can be said about a communication: it is never enough to have it partially documented. It is possible that you might be satisfied with only some aspects of a business entity being modeled initially; perhaps only some of the relationships are captured, or only the most readily evident attributes are documented, but think about this carefully before deciding to allow a business entity to only be partially documented as part of the initial work. Not documenting all the business entities initially, on the other hand, is a viable option. Just make sure you document all the business entities that are referenced in the rest of the initial model you are creating.

Finishing the Initial Work

You've done the modeling you said you wanted to as part of your initial work, but there's still some more work to do. What else did you commit to doing to consider your initial work "done"? Were you going to attempt to get a better understanding of your customers? Were you trying to re-engineer some aspect of the business? Now is the time to sort out what you still need to do in order to finish your initial work. Finishing your initial work will depend greatly on what you intended to get from your initial business architecture model.

There will always be some common tasks that need to be performed to consider any business architecture work done. You will need to do a gap analysis between your current state (whether documented or "understood") and the desired future state that your model indicates. This means a gap in interactions, processes, communications, and in business entities.

When your gap analysis is complete, you need to look at your current portfolio of projects. What is the business doing already to enhance and transform itself? How can you use the work that is already underway to assist in filling the gaps you identified? Perhaps the projects underway or scheduled will fill your gap? More likely, though, there will need to be more project work done beyond what is already scheduled, if the gaps you've identified are to be filled effectively. What you need to do is figure out what projects the business will have to undertake beyond what is already scheduled and then figure out the roadmap for the work. You also need to consider what to do with projects currently underway or scheduled that do not assist in filling your gap, or worse, that expand the gap between your current state and the desired future state. The best approach is to stop all the in-flight projects that are detrimental to your future state and try to rework their objectives. As for scheduled projects that are detrimental, they should simply be canceled.

The roadmap of project work will need to include everything that was already scheduled, as well as any work that needs to be done to fill the gaps. You need to not only consider your new work, but also the already planned work of the business as you figure out the order in which to execute the projects. Out of the entire portfolio of work, you need to consider what is foundational and what order it all needs to be executed in. You also need to take into consideration what the business needs are that will be fulfilled by the various projects that are part of the portfolio. If the business will see no immediate value from several foundational projects and will only perceive benefits after years of work, you will have a hard time selling the management team on the idea that you have the right roadmap to benefit the business. In fact, any roadmap will have to strike a balance between delivering immediate business value and building the foundation that the business needs to thrive in the future. This is the crux of the business architecture mandate—creating the right roadmap for the evolution of the business while executing the right projects in the right order. This mandate is true regardless of how much you attempt to do in your initial business architecture modeling work.

If you do anything less than the complete business architecture model as your initial work, there's another aspect of the roadmap that you seriously need to consider. You need to determine what effort will be required to get a complete business architectural picture of your business, and how you are going to achieve that picture. Are you going to build the rest on the back of future project work? This is an option, but you might risk doing the wrong project work because you don't already have a full business architecture model. Will you build it as a project on its own? Possibly, but understand that your business may undertake projects in the meantime that are not in their best interest because you lack a model. Your roadmap must include the work you need to do to complete the picture of the business that your model will provide.

Finishing the Business Architecture Model

The assumption in the early part of this chapter was that you would not create your entire business architecture model at once, but instead, build enough to get started on a portfolio of projects that will show the business a positive ROI for the work you've done. The business architecture model, however, is still only partially completed, and there is still work to be done. You need to get the model to the point where it reflects the entire business. This will mean doing a gap analysis between what you have modeled and your best understanding of what the entire business architecture model will need to contain. This gap represents the work remaining to get to a business architecture model that covers the entire business. You can either fill that gap with a single all-in-one project, or through accretion of content over time. Following is a discussion of the pros and cons of each approach.

Pros and Cons of the All-in-One Approach

All-in-one fundamentally means completing the picture of the business in one effort. This means that regardless of whether you are building the business architecture model in a top-down or bottom-up approach, you won't consider your work done until all aspects of the business are included in the model.

The value in choosing the all-in-one approach is that you build a *complete* model that you can use when it is done. While you might get some incremental value from parts of the model being available earlier in the accretion approach (see the following section), you will have a better roadmap and portfolio of work faster if you follow the all-in-one approach. Choosing all-in-one also means that you will not have to try to make interim project portfolio judgements based on an incomplete business architecture model; you will have the whole model in place, which will allow you to use it for all portfolio decisions from the start.

The drawback to the all-in-one approach is that you will have to take the time and considerable resources to deliver the entire model before it is considered done and therefore useable. It will typically take you longer to get value from the model using this approach.

Pros and Cons of the Accretion Approach

Accretion is the build-up of something over time by the application of smaller parts to some nucleus. The accretion approach to the initial business architecture model, then, is the approach that builds the complete picture over time by the application of small additional bits of the model to a nucleus of the model that was previously created.

When you use the accretion approach to create your initial model, you will have a usable model sooner than you would if you had to wait for the entire model to be built. You can start to influence the portfolio of projects earlier, and thus align work with the roadmap for evolving the business. You will also find that you usually get more sponsor support if you can show some value early, before the entire business architecture model is complete. Let's say that you want to build the model relative to your customer base first. You can then at least start to launch projects that will benefit the business relative to the business' customer base.

Of course, the danger of making decisions based on an incomplete picture is that the parts of the picture you can't see might hold information that would cause you to make a different decision if the information were available to you. You cannot be *certain* you are making sound decisions until you have the complete model in place, and if you've been following the accretion approach, you may launch work that you wouldn't have if you had the complete picture. You can't be sure about the usefulness and accuracy of the model until it contains the entire picture.

Ongoing Changes

The good news is that when your initial business architecture model is done (in whatever state of completeness you determined at the start of the building process), you have a base for continuous improvement work. Two things have to happen to ensure that your model remains useful to the business. The first is that you ensure all projects contribute to the model as they complete their work and deliver it. The second is that business architects need to be part of the business planning cycle (at least annually, or whatever other time frame the business determines).

Incorporating Project Content

Projects typically change some aspect of interactions, communications, processes, and business entities. Projects should not change goals, but they can often help implement changes to goals that the business wants to modify. These changes, of course, are the same things that the business architecture model is interested in. If you set the right policies in place, projects will produce content in such a way as to be useful to the model as well. Of course the flip-side is that the business architecture model should be the mechanism by which projects are launched, which means that the model should already have some of the content from the project just by virtue of the project having been launched.

When the business architecture model is used as the framework for launching a project, some of the content will have been created by the business architects during the planning work that lead up to the project being launched. The project, though, will typically elaborate on the work from the business architecture model, making it more detailed and more complete. The model might only identify, for instance, the fact that a new interaction is needed, what the primary flow of the interaction should look like, and that there are alternate flows needed for the interaction. The project, then, would be expected to finish detailing all remaining aspects of the interaction. Similar sorts of things might happen for a process, a communication, or a business entity. The business architecture model might provide some detail about one or more elements of one or more of these views, but you can expect that a project will then finish elaborating the content.

When the project finishes content for any of these views, you need to ensure that the project content gets back to the business architecture model. This means that the project will have to leverage the content you've started, follow the standards you've set, and then give you the updates when they finish their project. Once projects are used to the process of interacting with the business architecture—as a mechanism for launching the right projects and as a repository for their key artifacts after they go to production—you can be assured that your model will remain current and accurately reflect the realities of the business. This is key to being able to use your model as a picture of current state at any time, going forward, and for using your model as the starting point for further business architecture work. It is vital that the business understand the value they will receive by making the investment to ensure projects feed your model.

The Business Planning Cycle

As long as a business wants to continue to exist, it needs a vision, and as long as the business has a vision, it needs to plan how it is going to achieve its vision. Business architecture is about documenting that vision via its various views and then planning how to achieve the future state the views represent via the roadmap and project portfolio. Whatever the planning cycle the business has, business architecture should be front and center during the planning work.

The business planning cycle should be scheduled at least annually as input to preparing the budget for the upcoming fiscal year. This way the budget is determined based on the right portfolio of project work for the coming year. Depending on how dynamic the business environment is, you may need to plan with greater frequency than once a year. The roadmap may give you some clues as to the appropriate frequency for planning cycles in your business.

Whatever the frequency, the outcome of the plan needs to be captured in the business architecture model. Every planning decision made will have implications for the model, be it new goals, a change in product or service focus, or just a push to satisfy specific business needs. Any of these things might have an impact on goals, facades, processes, communications, and/or business entities.

More importantly, the business architecture model should be a significant input to the planning exercise. It is, after all, a snapshot of your business in its current state, along with the envisioned future state and the roadmap to get there. The business architecture model, by its very nature, is all about planning; it provides a framework for discussing what changes can be undertaken and what the impact of those changes to the business might be. Convince your business executives that they have a significant tool at their disposal, one that will help increase understanding and decrease time to effective decisions, and you will be a welcome attendee at the planning table.

In Your Business

Here are some things to consider in thinking about when you will be done with your business architecture work:

- How much business architecture modeling would you need to do in order to start positively affecting your business?
- How would you approach finishing the business architecture model after your initial work is done?
- What would be some appropriate ways to get your business architecture model used as a business decision-making tool?
- Can you see ways of tying business architecture into your business planning cycle(s)?

Summary

This chapter explored what it means to be done in the context of business architecture. While the business architecture model will evolve forever, there are stages when it can be considered complete, relative to the existing business vision. The chapter discussed the following:

- Planning initial business architecture work, including work on the five views (Goals, Facades, Communications, Processes, and Business Entities).

- Finishing up the initial work.
- Finishing up the model after the initial work is done, including pros and cons of both the all-in-one and accretion approaches.
- Recognizing that business architecture is not a one-shot deal—it needs to evolve over time.
- How to include business architecture into business planning cycles.

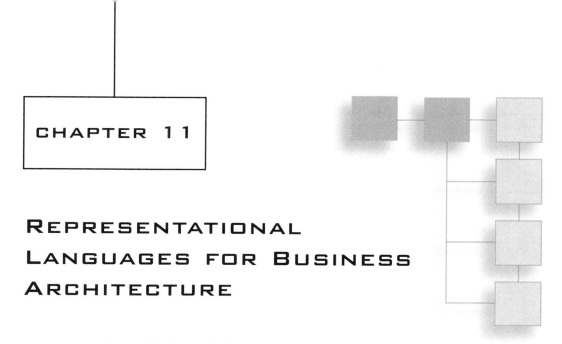

CHAPTER 11

REPRESENTATIONAL LANGUAGES FOR BUSINESS ARCHITECTURE

anguage is a critical part of all our communications. But unless we agree to a set of symbols, structures, and meanings, we simply cannot understand each other; we cannot effectively communicate. This is equally true when it comes to business architecture models. The models you create will be large, complex, information-rich artifacts. If it is not created using consistent language, no matter how accurate your model is, it will be useless as a means of communicating your vision of a future state for the business.

It is extraordinarily frustrating to be handed a document or diagram that has symbols you can recognize but the usage of those symbols doesn't match any structure you understand. The artifact doesn't follow language conventions, and so it requires clarification before it can be understood. There have been, in extreme cases, documents or diagrams where the creator of the content essentially had to travel with the artifact in order to explain it to each reader. While this may sound like a path to job security for the content creator, these folks are often sent packing if they don't start complying with standard language rules.

While language is very important for the artifacts that will make up a business architecture model, it is important to note that there is no single modeling language that will be able to capture all the complexity of the entire model. What is important, though, is to at least use a single language across an entire view of the model. Also important is to declare—explicitly—on each diagram what language is being used. This will remove ambiguity and give your readers all the information they need to understand what you are trying to communicate. See Table 11.1 for the basic modeling language options a business architect has to choose from.

Table 11.1 Modeling Language Options

UML (including UML 2)	The Unified Modeling Language (UML) is a diagramming language standard that is defined by a committee of industry experts, publicly available for use, and managed by the Object Management Group (www.omg.org). UML has a very rich lexicon of symbols and, using an extensibility concept called stereotyping, can support reasonably well all the views of the business architecture model.
BPMN	The Business Process Modeling Notation (BPMN) is a rich diagramming language specific to business processes. BPMN is, like UML, a language defined by a committee of industry experts and managed by the Object Management Group (www.omg.org).
	One of the burning questions of practitioners in the field of business process modeling is this: will BPMN and UML be merged in an update? You are just going to have to wait and see, or volunteer with OMG and be part of the decision.
IDEF	IDEF stands for Integrated Computer-Aided Manufacture (ICAM) Definition. Created as an initiative of the United States Air Force in the 1970s, IDEF is a loosely federated set of diagramming languages related to software and systems engineering. Diagram types supported include function modeling (IDEF0 diagrams), data modeling (IDEF1x diagrams), process modeling (IDEF3 diagrams), and others. While newer languages have replaced IDEF for new work, older businesses may have a rich legacy of IDEF diagrams available as input to business architecture modeling. This is often the language that most business people are familiar with.
ERD	The Entity Relationship Diagram uses a standard syntax and symbol set for diagramming basic relationships between entities (and by extension business entities). ERD is not a formal language as much as it is a diagram type. The standards for an ERD diagram also fail to include some of the more advanced relationships (generalization, aggregation) that a well-detailed Business Entities view needs to include.
Data Flow	Data flow does not represent a modeling language, either. Data flows were a very early set of symbols used by programmers and designers to show how data would flow through a system. This set of symbols can still be used for showing how information will flow in business processes. The symbols and syntax, however, are not rich enough to really do justice to all the details needed in a Business Processes view.

So then, what are the language options for each view? What is the preferred option and what conditions make one language more suitable than another? Let's look view by view at what the options are so that you can determine what will work best in your environment.

The Goals View Language

The Goals view poses some of the greatest challenges when it comes to language standards because it is one of the least established model views, despite its vital importance to the business architecture model.

Because goals are hierarchical and organizational in nature, a representation that is akin to an organization (org) chart is very useful (see Figure 11.1). There is no standard for creating Goals view diagrams, so language choice is really up to the business architect.

The UML class diagram is probably the best choice, since so much of the rest of the business architecture model is best documented using UML diagrams.

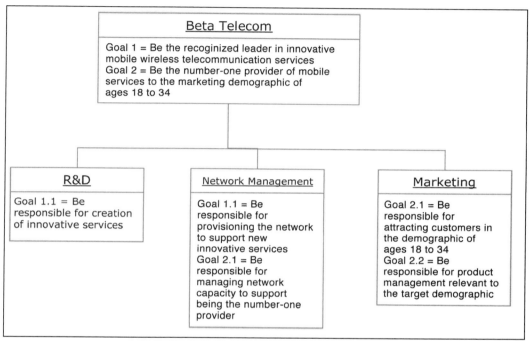

Figure 11.1
Sample goals diagram for a pretend company Beta Telecom.

We can build an org chart–like diagram using many different diagramming tools. Regardless of the tool we use, though, we need to set up some rules and guidelines to ensure that you model the business' goals in a way that is consistent and easy to read.

Each goal should be represented in a rectangular box. The box should, at the top, name the area of the business that will strive for the goal, and below the area name, listed in priority order, should be the goal or goals that the area will be striving for.

The overall goal or goals of the business should be shown at the top of the diagram. Each direct sub-goal should be at the same horizontal level below the main goal. Each sub-goal should be, again, on the same horizontal level, but below the sub-goal level. Because a sub-goal is a decomposition of a goal, you line all the sub-goals of a single goal close to vertically underneath it, while ensuring that all the sub-goals remain on the same horizontal level (see Figure 11.2).

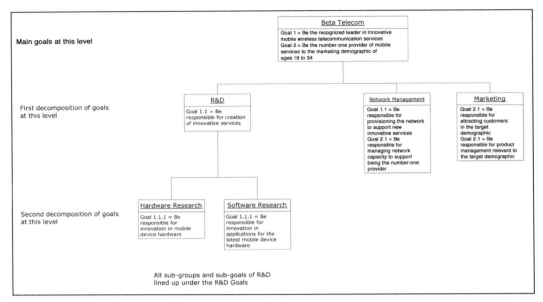

Figure 11.2
Goals diagram showing vertical and horizontal alignment.

Try to avoid decomposing goals to more than about four layers; beyond that you typically find the goals are actually becoming tasks. You link goals together with a simple solid line.

The Facades View Language

Facades are all about the interactions that the rest of the world will have with your business. You need to use a language that will allow you to represent what all the interactions are, who participates in those interactions, and under what conditions the interactions are allowed. UML is very well-suited to diagrammatically representing the interactions you and your audience will be interested in. The business use case (a stereotype of the use-case symbol) along with the business actor (a stereotype of the actor symbol), give you what you will need to diagram the interactions that make up the facades of your business. You will use these symbols along with relationships and packages to structure the diagrams and their contents (see Figure 11.3).

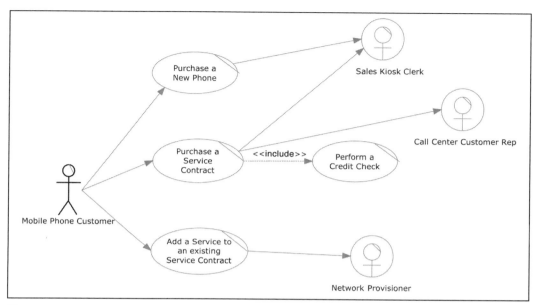

Figure 11.3
Sample business use-case diagram for Beta Telecom.

Remember, though, that a use-case diagram on its own does not convey sufficient information about an interaction. You will also need to document the flows of each interaction,
both when things go well and the primary actor achieves their goal the way you want them
to, and when they follow alternate behavior that either ultimately gets them to their goal
(succeeds) or doesn't (fails). This level of detail cannot be shown in a use-case diagram
because the definition of the syntax for a use-case diagram excludes any sort of representation of flow; the arrows on these diagrams simply represent communication between
elements. UML can still help you, though. The *UML activity diagram* is designed to show
the flow of activities, including the conditions for branching to an alternate path, return-
ing from another path, and even showing concurrent behavior. For each business use case
in your model, you will typically create one activity diagram. In the case of a very large,
complex business use case, you may provide one main activity diagram that shows the overall flow, and then supply one or more sub-activity diagrams that detail at finer granularity
one part of the overall flow of the business use case (see Figure 11.4).

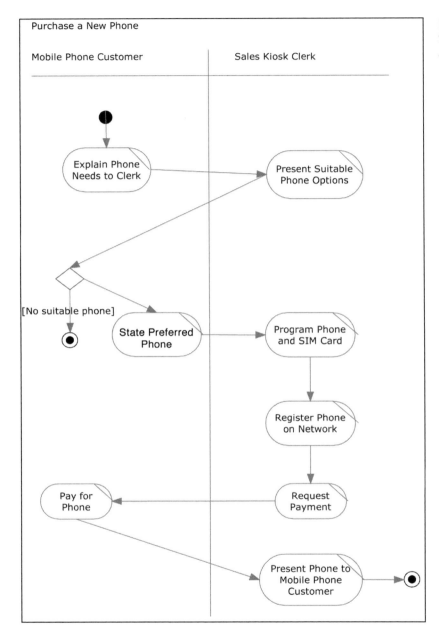

Figure 11.4
Sample business activity diagram.

Note that in Figure 11.4 when a phone is available, there is no guard condition on the flow from the decision. When there is no guard condition, this is considered the default flow and will only be executed if every other guard condition is false. There can be no more than one default flow out of a decision.

There is, arguably, still a need for a business use-case document above and beyond the activity diagrams that represent each interaction. You should create a separate business use-case document for each interaction or business use case in your Facades view. The business use-case document gives you a chance to collect and present information about the interaction beyond the flows: the goal of the primary actor, the pre and post conditions of executing the flow, the responsibilities of other actors participating in the flows. The business use-case document also contains a textual description of the flows, including all branching points. These textual descriptions of the flows benefit you in two ways beyond only providing the flows as activity diagrams:

1. You facilitate ease of understanding of what you are communicating with people who think textually rather than visually.

2. You give yourself a quality control check by writing the content two ways; whichever way you go first, when you create the content the second way, it helps you catch errors in what you documented first.

There is no other effective language for documenting your Facades view. IT architects have traditionally tried to represent business functionality using block diagrams that show functional decomposition of the business, but these sorts of diagrams are nowhere near as information-rich as the content you can produce using UML. These functional decomposition diagrams also fail to describe the intent and flows of the interaction.

One other approach possible with the Facades view is to document the interactions purely textually. Start with an index table that names each interaction, the primary user of the interaction, and their goal in using the interaction. In this scenario, you are still well advised to write a business use-case document detailing the flows and scenarios that are covered for each interaction (see Figure 11.5).

Actor	Goal	Interaction(s)
Mobile Phone Customer	Acquire a mobile phone	Purchase a mobile phone
	Acquire mobile phone service	Purchase a service contract
		Add a service to an existing contract
	Use a mobile phone	Make a phone call
		Use a 3G service
Government Licensing Agent	Ensure service is licensed	Review mobile phone company operating license
And so on		

Figure 11.5
Sample interaction index table for Beta Telecom.

The Processes View Language

People have been paying attention to process diagramming for quite some time, so there are several language options for creating content for this view. There are very traditional languages, like data flows or IDEF diagrams, and there are more recent options like UML and BPMN. While some of your users might be more comfortable with more traditional process diagram styles, you should really only consider recent languages as real modeling options.

UML offers a fairly rich syntax for diagramming process flows via the activity diagram. By liberally applying stereotypes to all the elements in an activity diagram, you can make it obvious to your audience that you're documenting a business process (see Figure 11.6). Please note that in this diagram, each activity has been stereotyped as a business activity to remind the reader that it represents a business process (and not a process within an IT system, which was the original intent of UML).

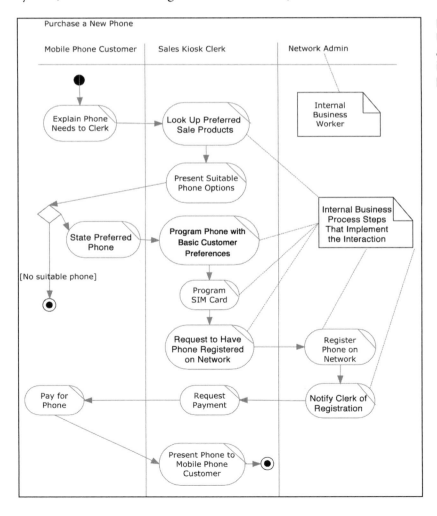

Figure 11.6 UML business activity diagram illustrating a process.

The advantage to using UML for your Processes views is that you will be using the same language as you did for your Facades view, which leads to the following benefits:

- You can use the same diagramming tool for both views.
- You can more readily demonstrate traceability between interactions and the businesses that support them because they are modeled in the same language.
- You only need to learn a single language.
- You only have to teach your audience how to read a single language; they already need to know how to read UML activity diagrams to read your interactions; they can apply that same knowledge to read your business process diagrams.

There are really only two disadvantages to using UML to capture business process diagrams, and only one of those disadvantages creates a real roadblock to success:

- UML activity diagrams don't look like the more traditional diagrams that process people are used to. Some critics object to these diagrams as being "too technical looking" or "not enough like the kind of swim-lane diagrams we're used to." Of course, with a bit of support through the learning curve, almost anyone can read these diagrams and see how much more information-rich they are than traditional swim-lane diagrams.
- UML activity diagrams can express most, but not all, business process content. UML does not easily express things such as time as a trigger or delay, messages as a means of invoking behaviors, and groups of related swim-lanes.

The first disadvantage can be overcome fairly readily; the second disadvantage is more problematic. If your business does not need to deal with some of the complexities that UML doesn't handle, then by all means, use UML as the language that you model business processes in.

If the disadvantages to using UML activity diagrams for your Processes view would negatively affect your ability to do your business architecture work, you can use BPMN. Please see Chapter 6 for a discussion of BPMN as a process modeling language.

The Communications View Language

Communication is all about what information needs to flow from where to where, who is involved in the flow, and what their role is in the flow. For example, consider the communications that occur when a customer orders a house to be built in a new subdivision. There will be communications with the bank regarding funds. There will be communications with the construction crew, which may include communications to sub-trades or building supply companies. There will be communications with local utilities. All sorts of communications may be launched as a result of a single interaction, and the orchestration of the various communications will be very important. For instance, as the home builder, you probably want to complete the communication with the bank that confirms your customer will be able to pay before you start communications with building suppliers to order the materials to build the customer's house.

So, then, how do you model all of this information about communications? There are two parts to the answer to this question. First, you need to be able to describe a single communication (like the lumber order that the home builder will send to the building supply company, including arranging for the shipping and unloading of the materials). This sort of information is well represented in a *UML communication diagram.* This type of diagram shows who participates in the communication and the order of the flow of information in a communication (see Figure 11.7).

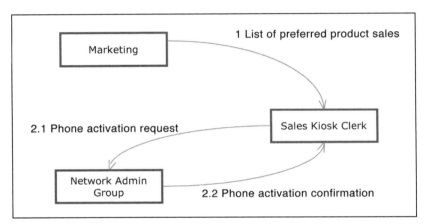

Figure 11.7
Sample communication diagram for Beta Telecom.

The second part of describing communication involves showing the orchestration of related communications. This is best done as part of process flows. Both UML and BPMN allow for the representation of communication objects as part of processes. This means that in your process diagrams, you can show the inter-relationships between and orchestration of communications within your business. (See Chapter 6 for more details on how to show the flow of a communication within a process.) If you're using some other language to represent your processes (whether by choice, as a result of a legacy of content, or by executive fiat), you will need to determine how you intend to represent the orchestration of communications (see Figure 11.8).

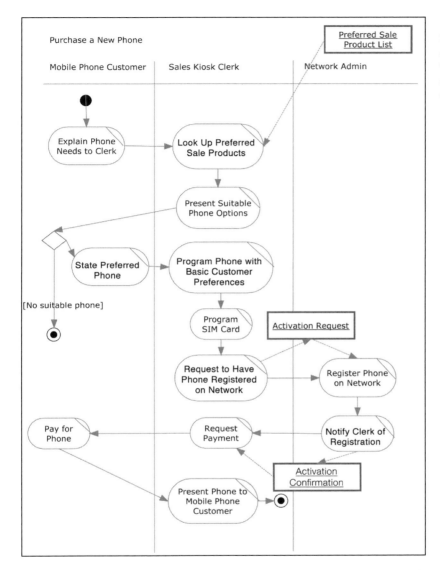

Figure 11.8
Sample UML activity diagram with communication object flow.

The language choice you make for representing communications needs to support the types of communications you will have to document, and will also need to help you demonstrate how the communications tie in with process flows and with interactions.

The Business Entities View Language

Business entities are another aspect of businesses that people have been paying attention to for quite some time. Whether they were referred to as entities, objects, business entities, or just "things" or information, businesses have long been aware of the need to understand what business entities and business entity relationships were important to them. As a result, there have been a number of languages developed over the years to model business entities. The earlier languages include IDEF and data flow diagrams. The most recent and information-rich language for modeling the business entity is UML.

When using UML, you create class diagrams, document the attributes and ignore "methods," and you employ stereotyping to turn your generic classes into business entity symbols on the diagrams. Classes are a concept from the object-oriented programming discipline in IT. Everything is an object, and objects are categorized into classes when they are all essentially the same type of thing (e.g., a rose growing in a garden is an *object* of the class *Flower*). Each class has *attributes*, which are additional facts or information about objects in that class (e.g., each object of the class Flower would have *number of petals* and *color* as attributes). *Methods* are the things that a class can do and are not relevant to the use of classes in a Business Entities view. (See also Chapter 7 for a discussion on classes and relationships.)

When you create a business entity diagram, regardless of which language you are using, start by naming the entities that you want on the diagram. You typically have to discover these business entities by reading through your other documentation and looking for nouns. Because nouns name things, and things are typically what you want to include in business entity diagrams, consider each noun you discover in your model and ask yourself whether the business will care about instances of this thing. If the answer is yes, then you've used the noun challenge technique to successfully discover a business entity that belongs somewhere in your model.

As you start to record the business entities in your model, you will hear about information related to them that is also of interest to the business. You will have to decide if the related information is an attribute of the entity, or if it is a separate entity that shares a relation-ship with the first entity. A good rule of thumb is that if there can only ever be one instance of that bit of information, it is an attribute, but if there can be more than one instance related to a specific business entity, then you have a separate entity that may have one or more attributes of its own.

An example of an attribute would be Hat Size or Age for a Retail Customer business entity; there will only ever be a single value of either Hat Size or Age for any Retail Customer. When it comes to Phone Number, though, there may be a number of different phone numbers you might want to record for a Retail Customer (business, home, cellular, and so on), so Phone Number is better off being a separate business entity with a relationship to the Retail Customer business entity. As you are defining and modeling business entities, you will dis-cover or surmise relationships between them. Be sure to capture relationships as soon as you are aware of them. The relationships will help you understand what needs to know about what else within the business. The relationships also help you discover rules about how many of one instance of an entity can be related to an instance of another entity. (For example, you may only want one representative from your business client to be associated with the primary contact of that business.) See Figure 11.9.

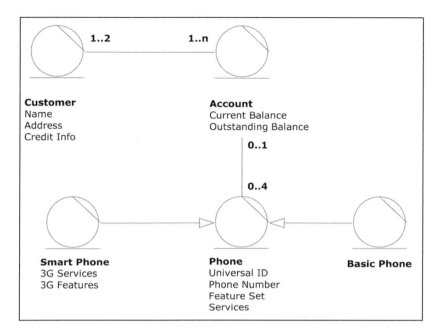

Figure 11.9
Sample UML class diagram stereotyped to show business entities.

Any of the languages named earlier can represent business entities and the basic relationships between then. All these languages can represent the cardinality of the relationships with varying degrees of accuracy.

UML, however, provides you with the capability to not only capture basic relationships, but also more advanced relationships like the fact that one business entity is a special case of another business entity (generalization), or a business entity is built up of other business entities (aggregation). If you are not using UML to model your Business Entities view, you will need to find some other way, appropriate to the modeling language you are using, to represent generalization and aggregation relationships. Realistically, generalization is an object-oriented technique that allows you to simplify your model, but you could create useful models without its use. Aggregation, on the other hand, is a very useful relationship at times and one that does not just represent notational shorthand. You won't use it often, but you will need to occasionally represent aggregation relationships somehow, at some point.

Realize that a Business Entities view can become very large and complex, and as a result it is seldom possible to represent it all on a single diagram. You will need to be able to split your model into effective, informational diagrams, so be aware that sometimes a single business entity may have to appear on more than one diagram. The actual business entity should only be defined once, regardless of how many different diagrams it may have to appear on.

Other Content/Languages

You may, on certain occasions, have to model additional information above and beyond what is captured in these five views. As an example, it might be important for you to capture all the stages an application form might have to go through from the time a potential customer requests it until the application is adjudicated and the potential customer is informed of the decision. This type of information is well-suited to a state diagram. Understanding what age restrictions apply to purchasing of certain products would be another example of information that doesn't fit the five views but might be of real importance to the business architecture model. In this case, you would be describing one or more business rules.

What you need to be able to do is identify when you have information that needs to be in the model but doesn't fit into the five views, and how you will capture that information when you do need it. The five-view model will capture the vast majority of information needed in most business architecture models. When you've got something that doesn't fit, you must ask whether it legitimately needs to be part of the model. If it does need to be part of the model, look at a very inclusive language like UML and determine how to best represent the information. If UML can't help you represent the information, look to the Internet for ideas about how others have captured similar information and build on their ideas.

After you figure out how you will represent this information, you need to figure out how to tie this information into your business architecture structure. Where will it fit? Where will you show linkage to elements of the five views?

Model Relationships

How will you tie the various views of your model together? You need some way of demonstrating to your stakeholders that a given process supports a specific facade interaction, which in turn helps achieve a goal. After all, alignment of the business architecture model is vital to getting the business focused on moving itself in the right direction. *Traceability* is the means by which you can demonstrate alignment.

Traceability is about showing how a lower-level thing is derived from a higher-level thing, typically by attaching an ID number to each of the things and building a matrix of relationships between the ID numbers. This can be done manually, though that is never a fun prospect. There are tools (typically called *requirements management tools*) that help manage the traces between elements, as well as aid in impact and coverage analyses. Regardless of the approach you take to tracing elements in your business architecture model, the most important thing is that the traces are done.

Coverage and impact analyses originally come from requirements management work done within projects, but they can readily be applied to the work of business architecture. *Coverage analysis* takes a look at a model to see if lower-level elements actually realize all the things implied by the higher-level content. As an example, you could do coverage analysis to ensure that all goals are supported by interactions in the facades by communications, processes, and business entities. You may also do another type of coverage analysis to see if all interactions are supported by processes. *Impact analysis* is about understanding what a change would do to your model (and therefore to the business). When a change is proposed, you look at what highest-level elements of your business architecture model (the goals) are implicated by the change. Once this is understood, you can use your traces to see what lower-level elements need to be investigated to see if they will also be impacted by the change. Any lower-level model elements that don't trace from the implicated goals won't be impacted by the change.

In Your Business

Here are some things to consider when thinking about representational languages for business architecture in your business:

- What would be the best way to document goals in your business?
- What would be the best way to document facades and interactions in your business?
- What would be the best way to document communications in your business?
- What would be the best way to document processes in your business?
- What would be the best way to document business entities in your business?

Summary

This chapter has discussed options for the language used to represent the various views of a business architecture model, including the following:

- Goals, showing horizontal and vertical alignment
- Facades and interactions, including ways of listing, diagramming, and documenting them
- Communications and how communication flows can be partially reflected in processes
- Processes and how to diagram them
- Business entities and how to diagram them
- Traceability and its use in coverage and impact analysis

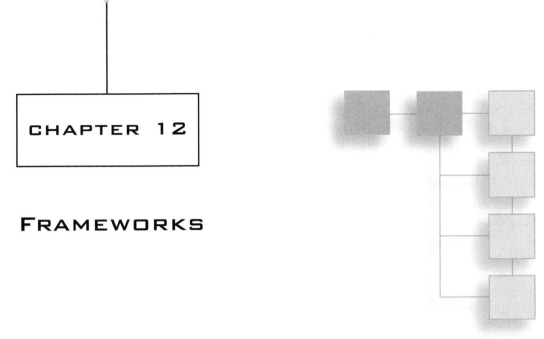

CHAPTER 12

FRAMEWORKS

Framework: *a basic conceptional structure (as of ideas)*. (From Merriam-Webster online: www.merriam-webster.com/dictionary/framework.)

A framework is a structure that can be shaped and utilized in multiple related circumstances to satisfy a given need. Architectural frameworks, then, are model frameworks that provide structure to enable you to represent the complexities of the concept you want to capture.

This book presents a framework for gathering information about your business into five views that, together, give a full view of the business. This framework does not, however, address IT architecture (the architecture of the technology systems that support the business). In order to be fully effective, both the business and IT architectures need to be aligned into a holistic view of the entire business. Business and IT architects need to share responsibility for ensuring that this alignment takes place.

Many frameworks have been developed to capture information technology architecture models. Historically, most of them started with a fairly narrow focus, concentrating only on the physical architecture of IT systems to support business. This meant capturing information about what applications were on what computer servers and what integrations existed between them (often in the form of file feeds in the early days). The focus was on how a system or application physically fit into its operational environment.

Over time, IT architecture matured, expanding its focus from just the physical layer to more abstract logical layers. Data, gaining recognition as a highly valuable resource, started getting much more attention; thus data architecture became part of the framework. As the applications grew more complex, application, or system, architecture was developed and expanded. Similar focus was also being given to infrastructure and the security aspects of IT.

All aspects of the technology that supplied IT solutions were being designed and constructed. As these various pieces of architecture were brought together, frameworks that would give them structure and tie the various levels together became more popular. IT architects adopted these early frameworks simply because it made their lives easier. They could easily see how to shape their architectural models that would represent the information technology of their business.

There was a gap, though, in the ability to fit IT architecture with the needs of the business. Business-IT alignment was (and often still is) considered a core problem in most large businesses. The answer to this vital issue was to take a look at the business itself and develop an IT architecture that corresponded to that business. This more holistic approach was dubbed *enterprise architecture,* and it invariably called for some semblance of business architecture. Unfortunately, there often wasn't a sufficient definition of business architecture to give the right level of business information. There were some good frameworks, however, that did begin to address the gap and move toward a holistic enterprise architecture even if they still were largely IT focused.

All the aspects of enterprise architecture have traditionally been done by IT architects, and their focus has been to understand just enough of the business to shape their IT architectural models, not on creating models that the business could use to shape itself. As business architecture matures, there is an opportunity to integrate the contents of a business architecture model with the contents of an IT architecture model to get to a true enterprise architecture model that is useful to both business and technology. This will mean that business architects and IT architects will have to work together to achieve a common goal.

Some of the popular IT enterprise architecture frameworks include The Zachman Framework, the POLDAT (Process, Organization, Location, Data, Applications, Technology) framework, and TOGAF (The Open Group Architecture Framework). Each of these architectural frameworks is noted for its usefulness, originally in the IT space, and now more holistically in the enterprise architecture space. If your IT team is using one of these frameworks, you may need to fit the contents of your business architecture model into it to get to that holistic enterprise architecture mentioned previously. This chapter explores the fit with these popular frameworks.

Business Architecture and The Zachman Framework

The Zachman Framework is widely noted as being one of the first frameworks to support the notion of enterprise architecture. John Zachman (originator of this framework that bears his name) recognized the business-IT alignment gap and addressed it by elaborating on his original framework to create one that covers all aspects of enterprise architecture.

The Zachman Framework is based on a six-by-six matrix that defines 36 distinct views of the enterprise, as shown in Table 12.1.

Table 12.1 The Zachman Framework

Zachman	What	How	Where	Who	When	Why
Scope	view	view	view	...	...	...
Business Model	view	view	...	...	...	...
System Model	view	...	...	...	...	...
Technology Model	...	...	...	...	...	...
Detailed Representations	...	...	...	...	...	...
Functioning Enterprise	...	...	...	...	...	...

The rows of the matrix represent different perspectives of an enterprise. Each perspective is unique; there is no implication that one perspective is in any way an elaboration of a higher row perspective. The rows should be thought of as orthogonal (or independent of each other). The columns of the matrix represent the fundamental questions that need to be answered for each of the perspectives. The intersection of a row and column in the framework, then, contains a view that represents the answer relative to a perspective that the business needs to understand for its architecture.

So which views of The Zachman Framework correspond to the views of the business architecture model, and how do we relate the Zachman and business architecture frameworks to get to something useful for the business? In fact, there isn't a single view-to-view mapping. What is found, instead, is that aspects of the business architecture views show up across many of the views of The Zachman Framework, but never completely within any one view. (Further information about The Zachman Framework can be found on the Internet, including www.zachmaninternational.com.)

Fit with the Goals View

Goals tend to answer the "what" question across the perspectives of The Zachman Framework. The most pertinent perspectives to answering the "what" question and supply business goal information are the following:

- **Scope**: The main goals will be found here.
- **Business model**: Sub-goals will be found here.
- **Functioning enterprise**: The operational organization onto which the goals are overlaid.

In each of these areas of The Zachman Framework, the Goals view of the business architecture model helps express what the business wants to be in the future.

Fit with the Facades View

"How," "where," and "who" are the key questions answered in the Facades view. Interactions are about who and how, while understanding where involves both the interactions and the facades. The perspectives that need to be looked at are the following:

- **Scope**: Where facades are defined
- **Business model**: Where you will find the interactions

In each of these sections of The Zachman Framework, the Facades view of the business architecture model helps express what the interactions with the business will look like.

Fit with the Processes View

Process comes from the "who," "how," and "when" questions. Process is all about who does what and when they do it. When considering the business processes, the perspectives needed are the following:

- **Scope**: Where high-level processes will be discovered
- **Business model**: Where the detailed processes will be defined
- **Operational enterprise**: Where the definition of the organization will define the "swimlanes" that parcel out who does which tasks within the process

In each of these sections of The Zachman Framework, the Processes view of the business architecture model helps express how the business will operate internally.

Fit with the Communications View

Any of the six questions can include an aspect of communications, which does not show up as a central focus in this framework. Communications pertinent to the business architecture will be found in the following:

- **Scope**: Inter-business communications can be inferred from this perspective.
- **Business model**: Inter- and intra-business communications can be found here.

In each of these views of The Zachman Framework, the Communications view of the business architecture model helps express how communications will shape the behavior of the business.

Fit with the Business Entities View

Business entities are the "whos" and "whats" of the framework because these are all the "things" that the business cares to have information about. They can be found in several of the perspectives because business entity information pervades so much of the business. You can find business entities in the following:

- **Scope**: Major business entities such as Customer are found here.

- **Business model**: Most business entities will be found here.

- **System model**: Business entities and their implementations in technology can be found here.

- **Operational enterprise**: Business entities like the various business worker actors will be found here.

In each of these sections of The Zachman Framework, the Business Entities view of the business architecture model helps express information that will need to be understood and/or manipulated by the business.

Whenever possible, consider creating your understanding of the business using the business architecture model, and when The Zachman Framework is used by the IT architects, supply them with pointers to the relevant sections of your model that they can put into their framework.

Business Architecture and the POLDAT Framework

POLDAT (Process, Organization, Location, Data, Applications, Technology) is another popular IT architecture framework that integrates aspects of the business into its concept of enterprise architecture, and it takes a different approach to framing enterprise architecture. Instead of explicitly asking the architect to consider six questions like The Zachman Framework does, the POLDAT framework simply implies them. POLDAT stands for the six "dimensions" of modeling that must be considered to get a complete picture. This framework is capable of considering the business at different levels of granularity, from a holistic overview of the enterprise to a very detailed look at specific implementation details.

The POLDAT framework is often shown as a hexagon or circle divided up into six equal segments (see Figure 12.1). When a change to any one of the six segments occurs, the business architect needs to look at the other five segments to determine what impact the change might have on them. Any change should be looked at holistically and impact to all six aspects of the model must be considered. So how, then, can the POLDAT framework be reconciled with the business architecture framework? See the following sections for more information.

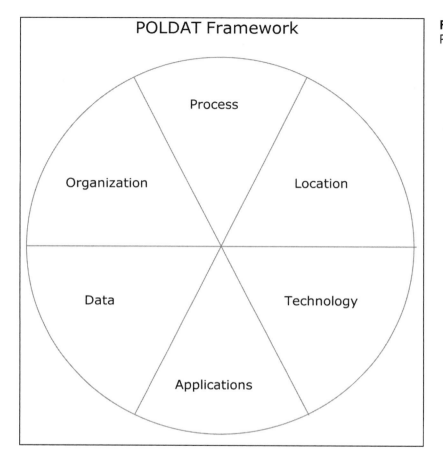

Figure 12.1
POLDAT framework.

Fit with the Goals View

Goals are not explicitly called for in the POLDAT model, but instead should be thought of as an overarching principle for all the architecture work. The Organization segment of the framework will provide the organizational model that the goals will be mapped to. You will need, therefore, to document your Goals view business architecture content outside of the POLDAT framework.

Fit with the Facades View

Facades are not explicitly called for in the POLDAT. Facades can be inferred from the Process and Location segments. The actual interactions within the facades are all inferred from the Process segment. The processes are the manner in which the interactions will be supported by the business; the Process segment will provide clues as to what the interactions are.

Facades and interactions are considered to be an important part of the business architecture model, so it is important that you still capture this information in a Facades view and use it to shape the rest of your business architecture model.

Fit with the Processes View

The Processes view of the business architecture model is a perfect fit with the POLDAT Process segment. POLDAT puts significant emphasis on processes, and business architecture also recognizes its importance. Ensure that you are creating processes that align with the goals and interactions of the business. Don't create a process for the sake of processes (which is possible if you only follow the POLDAT framework).

Fit with the Communications View

Business communications and communication flows can be inferred from the Process, Location, and Organization segments of the POLDAT. There is no direct focus on communications in this framework. Don't leave the understanding of communications to inference from other information. Make it explicit by creating the Communications view of your business architecture model.

Fit with the Business Entities View

Data has been called information without correlating structure. It is raw and of little value without context. Business entities are elements of information and can be mapped to the Data segment of the POLDAT framework. In some cases, the Process segment will also provide information about business entities.

What you can see from the discussion on POLDAT is that, though it is referred to as an enterprise architecture, in fact it doesn't have much content appropriate to the business, as you would want to have available in a business architecture model. If your IT department is using POLDAT, create the business architecture model as described in this book and let its contents guide them as they fill in their framework, which will be useful in the context of IT systems.

Business Architecture and the TOGAF

TOGAF (The Open Group Architecture Framework) is yet another framework for developing a holistic enterprise architecture. The Open Group has been in operation for years, providing ready access to publicly available intellectual property related to architecture and information technology. Their architectural framework has been around in some form or another since 1995, and as of this writing, it is at version 9. You can find more information about TOGAF on the Internet, including www.opengroup.org/togaf.

According to TOGAF, an enterprise architecture is built on four fundamental pillars:

- Business architecture
- Data architecture
- Application architecture
- Technology architecture

Internal to each of the pillars are contents appropriate to a comprehensive understanding of the related architecture. In the context of TOGAF, business architecture includes the following aspects:

- Product/service strategy
- Organizational
- Functional
- Process
- Information
- Geographic location

TOGAF's business architecture contents have the closest correlation with the business architecture model views proposed in this book, largely because TOGAF has specific focus on a business layer within its framework. Within the business layer, there is reasonable correspondence with many of the views of the business architecture framework.

Fit with the Goals View

Goals are not explicitly part of the TOGAF business architecture. Goals are partially represented by the strategy information about products and/or services. The Organization segment provides information about the operational structure of the business, which can be used to map goals.

Fit with the Facades View

The Functional aspect is where you will find the interactions of the business with the world around it. Facades are not specifically called for in TOGAF, but there is nothing stopping you from using them as a structure for organizing interactions within the Functional aspect, as is recommended in the business architecture model proposed in this book.

Fit with the Processes View

There is a direct, one-to-one mapping between the TOGAF process component and the Processes view. There is no surprise here, since process is one of the aspects of businesses that information technology architects have been paying attention to for almost the entire history of IT.

Fit with the Communications View

The Communications view has to be inferred from the Process and Organizational aspects of the TOGAF.

Fit with the Business Entities View

The Information aspect of TOGAF provides for the Business Entities view. This is another area where IT architects have placed significant emphasis since the inception of information technology.

If your business IT team is using TOGAF, as the business architect, you can either create the business architecture model as discussed in this book or fit related content directly into TOGAF and enhance it, where needed, with content that this book specifies but TOGAF doesn't.

Tying the Framework Concept Back to Business Architecture

You've now seen that there are frameworks for architecture that suggest they cover the needs of the enterprise. To varying degrees, this coverage is true. If your business IT team is using any one of these frameworks, you may (and likely will) be asked to align your business architecture efforts with the framework content. As you've seen, these frameworks don't always directly align with the business architecture work recommended in this book. What you will have to do is sort out how you want to handle the alignment issue in your environment. Keep in mind that there is a valid reason to do all the architectural work recommended, as you've seen so far and will see in coming chapters. If you are going to follow any of the frameworks in this chapter at the expense of creating all the content suggested by the business architecture model, consider what you might be sacrificing in the way of information and what it might mean in terms of future use of your business (architecture) model.

Even if you produce your business architecture model as per the framework suggested in this book, you will have to consider how the IT architects of your business will consume your content and apply it to their work. They should be creating their architecture in response to the needs of the business, as spelled out in your business architecture model. You need to work out with them how they will access your content and respond to it, and how you will ensure that they are, in fact, responding to it appropriately (that is, creating an IT architecture that truly supports the business architecture).

Business architecture may exist in isolation, but where the business has an IT architecture, the business architecture should relate to and shape that IT architecture. This would then represent a holistic or true enterprise architecture (see Figure 12.2).

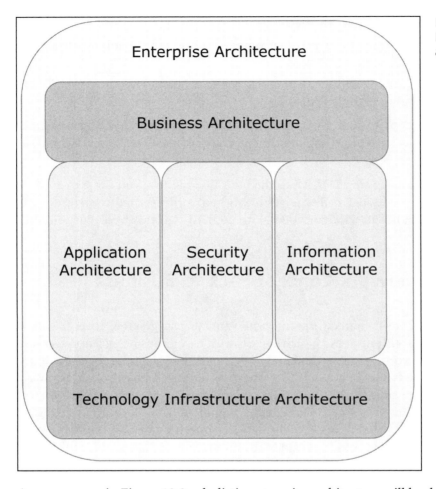

Figure 12.2
Enterprise
architecture.

As you can see in Figure 12.2, a holistic enterprise architecture will be driven at the top by a business architecture. Beneath the business architecture, and shaped by its influence, will be three interrelated architectures:

- *Application architecture* provides all of the architecture for the IT applications that the business will need to operate successfully.
- *Security architecture* provides a view of how security will be implemented across the business, including but not restricted to IT security.
- *Information architecture* provides an understanding of all the information a business will need, as well as how it will be stored and used throughout the business.

Underlying these three layers of architecture and supporting the entire enterprise is the technology infrastructure architecture. This layer of architecture discusses the physical implementation of technology to support the enterprise as described in all the preceding layers. Different architects with different, but related, skill sets typically create each of these layers, the business architect being one of them. All of these different architects need to work in collaboration, though, if their combined work is to be effectively aligned and of use as an enterprise architecture.

It is important that all these architectural aspects align to support the business. The business architecture should lead all changes, with the other layers responding as needed. Regardless of the framework you use, whether it is one of those listed in this chapter or some other one, keep in mind the fundamental principles of aligning the business architecture with the rest of the enterprise architecture and of having the business architecture lead the changes the business undergoes.

In Your Business

Here are some things to consider when thinking about frameworks and the integration of business and IT architecture in your business:

- Does your business use a framework for an IT architecture?
- Is your IT architecture informed by the future state vision for the business?
- What is the best way of aligning the contents of your business architecture with the IT architecture of your business?
- Is there value in aligning the business and IT architectures in your business?

Summary

This chapter introduced the difference between business and IT architectures, as well as how they can be aligned to create a more holistic picture, sometimes referred to as enterprise architecture. There was discussion of the following:

- Three frameworks for enterprise architectures (each originally from the IT industry)
- The mapping of the five views of the business architecture model onto each of the three enterprise architectures
- What to do about your business architecture efforts when you are being asked to work with an enterprise architecture framework
- How the business architecture should inform the IT architecture

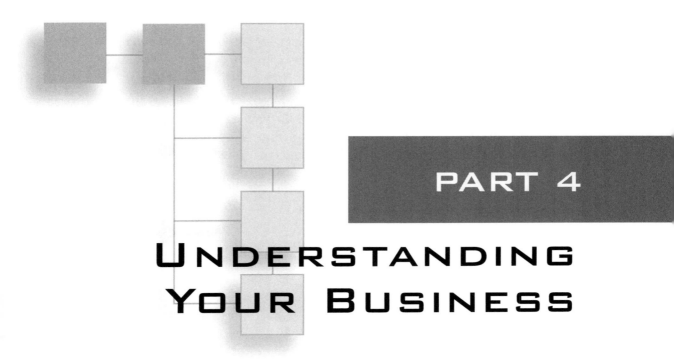

PART 4

UNDERSTANDING YOUR BUSINESS

Every business fundamentally exists to provide something, whether that something is a product or service, and hopefully it is also in business to make a profit while it provides that something. A business needs to clearly understand the product or service it is providing if it is going to succeed. The things a business can provide fall into three broad categories: products, services, and lower prices. Each of these three things can be represented in a *business structure model* that specifically describes what shape the business will take—that is, how the business will structure itself to providing support for the product or service. The business structure is a description of the way the business is shaped relative to one of the three categories. This business structure model can be expressed in the same way as a business architecture model, or a set of views that in total describe the business structure. (Think of it as an idealized business architecture.)

After you identify which business structure model is appropriate, you need to consider how each view of your business architecture model will need to look in the future to help your business succeed. Your future state will need to align with the business structure model you feel is appropriate for your business.

There may be times when a business wants to migrate from one structure to another. The business architecture model future state will need to reflect the new structure and the roadmap will need to reflect the work to be done to transform the business.

This section of the book is all about understanding the three basic business structure models and how to ensure that your future state aligns with the appropriate structure. Chapter 13 talks about the product-driven business structure model, where the business is all about providing products and making products key differentiators. Chapter 14 looks at the service-driven business structure model. Chapter 15 looks at the price-driven business structure model. Each of these chapters explores the use of the business architecture model in understanding the business structure. Chapter 16 discusses using the business architecture model to understand your business structure drivers and how to best align them with the appropriate structure, whether it's the structure the business is currently pursuing or another one the business would be better aligned with.

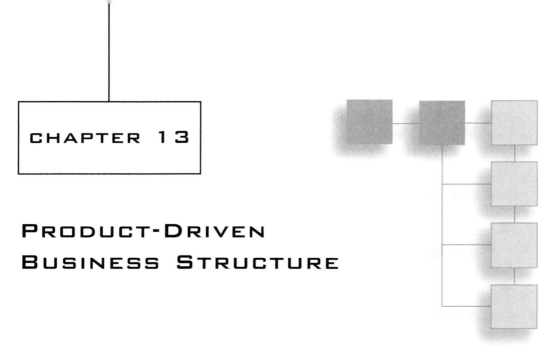

CHAPTER 13

PRODUCT-DRIVEN BUSINESS STRUCTURE

Many businesses sell products; these products are the "things" businesses make available to customers. The single concept that truly demonstrates that a business fits the product-driven business structure definition is that the business sees its product offerings as a key market differentiator relative to their competition and that they are organized to ensure they support that key differentiation. Product-driven businesses have departments dedicated to development or sourcing of products. They test their product offerings with target customers. They put support mechanisms in place to ensure that product satisfaction is provided to a significant majority of customers. In summary, the product-driven business lives and dies by focusing on delivering the right products to their market.

The product-driven business must still focus on service and pricing, but it will only do so in the context of its products. A number of examples will be given in the following sections of this chapter. Keep in mind that they are not meant to be an exhaustive or definitive list of product-driven businesses.

Goals in a Product-Driven Business

A business needs main goals that will support its product-driven focus if it is going to succeed. An example of a main goal that supports a product-driven focus would be something like, "to ensure that we are the leader in the creation and sale of an integrated business architecture modeling suite of tools." Clearly, this business is focused on delivering a product that will be a key market differentiator.

If the business has a main goal or set of main goals that either doesn't support a product-driven behavior or is ambiguous about that behavior, it is time for a discussion with executive management about aligning goals with an understanding of the business. Either the goals need adjustment, or the business isn't really product driven.

After the main goals are sorted out, it's time to tackle all the sub-goals. Keep in mind that not only do the sub-goals have to support the main goal (or goals), but they also need to align with the business being product driven. If you are trying to move the business to a product-driven structure from some other (possibly indeterminate) structure, it is advisable to get the entire Goals view model confirmed prior to any work in any of the other views.

Facades in a Product-Driven Business

If facades represent how others will interact with the business, what do the interactions need to look like in order to support the product-driven business? The goals you set in the Goals view give some solid clues as to how you might shape the interactions. If your goal is to provide the "recognized leading integrated business architecture suite of tools" as your product offering, you will need to make sure your sales interaction includes things like demonstrations of the integration as well as demonstrations of the full suite of functionality a business architect would need. You might need to set up integrations with your own research and development team to ensure they have input from real end users of their product as they plan future version enhancements. You may need to think of some service interactions designed to keep most customers satisfied enough to continue using your product and purchasing support and upgrades.

As you can see in Figure 13.1, even when your business is product driven, some thought has to be given to service and price. The primary focus, though, will be the product or products.

You may need to put some focus on supplier interactions to ensure that you are getting the right products at the right level of quality. Because your business is product driven, there's a good chance that very high quality is the standard you've set for products you make or source from suppliers because if you are all about products, product problems would be very detrimental to your business. You will need to ensure that all your quality-control interactions with third parties are well understood and that they align with getting the right level of quality for the products you are going to offer.

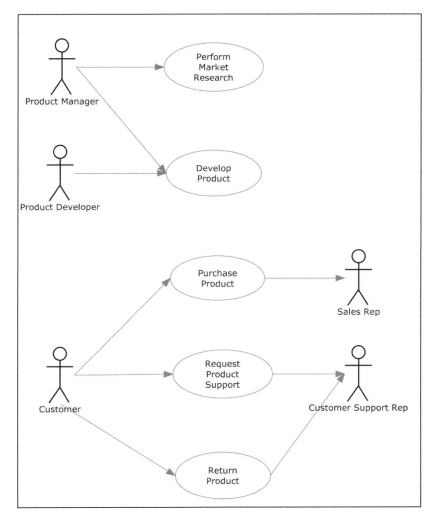

Figure 13.1
Sample business
use-case diagram
for interactions in a
product-driven
business.

Your regulatory and compliance facade will be all about having the right interactions with the right government and regulatory bodies to ensure that your sale of products is not impeded. You may need to have interactions with certification bodies, test labs, or independent adjudicators to ensure that your products meet the criteria necessary to allow them to be sold. If you sell physical consumer products, you may have interactions with consumer watchdog or recall agencies to register the products you sell, and in the worst case, to notify the public of a safety issue and issue a recall notification.

Obviously, you will have a complex Facades view for your product-driven business. Just be mindful that, although you will need some interactions that support service or price behavior, your interactions should be primarily about products.

Processes in a Product-Driven Business

If you've done your Facades view modeling well, it should be easy to ensure that your processes support a product-driven business. Remember that each process should exist only for the purpose of supporting an interaction (either completely or in part). This means that if all your interactions support the product-driven business structures and if you follow the rule about all processes supporting interactions, your processes can't be anything but aligned with being product driven.

The sorts of processes we expect to see in a Products view would be those concerned with developing or sourcing products, selling and cross-selling of products, and keeping customers satisfied enough to keep buying products from the business (see Figure 13.2).

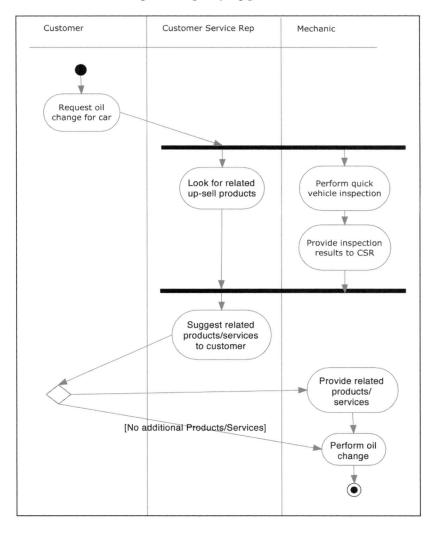

Figure 13.2
Sample business process for cross-selling products during a service call.

Processes will have to be put in place to support interactions from all facades, so in a product-driven business, expect to see processes for submitting new prototype products for testing, processes for rolling out new products or new releases of existing products, processes for registering products with appropriate regulatory bodies, and so on. The vast majority of the processes need to align with the production, sale, and support of the products your business offers.

What if your processes don't align well with products, but your goal is to be product driven? Maybe your facades are all aligned with being product driven, but the process subject matter experts (often referred to as SMEs) are still dictating processes that aren't product driven. It's time to go have another heartfelt talk with the business executives about the alignment. They may talk to the SMEs and reset their behavior. They may supply you with new SMEs to work with in the hope of better collaboration. They may turn around and say the SMEs are right, in which case you probably don't have the right goals and interactions defined. It's time for a much longer discussion with the executives at this point. You may find that the business doesn't really have the fortitude to become truly product driven. At least you will have you business architecture model as a reference for your conversation. It will help you demonstrate exactly what your concerns are.

Communications in a Product-Driven Business

As with the other views of your business architecture model, everything related to communications should align with products when your business is product driven. Expect to see communications related to product announcements, product order fulfillment, and product support.

If the preceding views are all properly aligned with a product business, it becomes a straightforward exercise to discover the communications that will be necessary and ensure that those communications will also align with being product driven.

If you are being told by SMEs about communications that don't align with products, you probably only need to have the business executives step in to reset the behavior of the SMEs or replace them. If you've gotten this far in your business modeling work and everything up until now aligns with being product driven, chances are good that your model is correct and the SMEs just don't yet fully understand the vision. You will not likely be in a position where you have to rethink your business structure model as a result of misaligned communications. The communications, in all likelihood, may need some adjustment and your model will be fine.

Business Entities in a Product-Driven Business

When you are dealing with a product-driven business, your main focus for business entities will be those related to products. Any business is likely to care about basic customer information, of course, but you will also likely care about what products your customer has and what other products they might be a prospective buyer of. You may need information about how the basic products you offer can be aggregated into suites of integrated products, and what that aggregation does to the pricing model. You may need a business entity model to represent who your competitors are and what their product offerings look like.

Your Business Entities view model will be product centric and should be built by thinking first about your product offerings and then considering what other information about the rest of the world you need to sell the products effectively.

At this point, your business is pretty much committed to being product driven, so if you see any misalignment between what you are modeling as business entities and a product focus, you need to start asking about the gap you've identified.

In Your Business

Here are some things to consider when thinking about the applicability of a product-driven business structure model:

- Is your business product driven?
- Does your business have the right level of focus on providing products to your customer base?
- Does your business architecture model actually prove the assertion that your business is product driven?

Summary

This chapter explored what a product-driven business structure model is. The impacts of being a product-driven business were investigated for all five views of the business architecture model. This chapter discussed the following:

- Looking for product-driven goals in the Goals view and what to do if they aren't there
- How to recognize product-driven interactions within facades and how to recognize interactions that don't support being product driven
- How to recognize product-driven focus in the Communications, Processes, and Business Entities views
- How your business architecture model helps you recognize when there is misalignment with the business structure model

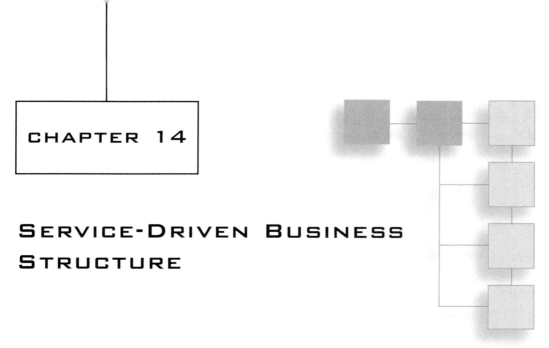

CHAPTER 14

SERVICE-DRIVEN BUSINESS STRUCTURE

Your business can follow the *service-driven business structure* in one of two fundamental ways:

- Your business may use superior service as a key differentiator in selling its products.
- Your business may sell services with or without any associated material product (consider consulting as an example of a service that is often sold without any product).

There will be significant basic similarities between these two sub-types of service-driven businesses, but there will also be some important differences. A business that sells services does not need to worry about product sourcing or production; a business that sells a well-serviced product still needs product creation as well as service management.

Understanding the future vision of the business will help shape your business architecture model from the appropriate sub-type of the service-driven business structure. Conversely, your current state business architecture model can help the business determine which sub-type it is best poised to successfully pursue, if the business is contemplating a change.

A number of examples will be given in this chapter, but keep in mind that they are not meant to be an exhaustive or definitive list of service-driven businesses.

Goals in a Service-Driven Business

Goals, as always, are key to building an accurate business architecture model when you are in a service-driven business. Again, goals must align with the business structure model if the business is to succeed.

When looking at the service-plus-product sub-type, you need to ensure that the main goals of the business focus on creating and maintaining products that are serviceable, and that differentiating services for the products is a primary consideration. Does your business still understand that it will have to create products that are competitive in quality, features, and price bases? Does the company understand what services it will need to provide to demonstrate to its existing and potential customers that these services truly are key differentiators? Does the business show the will to sustain this sub-type of service-driven business structure? You should expect to see main goals that reflect service superiority in your business if it intends to be service driven. If you are not seeing the combined focus on products and services that will differentiate the products from your competition, you will need to talk to the business executives about the misalignment you see and compel them to provide clear, unambiguous direction.

The Goals view will be a little different if your business is following the sale-of-services sub-type of the service-driven business structure. In this case, your business goals should all center on the creation, maintenance, and sale of services. There should be no focus on product development or sourcing, except as a possible by-product of the sale of a service. If you are being told the main goals of the business include things that aren't focused on development, sales, and delivery of service, you will have to talk to the executive management and sort things out.

Facades in a Service-Driven Business

If you are looking at services as a product differentiator, you will probably have facades and interactions similar to those of a purely product-driven business, but with a few key differences. You will want to make sure that you avoid defining interactions that are purely about the product without any consideration of the value-added services. You will also need to consider the interactions that are needed to provide the services related to the product.

As an example, say your business is selling cable boxes to decode digital broadcasts for older televisions that can only receive analog feeds. Your competitors sell similar boxes, and your key differentiators are that you will provide live-operator technical support and on-site installers (for an additional nominal fee). Not only will you need to document all the interactions necessary to sell the cable box, you will also need to consider what the interactions will be like to support your premium services. You've promised live support, so how will that work? Will it be to a call center over telephone lines, or will you insist on using Internet communication tools to keep operating costs down? How will you provide on-site support? Will you hire staff, acquire a fleet of vehicles, and so on, or can you outsource the work? How much can you outsource, and what will the interactions look like? You may need to analyze the pros and cons of multiple possible ways an interaction could be implemented. You may also have to tie different levels of the same type of service to differing products. You may offer both a basic and a premium digital cable box. For the basic box, support is only available via email for nine days from the original purchase date, while purchase of the premium box might qualify the customer to receive unlimited live support for the life of the product. You will have to capture what both types of service interactions will look like.

Your business might centrally manage the customer requests for service, but then, based on geographic location and type of service needed, the business will either provide the service directly or outsource the service to a qualified third party. There may need to be interactions with local service providers if you are outsourcing any of the on-site services you offer. Your business may also need to develop special interactions around reconciling the service orders with the outsourcer (see Figure 14.1).

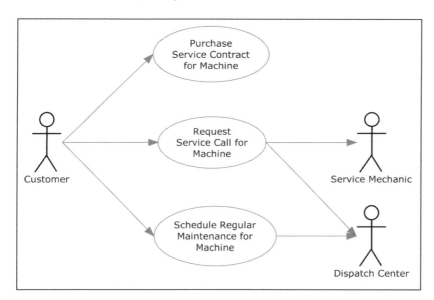

Figure 14.1
Sample business use-case diagram for interactions in a service-driven business—in this case, services for a product.

Not surprisingly, if the facade interactions you are documenting don't align with the Goals view, you need to talk to your business executives about which way they really want things to go. As a result of the executive conversation, you will either modify your Goals view or modify your Facades view. Either way, when you are done, you want to have fully aligned goals and facades.

If your business sells pure services (or primarily sells services and as an offshoot may supply products), most of your facades and interactions are going to look significantly different than if your business were product driven. You may find you have little or no interactions related to the creation of sourcing of products. You should expect, however, to have a considerable number of interactions related to the marketing and sale of services as well as interactions related to the sourcing of talent to create and deliver services. Will your service be a commodity service like an outsourced call-center operation, or will it be much more specialized like business architecture consulting?

As an example, consider the case of a business architecture consulting service. You probably won't have many interactions related to defining a generic service offering because the service will be so highly tailored to each engagement. You will probably want a lot of information around the interactions related to defining a statement of work for an engagement, precisely because each engagement's deliveries will be so unique. Your sales interactions might revolve around demonstrating value provided to past clients. You may need to think about what, if any, support interactions you might need to supply to your customers after the consulting engagement is over. (See Figure 14.2.)

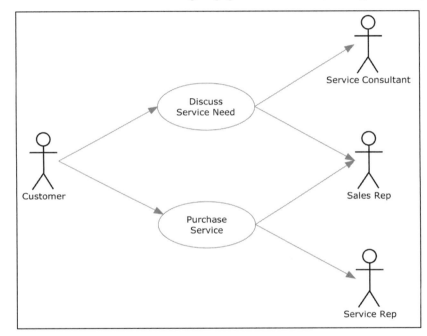

Figure 14.2
Sample business use-case diagram for interactions in a service-driven business—in this case, services only.

In Figure 14.2, the Service Consultant is seen as someone brought in early in the service engagement to understand the need, while the Service Rep would be the actor who provides the service during the engagement.

Service-driven businesses typically don't have product suppliers because products are not part of their usual offerings to customers. They will likely have secondary suppliers, such as printers, stationary suppliers, couriers, and the like, but the interactions are usually either insignificant enough or so controlled by the supplier that it isn't worth modeling them. But think about it carefully before ignoring the secondary suppliers. You may do enough printing (you are a consulting company, after all—most clients expect you to deliver volumes of documentation) that it is worth standardizing the printing interaction.

When it comes to government and regulatory interactions, there may be fewer for some service-driven businesses than for those that provide products, while other service-driven businesses are very heavily regulated (think of health care or educational services). Your service-driven business won't have to worry about certifying any products with regulatory bodies, so there won't need to be any of those sorts of interactions in your model. Your business might, however, need to worry about licensing interactions with certain government bodies. Service-driven businesses often operate in a larger geographical area than many product-driven businesses, so the service-driven business may need to worry about the governmental and regulatory interactions it will have to deal with in distinct jurisdictions. There are also, of course, the standard interactions that any business needs to have with the government for taxes, and so forth. While you may not bother to document the details of each of these governmental interactions (after all, the government dictates how they will go), you should at least note the existence of each of the interactions to ensure that you end up with processes consistent with the government mandated interactions.

Processes in a Service-Driven Business

If your Facades view model is accurate, it should be a straightforward exercise to discover the processes you will need for your service-driven business, whether you are dealing with the service as a key differentiator of a product or the pure service sub-type. As always, aligning the processes with the interactions of the various facades of the business is critical. You never want to have processes that don't support, at some level, at least one interaction.

When your business is about selling products with a heavy emphasis on services to support the products, you will have a very complex process model. You have to worry about all the same processes that a product-driven business would have, as well as many of the processes that a pure service business would have. The complexity is often rewarded by the success of businesses that adopt this operational model. The complexity also makes it all the more vital to have a Processes view model to help understand it.

Going back to the example of the business selling cable boxes, think about what process it would take to handle a customer request to have their box installed by a local professional. The business will need a process for capturing the customer request and for forwarding the request to an appropriate outsourcer. The business will need processes for handling complaints related to the service request, as well as potentially suspending the services of the outsourcer due to performance issues. There will need to be processes for approving an outsourcer for use as a service contractor by the business. Of course, there will need to be many other processes; these are just a few specific to just one customer interaction: requesting an installation (see Figure 14.3).

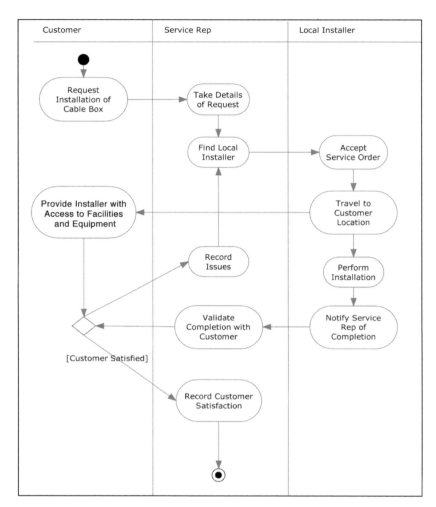

Figure 14.3
Sample activity diagram for ordering a cable box installation service.

Keep in mind that with these types of businesses, processes for services should all tie back to the products they support. It is a rarity to see processes that are service-only when the business is using services as key differentiators for its products. Most of the processes will be product-focused, with extra emphasis on ensuring service is better than that of the competition. You will need to understand what the justification is if your SMEs are specifying processes that talk about a service that doesn't tie to a product at all. Get clarification from senior management if needed.

Things are a bit simpler on the process front when the business is focused exclusively on selling services. You will, in these situations, have a Processes view model that does not reference products at all because there are no products to reference. (The only exception to this would be when a service-driven business will source products for its customers when needed during a service engagement.) The types of details seen in pure service process models are going to be quite different than those in product and service models. This is because the services, by their very nature, tend to be a bit more unique to each situation, whereas the products are the same in every instance (except for custom-built products, but even then the product will be exactly as per specifications).

As an example, consider a business that manages the IT infrastructure of other businesses. The service business will have some very standard processes for the routine things it has to do for its customers, such as monitor a live server, promote a new software application to production, or run a batch job. The business will also have some other processes that will not be as straightforward, such as those needed for things that the business will perform only periodically or at the specific request of its customers. These sorts of processes might include things like adding connectivity to a new customer facility; this won't happen all the time, but it might happen every so often (see Figure 14.4).

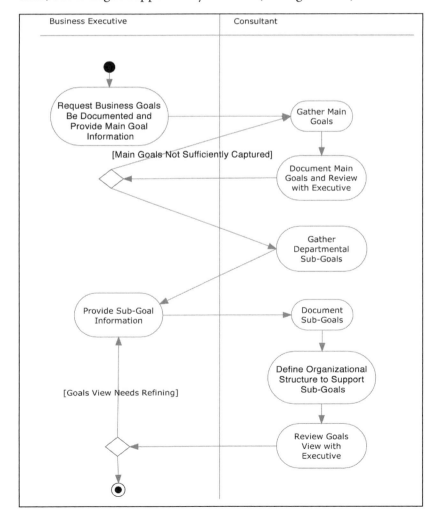

Figure 14.4
Sample activity diagram for a pure service.

You can easily imagine that this IT infrastructure service business may, on occasion, be asked by its customers to provide products. For example, if a server needs to be replaced, the customer may want the IT business to help find a new one. The business could also be asked to obtain or maintain server parts or network parts. Depending on how the service business wants to operate, it may sell the parts, it may help find the parts for a consulting fee, or it may require the customer to source the parts themselves. The business may even choose to have processes to reflect all of these options because it wants to apply different approaches to different customers. Whichever way the service business chooses to go, the process model will need to reflect that choice.

There's also a case to be made for pure service businesses to have *meta-processes*, which are essentially a set of processes for creating new processes they will need to serve their customers. Many service businesses may be engaged periodically to do something that they've never done before; if the business is smart, it will want to create processes around what it delivers in this engagement so that it can then start offering the service to other customers. The meta-processes, then, are all about creating these other processes that will be part of future offerings.

Processes are very important to service-driven businesses of both sub-types, so the documented processes must align with the interactions of the various facades of the business as well as the goals of the business. If there is misalignment, the processes will have employees of the business doing things that will not support the business, obviously this would have to be corrected.

Communications in a Service-Driven Business

Communications in a service-driven business will vary between the very complex (for businesses that use services as key differentiators for their products) to reasonably simple communication models when the business offers pure services. Regardless of the level of complexity, it is important to understand what communications might be needed by a service-driven business.

When you are modeling a business that uses service as a key differentiator, communications will be vital to the way the business operates. Just as the Processes view needs to reflect both aspects of providing products to customers and the services to support those products, these businesses will need communications that will support both the products and the services. Communications for acquisition of products, management of inventory, and customer orders will all need to be in place. Because the business is going to the trouble of developing services as key differentiators, it is wise to place significant emphasis on the creation of marketing communications to advertise that difference.

When the business provides services only, the need to capture communications is just as critical. Consider a consulting company, for example. Any time a consultant does something new or learns something new, the business will do well to document that experience.

Thus there will need to be a standard communication mechanism for a consultant to perform this sort of knowledge transfer so that the newly acquired information can be reviewed, institutionalized, and available to the entire business. There will also be a need for specialized communication between the consultants and the sales force because of this new information. The consultants will need to communicate to sales staff any new abilities that the sales force can offer to prospects; and the sales staff will need to communicate with consultants about prospective and confirmed sales (see Figure 14.5). The communications that the business should have in place should all contribute to the development or sale of the services the business is going to offer.

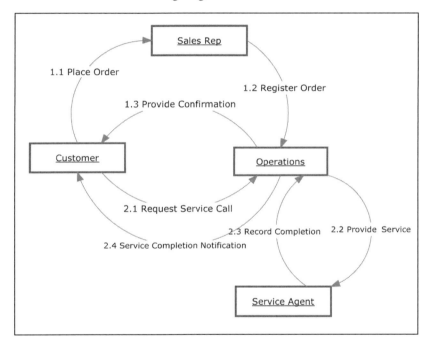

Figure 14.5
Sample communication diagram of a service sale.

Business Entities in a Service-Driven Business

Many of the business entities that a service-driven business will focus on are similar to those a business would focus on if it were product driven. The business will still need to define its understanding of its customers, its service offerings, and all the other information that helps a business operate. The relationships between business entities are just as important to service-driven businesses as any other. The business may need to build *business entity models* of its customers to better understand how its services will affect the customer information. This is modeling above and beyond what would normally be done with a product-driven business, or even a service-driven business that isn't focused on services alone.

If you are modeling a business with service as a key differentiator, you will need to capture all the entities pertaining to the products of the business, as well as all the additional entities that pertain to the services that support the products. You should expect to see several relationships between products and services.

When the business is selling services on its own, the business entities in the model will again need to capture things about the customer, but there will be no product definitions. There should be definitions of the services in the model, and the definitions of the services may be a close analog of the business entities that would define products in a product-driven model. The business entity relationships that define the services may need to be more flexible than would be the case with products because the services may need to be adjusted to the individual engagements.

In Your Business

Here are some things to consider when thinking about applicability of the service-driven business structure in your business:

- Is your business service driven?
- Does your business have the right level of focus on providing service to your client base?
- Does your business provide pure services or services as key differentiators for products?
- Does your business architecture model actually approve the assertion that your business is service driven?

Summary

There are two sub-types of service-driven model businesses:

- The product-selling business that uses service as a key differentiator
- The pure service-selling business

The business architecture models for each sub-type will have similarities, but they will differ fundamentally regarding whether there needs to be any focus on products or not. Regardless of the sub-type, service-driven businesses will benefit from the business architecture model, especially as it pertains to the definition of service properties and the execution of the services.

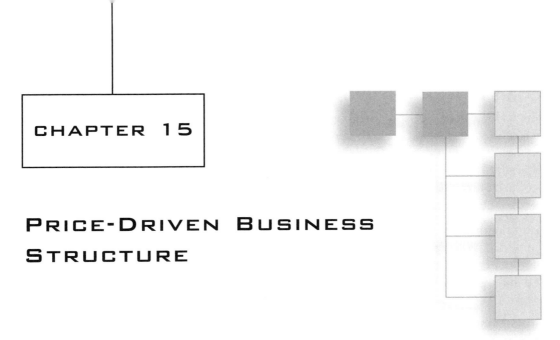

CHAPTER 15

PRICE-DRIVEN BUSINESS STRUCTURE

For some businesses, price is king. These businesses undercut the prices of all their competition in order to drive up their own sales volumes. Generally, these price-driven businesses are sellers of retail commodity products. In many cases, the business doesn't care what it is selling, as long as it has commodity products that can be sold for less than any competitors. You don't often see services offered by price-driven businesses because there are no cost savings to be gained by providing high volumes of services sales. The focus of these businesses, then, is to find the lowest-cost ways of obtaining and providing products, as well as to find as many cost-cutting efficiencies in the business as possible. These businesses have to be extremely profit-margin conscious because they will be selling similar products as others, but at lower prices. As already mentioned, price-driven businesses are typically retailers, but wholesalers occasionally adopt this business structure model as well.

Given these facts about price-driven businesses, what will their business architecture model look like? What things are they going to have to focus on to be successful? What will a price-driven business set as goals, need as facades, processes, and communications, and what business entities will represent the things that they will care about?

Because profit margins are so important to the success of the price-driven business, it is very important to understand how the business operates in order to find every opportunity for greater efficiency and cost cutting. The business architecture model is significant for finding efficiencies in processes, communications, and interactions, as well as finding ways to cut cost by understanding relationships between business entities.

Goals in a Price-Driven Business

The main goals of a price-driven business almost certainly will revolve around the notions of acquiring products at the lowest possible price, understanding and undercutting the competition's prices, and running as efficient an operation as possible. A marketing strategy is typically very important for these businesses, too. If they are going to sell high volumes of product, they need to reach the greatest number of potential customers with deal offerings as cost-effectively as possible.

After the main goals for the business are established, it will be time to document all the supporting goals for the various supporting roles of the business. More than any other type of business structure, it is vital that all the supporting goals align with and fully implement the main goals of the business. There is no room for discrepancy or misalignment when the profit margins are so very important.

Imagine what the goals might look like for a discount retailer that wants to provide all items in its store for less than two dollars. Its main goals might be something like "source product as cheaply as possible" and "provide a diverse set of products at a retail price of less than two dollars per item." Each department of this business is going to need goals that support the overall goals. The procurement department will have to find products that meet the needs of the public, are diverse, and are as low-cost as possible; the marketing department will need to find extremely cost-effective ways to inform as wide an audience as possible that the business has very low-cost product offerings, and it will probably also have to stress that consumers will still get decent quality for their money. All the other departments will have to similarly align their goals if the price-driven business is to succeed.

Businesses that are price driven typically understand very well how they need to align their goals if they are to survive, let alone succeed. Any time a goal is misaligned, it will take a simple, straightforward discussion with executive management to realign the goal.

Facades in a Price-Driven Business

When a business is price driven, it is usually focused primarily on price for products. Because of this, there will be significant similarities between the facades and interactions of the price-driven and product-driven Facades views. Of course, there will have to be some differences to account for the fact that the two business structure drivers are different.

While the price-driven business will need to have interactions with customers to generate sales, the customer interactions will be very simplistic to keep operational costs down. There might not even be any interactions to handle returns or exchanges; the business simply may not allow them. Sales may be very simplistic, with no effort devoted to an elaborate sales cycle because there would be too much cost associated with one. Often the primary form of customer interaction will be in the form of simply presenting the customer with direct access to a wide variety of product options for purchase with minimal assistance.

It is extremely unlikely that any customer support will be supplied in a price-driven business. There may need to be some form of *meta-service* interaction, essentially a means of pointing customers to where they can get service from product suppliers at minimal expense to the business itself. Service in general will exist only in the most minimal ways—these sorts of businesses view services as cost centers that don't significantly increase the quantity of sales.

As with the other business structure drivers, it makes sense that you will need appropriate interactions with government and regulatory bodies. There will be very little room for opportunities for these sorts of businesses to define unique interactions with these bodies, or even to dictate how the standard interactions will play out. The good news is that these types of businesses seldom actually create any products of their own—they simply resell products manufactured by others. This means that the product suppliers will typically be the ones to register the products and get them approved by the appropriate licensing bodies; the price-driven retail business does not have to worry about these interactions directly.

One half of the behavior of the price-driven model is selling products at prices below—often significantly below—any competition. The second half of the behavior of the price-driven model must be to acquire the products that the business will sell at the lowest prices it can possibly manage. In many cases, because the products are often commodities, it is reasonably easy to swap one supplier for another if there is a price advantage to be gained. This means that the interactions defined with suppliers need to be generic enough to be able to swap one supplier for another without having to fundamentally change the interaction itself. There are, of course, implications for the types of purchasing agreements you will need to put in place with suppliers. All of this means that to some extent, you may want to model a meta-interaction with suppliers that will establish supply interactions with new parties.

Processes in a Price-Driven Business

Processes, not surprisingly, will have to be as cost efficient as possible because they will all be viewed as cost centers in a price-driven business structure. There will be no room for elaborate processes or processes that concentrate on customer satisfaction beyond getting them commodity products at low prices. While the processes will not be elaborate, they will need to be as efficient and cost effective as possible. If the facades and all the interactions have been created correctly, it should be easy to identify each process that will be necessary; and while keeping the goals of the business in mind, it should be easy to create processes that align well with minimal expense and maximum efficiency.

Customer-facing processes will align with customer-facing interactions. This means that there will be very little in the way of processes that have significant interaction with customers. The processes will, instead, focus on processing customer purchases as efficiently as possible. There will be little or no sales support processes or returns management processes. (If the business won't allow a returned product interaction, there is no need for a supporting process.)

While it's not likely that the business will be able to influence what governmental or regulatory interactions it must have, the processes it puts in place to support those interactions can be defined any way the business wants, as long as it meets the government or regulatory expectations. This will mean doing things like simplifying accounting and financial reporting as much as possible. The business will need to look for ways to consolidate regulatory reporting so as to maximize efficiencies.

Then there are the processes to acquire products and make them available to customers. Because the business is price driven, it will require processes to source products as inexpensively as possible. You must also consider the set of processes for shipping products from the suppliers to the customers. Price-driven businesses will do everything in their power to offload the delivery processes to the suppliers themselves, only taking it on when there is significant cost savings to be had. There will also be a need to look at inventory processes. Wherever possible, the business will have to minimize the costs associated with warehousing products; this can be done by establishing *just-in-time delivery processes* whenever possible—where the supplier is responsible for having content on hand, and the business orders the content only as needed for its store. You can also utilize the concept of eliminating storerooms by keeping all stock on shelves where customers can access it directly. Other processes might include insisting that shipments to stores are scheduled during regular sales hours so that daytime staff can deal with the unpacking and shelf-stocking, thereby alleviating the cost of additional shifts to handle it.

Because price-driven businesses have such an overt, singular focus, it is very easy to see when the processes being proposed don't align with the business structure. When there is misalignment, it will pretty obviously be a result of the processes being wrong. It's very unlikely for a business to be structured as price driven by accident, so misalignment will likely be with the various view elements, not the structure itself. This means that it is easy to realign any errant processes by simply looking for ways it can be more efficient and focused on the delivery of low-cost product with minimal customer support.

Communications in a Price-Driven Business

It costs money to have communications. Of course, on occasion it costs even more to fail to have certain communications take place. The price-driven business needs to be focused on the judicious use of communications to reduce costs or increase profits. This means that there will be two primary focus locations for its communications: the purchasing of products from suppliers and the marketing of those products to the consumer.

Understanding how communications have to flow to order products with an absolute minimum of questions or rework is vital. If the business is working on a just-in-time product purchasing mode, the time wasted clarifying order details is time that store shelves sit empty, which in turn leads to lost sales and lost future potential, as customers check out your competition in order to meet their purchasing needs. There's also the cost of handling questions from the supplier. Somebody has to receive and interpret the question, and then chase down and provide the answer back to the supplier. The worst-case scenario is that one answer leads to another question, which when answered, leads to further questions, and so on. Clear, unambiguous purchasing communications, then, are imperative if the business isn't going to waste its precious profit paying to answer questions with information that it should have supplied in the first place.

Then there's the question of how communications should flow from individual stores. Should each store independently order direct from the supplier, or should stores aggregate their orders at a central location and have that location pass the orders on when they are sufficiently big enough? The former approach means that each store can control its own inventory levels more accurately, resulting in better client satisfaction, while the latter approach allows for more centralized control of purchase volumes and possibly shipping economies of scale. Either way, the communications flow and content needs to be worked out effectively.

Marketing will typically be looked at as a pure cost center for price-driven businesses. This means that the marketing group is going to have to find very creative ways to communicate with the potential market of the business to let potential customers know what wonderful deals they can get and how to locate the stores where these deals can be found. These communications have to be as economical as possible on two fronts: they need to tell the customer vital information as inexpensively as possible, and they need to create the communications that the customers will see as efficiently as possible.

You must also consider communications about policy and the like that the business will want its store employees and its customers to know about. Policies and standardized behaviors are very important if costs are to be controlled, so communicating the policies as effectively as possible becomes very important to the business.

Business Entities in a Price-Driven Business

Business entities may be relatively simplistic in a price-driven model, depending on some basic assumptions that the business may want to make. Given that most of these businesses have a retail consumer focus, the business may simply state that, statistically, its customers are all similar enough to not have to worry about an elaborate informational understanding of them. For instance, it may never collect name or mailing address information about its customers because it would never need to act on that information.

Depending on how elaborate the business' inventory control structure is, it may need to keep some very basic information about each product, such as its SKU (Stock Keeping Unit) number, supplier, cost, typical fulfillment duration, any special ordering details, and so on.

Sales tracking and profit margin information are going to be highly valuable to this type of business. Management is going to put a lot of focus on this information in regular reports, as well as being able to create special reports about it on an ad hoc basis. The price-driven business entity model will have to include as much information about product sales as possible, such as product sold, location, how long the product was in stock before being sold, when the product was paid for by the business relative to its sale date, and so on.

There will, of course, also need to be information related to suppliers used by the business. Invoicing terms, standard shipping rates, drop shipment costs, and so forth—all of these things will need to be tracked, as well as a generic description of what a supplier needs to be. This latter set of information is useful when it is time to look at swapping one supplier of commodity products for another.

Alignment of business entities with the price-driven business structure should be a very straightforward exercise if the other views have already been aligned. Use the noun challenge technique to find the business entities, most of which, by virtue of having come from aligned views, will themselves be aligned with the business structure. By keeping an eye on the goals of the business while performing the noun challenge, it should be easy to ensure that this view is fully aligned with the structure. There should be no special need to go back to executive management if you see minor misalignments at this level. You can simply make the appropriate adjustments yourself.

In Your Business

Here are some things to consider when thinking about applicability of the price-driven business structure model in your business:

- Is our business price driven?
- Does your business have the right level of focus on providing lower prices to your client base?
- Does your business architecture model actually approve the assertion that your business is price driven?

Summary

This chapter has outlined the unique requirements of the price-driven business structure. There was a specific emphasis on ensuring that cost cutting was focused on, as well as emphasizing that the actual products might not matter as long as they are commodities that the business could provide to consumers at low cost. There has been discussion about how this structure should shape the five views of the business architecture model:

- Goals focused on cost reduction and low-cost product delivery

- Facades to ensure interactions that minimize overhead costs and find appropriate suppliers
- Processes and communications that took into account concepts like just-in-time stock delivery and eliminating stock storage
- Business entities to represent the competition and the product pricing models
- Discussion of how to detect misalignment in any one of the views, and basic steps to be taken to resolve misalignment in any of the views

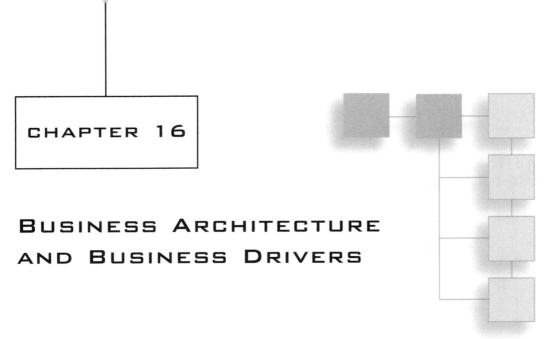

CHAPTER 16

BUSINESS ARCHITECTURE AND BUSINESS DRIVERS

Chapters 13, 14, and 15 defined the three basic business structure models and how to recognize them. There was information about how the business structure would affect the various views of your business architecture model and what the correct content for your model would look like, based on which business structure model your business pursues. So what if your business thinks it is aligned with being product driven, but your business architecture model is showing you that the business is really service driven? What if the business is well aligned with its current business structure model, but wants to investigate a switch to a different structure? This chapter is about taking that basic understanding of the various business structure models and using the business architecture model to align your business to the appropriate structure.

Determining Which Structure Model Drives Your Business

Businesses that don't have a clear understanding of what is driving their structure will struggle to shape themselves and their aspirations for the future. A clear understanding of what they will be making available to their customers fundamentally is vital to the future of all five views of the business: Goals, Facades, Processes, Communications, and Business Entities.

In the situation where a business doesn't know what structure is driving it, or if the structure the business thinks is driving it doesn't align with observed behavior, the business architecture model can be of great assistance. The current state of the Goals view can be used as a discussion point with business executives. You can knowledgably discuss the misalignments you see and ask for clarification; your documentation will help the executives see what you see, and it can help them to understand and share your concerns. After the executives see the problems you identify at the Goals view level, you can demonstrate to them how those same problems cascade down to the Facades and Processes views. You may even want to highlight concerns within the Communications and/or Business Entities views as well. Astute business executives will quickly see the implications of what you are showing them, and they will want to fix the misalignment issues quickly. This is where you can demonstrate further value of your work by showing how the future state views of your model can not only document the problems as fixed, but also provide the roadmap for fixing the problems (see Figure 16.1).

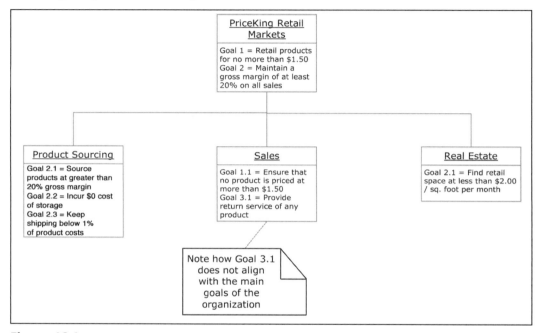

Figure 16.1
A sample of misaligned goals in a price-driven business.

Even when the business understands the drivers that inform its structure, the business may not be as well aligned as it needs to be. Again, showing the business executives the current state model will open the conversation about any misalignments and what to do about them.

Finding misalignment is generally a simple case of inspection and common sense. There is no special trick to it. If your business declares itself to be product driven, look for goals that support a product-driven structure. If the goals are all about defining services or about providing adequate product at price points below the competition, there's likely misalignment. It's that simple. Remember, though, that you need to confirm the existence of misalignment between the structure model and the Goals view. The hope is that the business will be pretty well aligned at this level. It's when you get into the lower-level views of the business architecture model that you are more likely to see misalignment with the structural driver of the business. Even with these lower-level views, inspection is going to be your single most valuable tool for detecting misalignment. Look at your facades, your processes, your communications, and your business entities. Every element within each one of those views needs to support the structural driver of the business, and if a model element doesn't, ask what its purpose is. Often these conversations will not be easy. Occasionally, you may be perceived as nosy and getting involved in things that some people consider to be none of your business. This is when support from senior management is vital, including managing the behavior of those in the business who are not cooperating with you fully. You can also explain to these people what the purpose of your work is and how it will benefit them, which will help them understand why it is in their best interest to cooperate. When people are cooperative, it should be relatively easy to find misalignment through inspection and discussion.

Determining How Well Your Business Is Currently Aligned

Often a business isn't well aligned with either a business structure model or a business architecture model (see Figure 16.2). There may have been a time when the business was better aligned, when the business had much better focus, but time and entropy have a way of causing a business to misalign and lose focus if explicit effort is not made to keep things on the right track.

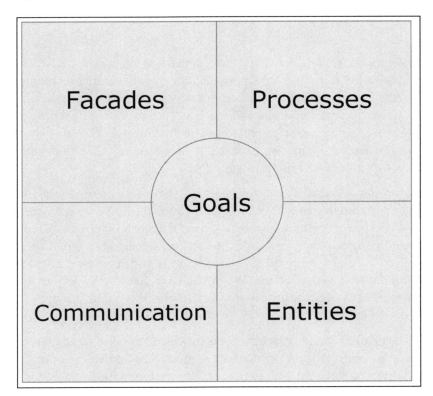

Figure 16.2
Business architecture model framework.

The first thing to do when evaluating alignment is to look at the goals as they relate to the driver of the business. Do the goals match the driver? If not, why not? The goals might be right and the driver is wrong, or it could be the other way around. Either way, executive management must be part of the solution. It is up to them to provide guidance as to whether the goal or the structural driver is correct. After you establish which one is correct, you will need to document the future state of the other to support it. This will begin to shape the future state of your model and the future state of the entire business.

When the future state goals are understood, it is time to look at how well the facades align with the goals. Do you have the right facades? Do you have the right interactions within any of the facades? What makes an interaction "right"? An interaction is right when it is part of the correct facade and it supports at least one goal of the business in some recognizable way. In other words, an interaction is "right" if it aligns with the Goals view. Here again, alignment is detected by *inspection* (the act of looking at the model content to find alignment issues, or specific interactions that don't support a goal) and by conversation with those responsible for the interaction that is taking place in the course of business. During this analysis, you need to keep your eye on the alignment between the business structure drivers and the interactions themselves. Although aligning the goals with the business structure drivers will have already caught the majority of alignment issues (and the same with the facades and interactions with the goals), it makes sense to double-check key interactions to ensure they directly support the business drivers implied by the business structure model.

This analysis of facade alignment will take time, of course, depending on the size and complexity of the business facades, but it is crucial to do this alignment work before proceeding to the rest of the model. After—and only after—the Facades view is fully aligned should you consider aligning the Processes, Communications, and Business Entities views with the business structure drivers. Because you've been so careful to ensure that the higher levels of your model align correctly, all you need to do now is ensure that your remaining views align with the Facades view. Then your whole model should align.

Inspection is again the primary analytical tool for checking alignment of these various views with the facades and the interactions they represent. You will usually want to start the remainder of your analysis work with the Processes view. Each process needs to support a facade interaction. Because all of your facade interactions are already aligned with the business structure model, you have a good chance of keeping your processes aligned just by ensuring that they support an interaction. When you have that level of alignment in place, it is important to go back over the processes to ensure that they really do support the business structure model as well.

For example, consider the case of a price-driven business in which there is a facade interaction for providing product information to customers. A process could be developed to support this interaction that would require staff to man an information booth at each store location and answer customer inquiries as they arise. This process would fully support the interaction that was specified, but it certainly would not satisfy the business driver. In order to support both the interaction and meet the needs of the business driver, the process might be to simply have staff stocking shelves or processing customer purchases to briefly answer customer inquiries and/or direct the customer to a website that contains all the product information they should need. In this way, the business is keeping the cost of answering the queries down as much as possible, while still ensuring that the query interaction can be handled in a way that the customer feels is reasonable. Once you start considering business drivers, it is no longer sufficient to ensure alignment between views of the business architecture model—there must be alignment with the business driver as well.

When the Processes view is fully aligned, you can begin to consider the Communications view. Inspection—as in the other views—is the primary tool for alignment inspection here. You want to ensure that all communications conform to the business structure model and the other views. If you imagine a service-driven business that is using services as a key differentiator for their products, the manner in which a request for customer assistance is communicated will need to be carefully crafted. This communication needs to have all the information about who the customer is and what product they have, as well as what level of service the customer qualifies for and what service professionals might need to be involved in satisfying the customer need. These latter aspects of the communication are what will help ensure alignment with the business driver as well as the other views of the model.

The Business Entities view will also have to be aligned with the other views of the business architecture model as well as the business driver. The business entities reflect the information that the business needs to understand and manipulate, and the types of information and the relationships between the information may vary in subtle but important ways, depending on the business structure model that is driving your business. A product-driven model might pay particular attention to the definition of its products as business entities, as well as the relationships between those products and which customers have the products, which version they have, what support agreements are in place, and so on. A service-driven business, on the other hand, might not be as concerned with which clients have purchased which services in the past, and there's probably no concept of a "service version."

Determining What It Will Take to Align Your Business

What you've been doing as you analyze your alignment is to define a component of your future state business architecture model. You should only think of the alignment work as a component of the future state work because there is more work that could, and often must, be done to get a full understanding of where the business wants to be in the future. There may be a desire to expand (or contract) your product offerings. Your business may want to enhance the customer service experience. The business may want to expand its online presence as a means of (hopefully) reducing costs. These are just a few of the possible examples of the kinds of issues beyond business alignment that might become part of the future state model. These issues also need to undergo alignment scrutiny as part of defining them in the future state model. You certainly wouldn't want to include in your future state model a shift to going completely online if one of your stated goals is to enhance one-on-one service interaction with your customers.

After these other issues have been considered and included, you have arrived at the desired future state. This future state model will outline where the business wants to be in the long run. The next task is to develop the roadmap for getting the business to that future state. This is the point where you need to do a gap analysis against the current state of the business, whether the current state is documented or just implied. The gap analysis will tell you what must be done to reach the future state, to achieve alignment of the business with its business structure model and with the business architecture so that the entire business is working toward the same goals in the most appropriate ways possible. Now you know what it will take to align your business. The way the business will get to that point is an important planning question that needs to be answered. Business architects need to be part of that discussion because they are the ones with the holistic picture of the future state and the understanding of the gap.

So, how will your business close the gap between the current and future states? Can it be done in one initiative? What will the impacts be in this case? If more than one step is necessary, how many steps are appropriate? You are defining your roadmap and a first cut at your portfolio of projects now. As you make these decisions, you have to consider the tradeoffs between the amount of change the business can adjust to successfully at any one time versus how expensive it is for the business to be out of alignment with its business architecture model and its business structure model. You will also have to consider the cost of making the necessary changes and how you will provide the resources to do the work. All of these things will impact the planning decisions you and the business executives need to make about how to fill the gap. Don't forget that you will also have to consider priority and prerequisites as you do this planning; some work simply has to be in place before other work can be executed.

Using Standard Frameworks for Your Future State

There is a considerable amount of work that must be done to get to a "complete" business architecture model that will be of real use in shaping the future of the business. Do you have to do all of this work on your own? What if the business doesn't have the vision or understanding needed to create the future state? They may "feel" they need to change but have no capability to undertake the work on their own. How do you go about solving this sort of problem?

Most consulting firms (either business architecture or general business consulting) will be glad to participate in producing your business architecture model. You needn't turn the work over to them, though, in order to get help. Many of them will sell you a framework that can serve as the basis of your model, at some level or another. Frameworks of this sort are of varying levels of value as you create your model. Some are a fairly complete generic business architecture model; others are more tuned to businesses in a specific industry.

Most frameworks will cover only one or two of the facades, though. There is a concept called the party model, which can be configured for various industries. The *party model* is essentially a Business Entities view that consists of all the "parties" that interact in the course of business operations. There are other frameworks that describe the main interactions needed by a business in a given industry, and may even include suggested organizational structures to operate effectively. However, you will be hard pressed to find a framework that would include a Goals view that is suitable to your business.

What is most unlikely, though, is that you will find a single framework that covers all views of an effective business architecture model. You will likely have to create one or more views yourself. Even if you find a framework that covers all views, you will need to adjust it to make it suitable to your business. A framework by its very nature is generic; it needs to be adjusted to suit a specific circumstance.

A framework is a good place to start for businesses that are either interested in leveraging the learning that consulting firms have acquired, or for businesses that need a base model to start from, either because of time pressures or because they lack the information to create a model from scratch internally. Of course, there is the up-front cost of purchasing a framework. You, as the business architect, and the business executives will have to do a cost benefit analysis, weighing the pros and cons of starting with a purchased framework versus starting from scratch on your business architecture model. If the business is entertaining the thought of starting from scratch, it needs to consider the price it will pay by not having a business architecture model in place as quickly as if a framework were purchased (costs of being less efficient, not having fully aligned views, and so on).

In Your Business

Here are some things to consider when thinking about alignment with a structure model in your business:

- What business structure model drives your business?
- How well is your business aligned with the structure model that drives it?
- What would it take to get your business fully aligned with the structure model that is driving it?
- Would a business architecture framework benefit your business as a starting point in getting it aligned with the appropriate business structure model?

Summary

This chapter discussed how to determine the degree of alignment between a business and its business architecture model, as well as the business and the structure model that drives the business. Some discussion points were as follows:

- Determining how well your business was aligned with the appropriate structure model across all five business architecture views: Goals, Facades, Communications, Processes, and Business Entities

- Determining the gaps between where your business is and where it needs to be in order to be correctly aligned with the business structure model

- Consideration of a standard business architecture framework as a means of jump-starting your business architecture modeling work and how it might help you get your business aligned more quickly

PART 5

PRACTICAL USES
FOR YOUR BUSINESS
ARCHITECTURE

Just what can you expect to accomplish with your business architecture model to justify your business' investment? Part 5 discusses some of the basic ways to use your business architecture model to create value for your business. Part 5 is all about shaping your business using the business architecture model as a plan that will drive change.

The business architecture model should become the central reference for your business. It should tell you all you need to know about the state you are currently in, the latest ideas about a future state, as well as act as a "what-if machine" to test possible scenarios for change. Part 5 of the book looks at different ways you can utilize what-if tests to forecast whether an outcome is desirable, and once that has been determined, how to make the shift. Part 5 also discusses how significant, fundamental changes, such as a business acquisition, can be aided by the application of this model.

Chapter 17 looks at using the business architecture model as a tool when the business is considering shifting its structure model. Chapter 18 examines acquisition and the role of the business architecture model (whether your business is acquiring others or is being acquired by another). Business architecture applied to business reengineering is the topic of Chapter 19. Chapter 20 discusses how the business architecture model feeds into the roadmap and planning work. And finally, Chapter 21 discusses the relationship between the business architecture model and projects.

From here it's up to you to expand on the use of the business architecture model to reap even greater benefits for your business.

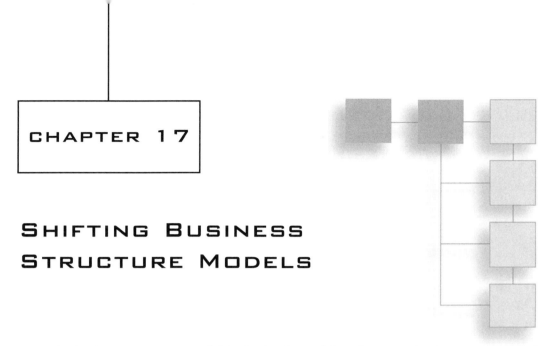

CHAPTER 17

SHIFTING BUSINESS STRUCTURE MODELS

The business structure model is the business driver for organization structure and behavior. The sooner a business determines what their business driver is and aligns with it, the better off the business will be. A business that is aligned with its driver reduces wasted effort; it does things with purpose and avoids inessential activities. The aligned business has a framework with which to test possibilities and make informed decisions. Alignment with a business driver demonstrates a managerial maturity that the business can leverage for a number of purposes, including recruiting new executives, seeking financing, acquiring another business or becoming an acquisition target, and becoming a recognized industry leader.

As you'll remember from Part 4, the three fundamental business structure models are the following:

- Product-driven model
- Service-driven model
- Price-driven model

Determining which structure is driving your business today may not be as straightforward an exercise as it would appear on the surface. In many cases, businesses declare themselves to be driven by one structure but in reality are driven by another, or more commonly they are driven in a haphazard way by some combination of structures. This sort of failure in alignment is costly and counterproductive.

If a business wants a reasonable chance to succeed, it must sort out which is the appropriate business structure model and then aim for that structure. The business architecture model can drive the discussion about current misalignment issues and also aid in discussions about the best structure to adopt. A clear understanding of current goals and facades will provide a picture of what the business is most capable of in its current configuration; it will be easy to see if the business is best poised to be driven by a product, service, or price business structure model. Once this analysis is done, the business executives can then make an informed decision about which structure they want to align the business with in the future. They may decide that the business is better off aligning with the structure it is currently best able to support, or they may decide that the business should align with the structure they initially intended to align with. They may also decide that now is the time for the business to shift to a different structure because it needs to do some transforming anyway. Regardless of the ultimate decision, the business architecture model is the reference tool you should use to determine the work the business will undertake to successfully make the transition.

Migrating from One Business Structure Model to Another

Consider this scenario: a business is well aligned with a structure model and with its existing business architecture model, but there is a significant opportunity under another structure—so much so that the business is willing to undertake the huge shift required to remake itself under a new business structure driver. The decision to make a change like this should never be made lightly; the cost to shift is almost invariably significant. So how does a business make the decision to shift its structure? How does it determine if it has a reasonable chance of not just surviving the shift but actually thriving? The business architecture model is a vital tool in investigating the gap between the way the business is currently set up and the way it would be set up to suit the new business driver. This is, really, just another type of gap analysis exercise using your model as a reference point.

The first thing to do when evaluating a shift in business structure models is to consider what the goals need to be going forward. At this point, you are just trying to develop an overview of the future state you might pursue, you're not going to build a full, detailed model yet. Describe the high-level goals that the business will need to achieve, and possibly describe one level of decomposed goals beneath those high-level goals. You want to understand the changes to the business' organizational structure that will be implied by the shift in goals. Will the business need to add a customer service department? Will the business need to add an R&D group to develop products? You do not need to go any deeper than this now. You just need enough information for the shift analysis.

Next you need to understand the key changes in all the facades of the business. Consider how your interactions with your customers will change as a result of the new business driver. Will the business need to treat their customers differently? The answer is almost invariably yes, if the shift is between product and service or price and service.

In order to effectively perform the shift analysis, the business needs to understand the key ways that the customer interactions will be different. Look only at the interactions that happen very regularly, as well as the ones that are new or significantly different than they are under the existing driver. Will you be adding products to your customer offering? What about the level of service that will be offered? Will the business need to interact differently with its customers as a result of these proposed changes? What are the most significant changes to the customer interactions that the business is likely to undergo to support the differences in interactions. Consider the ways interactions with suppliers, with government and regulatory bodies, or others would need to change. Look for the key differences in these facades and clearly outline the implications for the business in the future. Again, you don't want to model the entire set of interactions yet; you only want enough information to do the shift analysis. The same level of work should be done for each of the remaining facades of the business. You only want enough detail to understand the nature of the change the business will undergo—you don't need to model the whole change yet.

Wherever you discover interactions that have to change as a result of the shift to a different business structure model, you need to understand the changes to processes that will occur as a result. This is where traceability from interactions to the processes that support them is of great assistance to you as a business architect. Find each process that supports a changing interaction, and consider how the process will have to change. Will you need to add or remove steps? Will there need to be any completely new processes? Will any processes have to be decommissioned? You can either modify the processes at this point or simply note the necessary changes. The point is to understand the change that the business will undergo, not actually institutionalize the change yet. Don't do work beyond that which will help you understand the extent of the change in structure.

Finally, you will need to consider changes to communications and business entities relative to shifting from one business structure model to another. You will not typically need to do extensive analysis of either of these views. You can safely make some assumptions about the fact that there will need to be change; 25 to 50 percent of the communications and business entities the business will deal with will likely need to be remodeled as a result of the change the business is contemplating. (This estimate is based on the experience of a number of projects I have encountered.) Use this as a rule of thumb, but do spend a bit of time validating that the specific shift your business is contemplating isn't going to be significantly different than these approximations. The point of the exercise is to understand the cost of the change. In most cases, this can be understood without doing any actual modeling in either the Communications or Business Entities views.

After you outline the changes that the business will undergo in all of the views of the business architecture model, you need to understand the cost of making the shift. The best way to do this is to treat the proposed changes as a possible future state for the business, and then create a roadmap of projects that will get the business from where it is now to the desired future state. All that is left is to estimate the costs associated with each project. Don't forget that this will be total cost, including restructuring , training, changing supplier agreements (and possibly early termination of some existing contracts), and so on. This is not just a typical IT project where some new software is installed and that's the total budget for the work. With these transformational projects (moving the business from one business structure model to another), the IT change is typically only a small portion of the total project effort and cost.

Creating the roadmap in this situation is a bit different than has been discussed in previous chapters, in which you've always had a complete future state model to work from as you build your roadmap. In this case, it isn't in the business' best interest to build the full future state model yet because the business is just running a what-if scenario; the executives have not yet committed to making the change. You, as the business architect, have less information than would be expected with a full future state model, so how do you go about building a roadmap? Start with the changes you know will take place, and figure out what it will take to get the business to undertake those changes. Then you must make assumptions about what else is likely to change and what those changes might imply. Document your assumptions clearly, and make sure that the assumptions become part of the proposed roadmap that you deliver. Can they be done as part of other changes you already envisioned? Are any of these assumed changes foundational, and would they need to be completed before any of the other changes? How are you going to accomplish all the necessary changes? Make sure to have others consider your proposed roadmap and provide constructive feedback. They might see something you missed. Again, document any assumptions your reviewers make if the assumptions change the roadmap.

Now you can make a projection about the projects that the roadmap indicates would need to be undertaken. Be very holistic about these projections; consider all aspects of the change, including the people change component. Then work with the executives to set an appropriate amount of contingency above and beyond what you would normally apply to account for the assumptions and the incomplete future state model you've been working from. When all this is done, you will have a pretty good picture of what it will take to move your business from one business structure model to another. The executives can—thanks to your model and your work—make an informed decision about the future direction that the business should take.

Hybrid Business Structures

Because the cost of making the shift from one business structure model to another is expensive and disruptive, some businesses will instead consider the shift from a single business structure to a hybrid. Depending on the nature of the transition, this may be less costly and typically won't be as disruptive as a complete shift.

While any hybrid combination is possible in theory, some of the combinations won't make sense for most practical applications. As an example of a poor hybrid combination, consider a mix of product-driven and price-driven business structure models. The product driver expects that the business is focused on delivering the right product to the customer. The product will be of good quality, quite possibly developed by the business itself. The price driver says that the product isn't all that important and quality is of little importance. The point of being price driven in this context is that commodity products of modest quality be made available to mass markets as cost effectively as possible; the development of the products by the business itself would be contrary to this behavior in all but the most exceptional of circumstances. Far more common is the hybrid of a service-driven business adding a product focus, or a product-driven business adding a service focus.

Service-Driven Business Adding a Product Focus

The easier of the two common hybrids is the service-driven business adding a product focus. This usually happens as a result of the business being asked to provide or develop a product as part of a service engagement. The business may choose to act as soon as the first such request is made, or it may choose to wait until there are a few requests and believes it can reasonably expect more requests in the future. When the business has made the decision to investigate adding a product focus to its service structure model, the business architecture model will come into play. In fact, the business architecture model might even be the means by which the business realizes it has the opportunity to switch to a hybrid structure model.

The first step is to examine the Goals view to see how the main goal or goals might be affected by the change. Do you want to have such a significant focus on products that they warrant consideration as part of your main goals? If you are simply going to augment services, you probably don't need products at this highest level of goals, but if you intend to significantly shift the business toward selling products as well as services, you probably need to adjust your main goals to consider this shift. After consideration of the main goals, you need to look at the goals of the various departments of the organizational structure. You are certain to have some new or adjusted goals here as you will now need to develop, supply, and support products, something that the business has only done on an ad hoc basis in the past. Make sure you determine what the necessary goals will be and who will need to achieve those goals.

After you sort out changes to the goals, it is time to investigate the changes to the facades that will be needed to achieve the goals. This will mean understanding what additional interactions will be needed for sourcing, supplying, and supporting the products. The business also needs to understand the adjustments to the interactions that provide services to customers so that there will be a better integration between the services and the new product offerings. After all, the point of a hybrid business structure model is to provide the integration of two or more drivers. Think first about the customer facade and all the ways it will need to change in order to support the availability of products on a regular basis. Then think about the supplier facade. Your service-driven business may not have even had a supplier facade in the past; it will definitely need one now. Then it's time to think about the implications from a regulatory perspective. Will the business need to test products?

Will the business need to report products to standards bodies? This is more likely to be the case where the business is actually going to develop products, but even if the business is just making products available from a third-party supplier to sell to its customers, it may need to consider these same regulatory issues.

At this point, you typically have enough information to understand whether the business really should pursue the hybrid model at this time, as well as an idea of the cost implications of making the change. If the business executives decide to make the shift, you can continue to pursue the business architecture modeling exercise related to the shift to a hybrid business structure model.

After you understand the impacts to the facades, it is time to outline the process impacts. You can expect significant changes to the processes, both the addition of new processes and adjustments to existing ones. This is due to the fact that you will have some modified and some completely new interactions at the facade level. For each interaction that you predict will change, look at the processes that currently support it. Where will you need to add or adjust steps to deliver products with the services the business already offers? Will there be product-specific processes to support customers just buying a product without any service engagement involvement? Will there need to be processes to support repairs, returns, or other product-specific interactions? Who will support those processes, and will there be any net new job roles? There may need to be explicit steps as part of each service process to ensure that products are sold and provisioned. It will require considerable change to processes to successfully make the shift to a hybrid model, so be very analytical about each existing or new process to understand what it will look like in the future state. Remember that this work will have a significant impact on the future behavior of the business, so don't rush or make unsubstantiated assumptions.

After the processes of the future state are understood, you can consider the impacts to the Communications view. Here again, you need to consider all the new communications that will be needed to effectively support the shift. Pay particular attention to the communications needed to acquire products, to sell the products, and to support the customers who have purchased the products. Use the Processes view as a means of analyzing the necessary changes to the communications. Don't forget that the communications will include modifications to existing processes or the addition of net new communication processes.

Finally, consider the impacts to the Business Entities view. What new things will the business need to have information about? What relationships between business entities will be needed now that weren't needed before? One of the most obvious areas to consider would be the definition of the products themselves. What information will the business need about the products? Will there be products that are aggregations of other products? Will there be products that are part of a generalized category of products? What sorts of relationships between products and customers will the business need to know about? In some cases, there may be restrictions on the sale of products or the number of like products that need to be understood (i.e., at least one customer must be related to a credit card product, no more than four customers can be related to the same credit card product, and so on). What about relationships between products and suppliers? Is there a primary and a backup supplier for critical products? Are there special rules about acquiring some products from some suppliers (e.g., supplier X needs one week lead time on orders of more than 100 units of product Alpha)?

Product-Driven Business Adding a Service Focus

There may be situations in which a business discovers an opportunity to grow by offering services along with its products. Sometimes the realization comes from customer requests for services related to the products they have purchased or are considering purchasing in the near future. Sometimes the business recognizes that it has an opportunity to differentiate itself from its competition selling similar products. Regardless of the impetus for the hybrid shift from product-driven to a product-service focus, it will be a significant undertaking and should be done in conjunction with a business architecture model.

Start by looking at the main goals of the business and determine how they will need to change to reflect the inclusion of services with the products. Depending on the extent to which the business is considering the shift (services as a secondary offering, services as a significant offering as the products themselves), there may or may not be any impact on the main goals. Once this is sorted out, consider the impact to secondary goals and the organizational structure implied by those changes.

When the impacts to goals are understood, consider the impacts to the various facades. Look first at the interactions with customers and think about how they will need to support the services the business is considering. Will the services be available seamlessly to the customer, or will the customer need to explicitly apply for them? Will there be new or different sales cycles to support offering services to the customers, or will services just be offered as part of product sales? Because the business is adding services, there may not be suppliers of those services, so there may not be any impacts to supplier interactions. However, if the service work will be outsourced to local providers, there may be considerable new supplier interactions to support this outsourcing. There is likely to be very little change to the government and regulatory facade, but consider it for your specific business in your specific location before you state definitively that there is no change for your business.

This, again, is the point at which there should be enough information for the business executives to understand the implications of making the shift, as well as a basic understanding of the associated costs. Once they make the decision to pursue the shift, the work on the remaining views of the business architecture model can continue.

After you have a managerial commitment to proceed with the hybrid shift, commence work on the Processes view. There will be considerable work in this area. You will need to look at each interaction from the Facades view that you need to change and consider all the processes that support the interaction. How will each of these processes change? Will the same business groups that support the sale of products support the sale of services? Will there be new processes to provide the services? What about customer complaints related to the services, will they be handled in the same way as product complaints? Will they be resolved the same way as product complaints? If there are changes to the supplier or government and regulatory views, you need to consider the impact to processes that are required.

The Communications view also needs work to achieve this hybrid shift. Will there be communications to local service providers if you are outsourcing some or all of the services? Will the provisioning of services need new internal communications? There are a number of possible changes to this view that need to be considered.

Then there are the changes to the Business Entities view. Think about all the new information that the business will need to keep track of as a result of adding services to their offerings. The first thing to think about is the extent to which the services themselves will need to be defined. Are there relationships between the services offered and the customers that partake of them that will need to be tracked? Are there relationships between services and products that the business will need? (Perhaps some services are product-specific and therefore can only be acquired if certain products are purchased.)

Making the Transition

After you consider all the implications for change across all the views of your business architecture model, you will have a future state vision. This is the same as any other future state vision you could create with your model, and the process for enacting this type of future state is no different than the process for transitioning to any future state. Create a roadmap and plan the projects that will need to be delivered to get where your roadmap says the business should be going.

These types of transitions are usually so significant that accomplishing them in a single step is too much change at once. The business will have to shift through a program of related projects, each designed to get the business further along its envisioned path. Consider what work needs to be done first, what is the foundational work that other, later projects will build upon and elaborate? How will these changes and projects impact your staff? How will they impact your customer base? How will sales and marketing be leveraging the changes you are making to increase customer satisfaction and drive uptake of offerings?

Think about building some feedback processes, or beta-testing your changes to see whether they are having the desired effect both internally and externally. (Beta-testing is the concept of trying out a solution with a representative set of people before making it generally available.) You may need to apply corrections to your future state model before you reach the end of your roadmap.

In Your Business

Here are some things to consider when thinking about shifting business structure models:

- Is there a real justification for your business to be making the shift, and can the justification be demonstrated with the business architecture model?
- Have you planned the projects that will shift the business?
- How will you ensure that the changes the business plans to undertake will be successful? (Think beta-testing.)

Summary

If your business is considering any fundamental change to its business structure, you can play an instrumental role as the business architect. Bring your model to discussions with executives about the transition they are considering and discuss the possible impacts related to their vision. Help them to understand the value of the transition and also its impacts. Be part of the analysis and the decision-making process related to this transition. Use what you've learned from this book, and especially this chapter, to shape what you should be considering as you analyze impacts to the business across the five views. This chapter covered the following:

- The implications of migrating from one business structure model to another
- Hybrid structures
- Planning how to make the transition

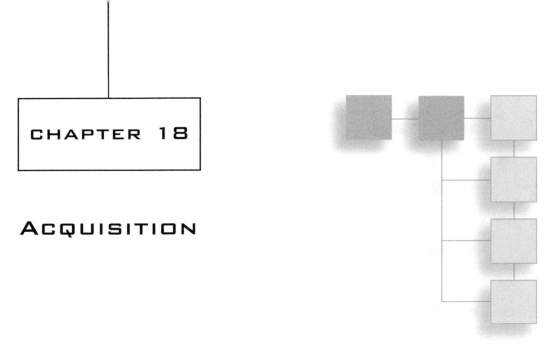

CHAPTER 18

ACQUISITION

One of the fastest ways to grow a business is through the acquisition of other businesses. Your business will instantly have new products and/or services, new facilities and resources, new operations, and new customers. The integration of two businesses is never easy, though. Figuring out where gaps and duplications are and how to resolve them can be complex and time consuming.

There are other times when the intent of the shareholders of a business is to be acquired by another company. The intent of the founders of these sorts of businesses is usually to create a product that other companies would want to provide to their own customers, and then sell the business itself to one of these companies. The founders can create a significant return on their start-up investment if they have the right product and can make their business look attractive to potential buyers.

In either of these situations, the business architecture model can help. A picture of the operation of the business can help you sort out how to fit a newly acquired business into yours, or it can help you make your business more attractive and useful to an acquiring business. In either case, the business architecture model is the blueprint needed to help you understand how the business operates, how it is built, and how it can be added to or made part of a larger whole.

Acquiring a Business

There is little point in acquiring a business just for the sake of owning it. Acquisitions made without due consideration lead to problems, and occasionally the failure of the acquiring business over a modest period of time. There should be careful thought and planning in place before an acquisition is even considered.

The best reason to consider an acquisition is because of a gap in your existing business. This gap could be the result of a problem the business faces or an opportunity the business wants to take advantage of. When the gap or gaps are well understood, they will frame what, at a minimum, the business will want to achieve by making a business acquisition. The business might decide that it is in the market to purchase a service operational group to complement its existing product offerings. The business may decide that the best way to enter a market segment is to purchase a competitor that is already selling in that market. The business may decide that its growth is dependent on acquiring products that complement its existing product offerings.

Assuming the business finds a target to acquire, analysis needs to take place to ensure the purchase makes sound business sense. The business architecture model will play a significant role in this *due diligence analysis*. Usually acquiring businesses will perform financial and legal due diligence work once a target business is identified, which typically involves auditing the books of the target and ensuring that the target is the business it represents itself to be, as well as investigating any legal encumbrances the acquiring company should know about. Similar due diligence analysis should be performed to determine how successfully the target business will fill the identified gap of the acquiring business.

Due Diligence Analysis on a Target Business

You identified the gap you were trying to fill when you created your roadmap. This gap documentation should be in the form of a list of changes that needs to be applied to one or more views of your current state business architecture model to get to the envisioned future state. You will use this gap list to analyze the acquisition target.

Don't worry about the Goals view. The target business will simply be forced to adopt your goals as part of the transition. Generally, the goals of the target business won't help fill your goal gap in any material way.

Start by looking at the facades the target business has. What interactions does it have with its customers? Will any of these interactions be of use to your business? Will these interactions help fill your identified gaps in customer interactions? Take a similar look at supplier and other facades, again asking how each interaction might help to fill any gaps in your business. You probably don't need to look at the government and regulatory compliance facade for direct gap-filling interactions. You do, however, need to look at these interactions to ensure that the target business has all the interactions that you will need in order to support the products and/or services it represents in your jurisdictional environment. (In other words, will you be able to start selling its products and/or services without building any new interactions with government or regulatory agencies in your area?) If the target business will not completely fill the gaps to your envisioned future state, note what gaps will still exist after the acquisition. If the target fills the gaps and then some (and there are many cases where this will be true), list the net new interactions your business will have available after the acquisition, as well as any interaction overlaps between what your business already has and the target business already has. If the acquisition goes through, you will need to integrate the additional interactions into your Facades view and have a plan to eliminate the duplications.

You should also take a close look at the processes supporting some of the key interactions (particularly the interactions of the target business you'd like to preserve after the acquisition). You want to look at how well the target business executes its processes and how well those processes support the interactions. These processes will have to be integrated into your business, so look for issues related to that integration. Will you need teams or departments that don't currently exist in your business? Do you expect that the teams or departments from the target business will transition into your business? (This could be a problematic issue if you will be relocating the people involved.) List any concerns related to the processes, including those previously discussed, and also consider duplication—within its processes and between its processes and yours.

You also should take the opportunity to look at your process gaps that are unrelated to the preceding interactions to see if the target business has processes to help fill those gaps. You are looking to see whether the target business already has ways of doing things that you know your business will need to do in the future. After all of the process gap fit analysis is complete, compile a list of all the processes that are partial fits (they do some of what you need) and what it might take to finish filling the gap, as well as list all the processes that overlap with processes your business already has. (You are going to have to eventually eliminate these overlaps.)

Typically, you won't worry too much yet about how many gaps the target business can fill in either of the Communications or Business Entities views. At this point, you are just investigating whether the target business should be acquired, and filling the communications and business entity gaps isn't a critical part of the gap fit analysis. If you do choose to acquire the target business, however, you will need to do more work later to understand its current state and plan for integration, including integration of Communications and Business Entities views.

In order to accomplish all of this due diligence analysis, there is an underlying assumption that the target business can provide your business with the information you will need. In the ideal case, the target business will have a current state business architecture model that you can simply leverage to do your analysis. In many cases, though, you will likely have to create a partial current state model from some basic information the target business can provide for you. It may have procedure manuals from which you can deduce processes. It may have product lists from which you can deduce many interactions. The point is to gather enough information about the target business' current state to be able to do your analysis. You do not want to fully document its current state: if you don't acquire the target business, then it will be a largely wasted exercise. But if you do acquire it, the current state model will be of some value during the integration/assimilation work, though will quickly become throw-away content afterward.

Planning the Integration with an Acquired Target Business

As a result of all the due diligence, including your analysis work, your business has decided to acquire the target business. Now what do you do? Your due diligence analysis work will be of significant value in this stage of the acquisition. You have a list of the interactions and processes from the target business you want to leverage, you have a list of the gaps that will be partially filled by target business interactions and processes and what will still remain as gaps, as well as a list of the interactions and processes that represent overlap or duplication. First you need to figure out if you are going to attempt a "Big Bang" integration (all at once) or if you will be integrating in stages. Your next step is a planning session; the planning will be driven by your priorities relative to integrating value, filling remaining gaps, and eliminating duplication waste. Setting the priorities will depend to some extent on how close you are to the envisioned future state in each of these three areas. If your business could begin selling new products you've acquired without extensive integration between the acquired business' interactions and processes and your existing business, then the right business decision might be to get on with selling and deal with formal integration later. If there is only a small amount of duplication of effort and it isn't likely to impact customers significantly or often, the right decision might be to allow the duplication to continue in the short term while higher priority issues are dealt with.

Sort out the business integration priorities and perform any modeling that will help you build the roadmap to get the two businesses integrated and moved to the envisioned future state. Hopefully, this work won't include any major changes to the Goals view; ideally, it should remain reasonably stable through the integration. The exception to this will be integrating new departments into the view and setting appropriate goals for them that will align with the main goals of the now combined business.

Update and adjust your current state models for the Facades and Processes views to reflect the integration. This integrated current state will be informed by the due diligence analysis work you did prior to the acquisition and may need to be augmented by further research now that the acquisition has taken place. This is the current state as of the time of the acquisition of the other business—you should reflect all the imperfections in the fit at this time because the gaps and overlaps all need to be represented if you are going to fully understand the integration work that needs to be done. You may need to adjust your envisioned future state model as well to reflect the interactions and processes of the acquired business that you intend to keep using, but that weren't part of your model prior to the acquisition.

At this point, you need to have a clear understanding of the integrated Communications view that you will be dealing with. Again, model the current state of both businesses in the same view, showing all the gaps and overlaps. You need to see what the acquired business routinely communicated to its customer base, as well as all of its internal communications. You need to analyze which of these communications will continue, now branded as part of your business, and which will either be adjusted or done away with entirely. Your current state of the Communications view will show all the overlaps, collisions, and gaps in communication that resulted from the acquisition. Adjust your future state Communications view as necessary to reflect the communications inherited from the acquired business that you want to preserve or adjust but that weren't part of your previous future state.

Then there's the Business Entities view. The acquired business needed and managed information just as your business does. It probably had many similar business entities that it cared about, and some that were unique to it that your business never bothered with in the past. For your current state model, integrate all of its business entities with yours without worrying about duplication or relationship differences. The future state model of the Business Entities view is where you will work out all the discrepancies between what information the two businesses initially managed and what information the combined business will collectively care about going forward. Pay particular attention to issues like similar names (e.g., "customer" versus "client") to ensure a clear understanding of whether there are two distinct things being captured or just one. Also pay attention to the attributes of the various business entities. The attributes can help you understand whether you are talking about the same thing with two different names or two distinct things. If the same thing is referred to by two names, you're going to have to create a single business entity for the future state. That single business entity may have to be adjusted to include appropriate attributes from both of the prior versions of it. When looking at the attributes, you will again have to sort out whether you are looking at two distinct attributes or the same attribute but with two different names. In the case where it's really one attribute with two names (one name for it in your business entity and a different name for it in the acquired business' business entity), just use your attribute name; don't worry about what the acquired company used to call the attribute.

Keep in mind that one of the primary reasons for acquiring the other business was likely to gain its product or service offerings. (Another important one is purchasing a business to acquire its booked business and customer base, but this isn't germane to the business entity discussion.) Definitions of those products or services will be vital, and the definition is often best captured as part of the business entity model. Make sure that you focus especially on understanding and modeling the products or services that were acquired.

After you update the current state of your model and make any corrections to the envisioned future state, it is time to plan how you will get to the future state. This planning is no different than the planning you are used to doing for any type of work to get from a current state to a future state. Make sure you pay particular attention to whether the integration of the two businesses should be done in a single step or in multiple steps. Your planning needs to include what you will do with redundant aspects of views: redundant interactions, processes, communications, and business entities. How will you phase out the redundancies?

Prepare your roadmap and have it confirmed by all the executives. After you have the roadmap sorted out, determine the projects that will be necessary to move the business to the desired future state. As with any planning exercise, look for the foundational projects and get them done first. Then the business can execute additional projects that will move it further forward.

Being Acquired by Another Business

As you've seen throughout this book, there are many good reasons to have a business architecture model. It is useful as a means of understanding and growing your business, and it is useful as a means of fundamentally shifting your business. It is also useful as a means of acquiring a business, as well as a means of explaining and making your business attractive to another business that might be interested in acquiring yours.

There may come a time when you want your business to be the target of an acquisition. When this is the case, there are a number of things you need to do to make your business look attractive. One of the things you may not have thought of is that you can provide solid, clear documentation about the way your business is organized and how it functions to a business interested in acquiring you in the form of a business architecture model.

Preparing to Be Acquired

Hopefully, you've been operating with a business architecture model and a business roadmap for quite some time. If this is the case, then when the decision is made to try to sell the business, you need to do nothing more than ensure the current state model is accurate.

However, things become a bit more challenging if you've never had a business architecture model, but you now see the value in having some documentation about your business to share with prospective buyers. Do you need to create an entire model now? If not, what modeling work will be sufficient to adequately inform an interested business? What will an acquiring business want to know about your business?

An acquiring business will not be interested in your business' goals, nor will it be particularly interested in any envisioned future state, except as far as you've begun work to move toward a future state. These things just won't matter because the acquiring business will want to have your business support its goals from now on—the future state it will care about is its own and how your business will fit into it. Of the business architecture views available, an acquiring business will be primarily interested in your current states for facades and processes, but will also typically show interest in your current states for communications and business entities. Remember that this work may help you make your business more attractive, but it will not appreciably increase the value of your business from a buyout perspective, so don't invest more than you need to create your model.

Start by creating a customer facade current state model, including all the typical interactions your business has with customers. You should draw UML business use-case diagrams to provide a visual inventory of these interactions. You may want to only write business use-case documents for the most common interactions, however. After you finish the customer facade, run a similar exercise for each of your other facades, again diagramming not the whole facade, but just the most common interactions.

Processes are important to an acquiring business; it is going to want to understand how you operate and what your staff does each day. The Processes view will give it the information it needs to answer these questions. Rely on the current state work you just did in the Facades view to guide your work in documenting the Processes view. Start with the processes that support the interactions in the customer facade that you considered sufficiently important to document. For the processes themselves, begin by working out how the process is supposed to work when everything goes correctly (in a use case, this is often referred to as the "Happy Path"). After you sort out the way it should go, indicate on the process diagram the places where activity can branch off of the Happy Path into some alternate behavior. After you indicate all the branching points for the process, diagram the branches that occur frequently or those that require significant work when the branch is invoked. Don't bother to diagram the branches that aren't common or that are trivial to execute. You are still trying to get the most valuable content created with a minimum of effort.

The Communications view will need your attention next. Normally, the communications are documented based on what you've already modeled in the Facades and Processes views, but in this case, because you did a very minimalist pass at modeling these views, you will have to do some extra work on the Communications view. Start the work by discovering the communications in the interactions and processes you did model. Create the communications diagrams from what you discover here. This should work to give you the majority of the communications that will matter to an acquiring business, but it may not be enough. You also need to look for other communications, particularly with customers. Look for things like contracts or agreements that you share with your customers. Look for marketing information. There might be, in these areas, communications that you need to include in your minimalist current state model to hand over to the acquiring business.

When you get to the Business Entities view, start by looking at the things of particular interest to an acquiring business. This will typically include modeling your product and/or service offerings, so make sure to model these things first. After that, look at the interactions, processes, and communications that you determined were important enough to model in the other views of your current state model. Just as with any case where you are looking for business entities, use the noun challenge technique to find the information that the business needs to track. After you find all the business entities that matter, depict the relationships that will help an acquiring business understand the information your business keeps track of. Don't forget to add cardinalities to the relationships, where the cardinalities represent important restrictions on the relationship. You'll especially want the cardinality information when you are merging two businesses because the cardinality of relationships represents business rules, which you will need to understand if you are to make informed decisions about upholding or changing. You will probably find that by the time you model these business entities and their relationships, you will have captured pretty much all the business entities that your business needed. While you've managed to take a minimalist approach to documenting interactions, processes, and communications, even when trying to go minimalist with the business entity approach, by the time you get the ones that matter, you've captured pretty much all of them.

Having this information about your current state will be of great value to acquiring businesses as they try to understand what your business is and how it could be valuable to them. They can see how you interact with the world and determine whether any of those interactions will be beneficial to them. They can look at your processes and easily comprehend how those processes will fit with their own processes. They can see if there will be any issues with the communications you have in place. They will quickly be able to understand your products and/or services as well as other information your business has been interested in. Your minimalist current state business architecture model may be a real value-added package if the acquiring business is considering several possible target businesses.

Demonstrating Value During the Integration

Now that your business has been acquired, how can you help smooth the integration process? What can you bring to the table to support the integration work and maybe at the same time demonstrate enough value personally and in your team that your business architecture group will be an obvious and necessary part of the new structure that is the outcome of the integration? The first and most obvious thing that you bring to the table is your existing business architecture model. Whether you had a full-fledged model already in place or you produced a minimalist version to help explain your business as a target, the modeling work you did will now be very valuable in determining how your business will integrate with the acquiring business.

As the integration planning talks begin, find out if the acquiring business had a business architecture model of its own prior to the acquisition. If it did, the integration planning will be fairly straightforward. You can simply take your two models, merge the contents into a new current state, and then figure out how to fill the gaps between that new current state and the future state envisioned by the acquiring business. After you have the gaps and overlaps sorted out, you can create your roadmap and plan the projects that will implement the change. Figure out if the integration can take place as a single initiative (Big Bang), or if it should take place over the course of several initiatives. You need to understand what the acquiring business wanted to achieve by taking on your business in order to understand what aspects of the integration you should tackle first. Was it looking to offer your products and/or services as a key part of the deal? If so, you need to find ways to help make that happen early in the integration, even if you have to put temporary fixes in place to support the sales work. Try to ensure that the plans you suggest align with the needs of the acquiring business— after all, it is the new owner.

When the acquiring business does not have an existing business architecture model, you face a larger challenge in trying to integrate your business with it. You will not have any current state model of the acquiring business to merge with your own current state model. You will need to understand what its motivation was in acquiring your business and ensure you integrate that aspect first. Typically, this will entail running the two businesses in parallel, almost as if they were still separate entities, but reporting to the same management. While this is going on, you need to do some minimalist modeling of the acquiring business so that you will understand how it operates and how that compares to the way your business operated prior to the acquisition.

Start by looking at the customer facade of the acquiring business. Look at interactions it has that are related to interactions your business has. You want to understand where there will be overlaps or gaps in the way things are done. Diagram the overlapping and the missing interactions and document them using business use-case documents. This will give you an idea of what the future state needs to look like based on the implied current state of the acquiring business and on your documented current state. You're not going to model any more than the interactions that need to change at this point. If the acquiring business sees value in the work you are doing (and it should), you will very likely be given the chance to do much more business architecture work for it after the integration work is done.

After you sort out the interactions that need to change, you need to figure out how processes will need to be changed or created to support those interactions. This means you will develop future state processes for every interaction you identified in the first part of the integration modeling exercise. Where you have duplicate processes or overlapping processes between the two businesses, look for the most efficient process and promote it as the future state. Be aware, though, that even if the most efficient process is actually from your business, the acquiring business may still want to keep its process anyway—you'll have to prove why it is worth changing the other business to your way of doing things. You can often accomplish this by highlighting the efficiencies gained as well as discussing concerns about the lack of documentation of the other process, that it is therefore less likely to be repeatable and successful over the long run because of the lack of documentation. In order to do any of this comparison, you will have to do some minimalist documentation of the acquiring business' key processes. Start by identifying the key processes using the interactions of theirs that you modeled in your earlier efforts. Only model the Happy Path for each of these key processes, and also identify branching from the Happy Path. You don't need to model any more than this yet because you might not keep their process. You just need to understand it well enough to do some basic comparisons between it and your own versions of the processes.

Do a quick, cursory inventory of the acquiring business' communications just to expose any important overlaps that you need to worry about. Overlaps might include things like handling a purchase order two very different ways, depending on whether the order was taken by one of your sales staff or by one of theirs. These sorts of things lead to very inconsistent and upsetting customer experiences, which you obviously want to avoid. Many customers will be reasonably forgiving in the very early days of the integration between two businesses, but they will not be forgiving for long, and they won't be very forgiving if they had a bad relationship with one of the businesses in the past. Do your best to ensure that communication mechanisms don't lead to unhappy customers in the early days of the integration work. You will have to figure out the acquiring business' communication flows from the minimalist current state process modeling you did of its business, along with looking at any inventory of customer communications you may be able to find or create. Look for contracts, statements, notices, and so on to see what the other business used to communicate with its customers. Spend a bit of time understanding which of your suppliers will still be used after the integration and make sure you make available any information about the way your business used to communicate with them. Don't worry too much about how the acquiring business communicated with its suppliers; it is reasonably safe to assume those communications won't change just as a result of the integration. The same can be said about communication with government and regulatory agencies.

If the acquiring business didn't have a Business Entities view model, the best thing you can do is share the model for your business. Start from there, and based on what you discover in the facade, process, and communication work you've done, expand it to include the information that wasn't captured before but will be needed by the newly integrated company. By the time you get through this exercise, you may almost have the entire set of business entities that the fully integrated business will ultimately need.

Now that you've helped capture basic current state information about the acquiring business and you've mapped out an interim future state that resolves any immediate gaps and overlaps, you are in a position to plan the work necessary to make the integration happen. Start first with any foundational changes that will need to take place, and then move on to the projects that will build on that foundation.

The danger with this type of integration is that if you do not have a complete understanding of the goals of the acquiring business, you really can't tell how well aligned your work will be with the future it envisions. The sooner you can help the new executives see what you are doing and how it can be valuable to them, the sooner you can develop a more complete future state business architecture model that will start with goals and strive for alignment through all its views.

In Your Business

Here are some things to consider when thinking about acquisition in your business:

- Is your business looking to grow through acquisition?
- Is your business trying to be acquired?

- Is your business in the middle of a merger (acquiring or being acquired)?
- Does your business have the information it needs about itself to make the work of merging with another business as easy as possible?

Summary

In this chapter, you've seen how a business architecture model can be useful in a business acquisition. Whether your business is acquiring another business or you are trying to be acquired, the business architecture model can be a useful tool for easing the work that is involved in a merger. There was information about the following:

- Using your model as an evaluation tool for target acquisition businesses
- Using your model as an integration tool when merging with an acquired business
- Using your model to make your business a more attractive acquisition target
- Using your model to ease integration with a business that has acquired it, regardless of whether the acquiring business has a model of its own or not

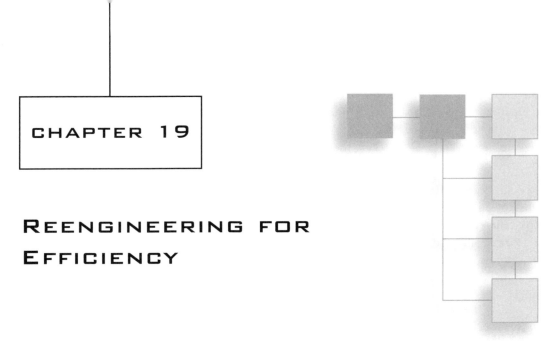

CHAPTER 19

REENGINEERING FOR EFFICIENCY

There are several reasons why a business may believe it isn't running at peak efficiency. A business may compare itself against industry metrics, it may have input from a consultant, it may have internal metrics, or just anecdotally it may believe that things are not running as efficiently as they could be. It may be imperative to find greater business efficiencies because of increased competition or new operational constraints.

To successfully find efficiencies, you must understand very clearly how the business operates now (current state). Only with this understanding in place can the business find where there are inefficiencies and correct them (future state). The business architecture model can provide this current state model and can also capture the changes the business will have to undergo to become more efficient in a future state model.

In the past, many reengineering initiatives typically focused just on the processes of the business. While many of these historical initiatives were at least partially successful, a more holistic approach, one that considers all views of the business architecture model, will find greater opportunities for efficiencies and will position the business to achieve greater success.

You will need a current state model in order to do this reengineering work. You may be able to take some shortcuts to creating some views of the current state model if you have no model yet. How and when you can take a minimalist approach to some views' current states will be discussed in the following sections.

Reengineering Goals

The drive to reengineer for efficiency should come from a goal set by the business executives. Reengineering typically has significant impacts to sizable portions of a business, even when it is just one area that is driving the change. Keep in mind just how interconnected business areas are, both internally and with the rest of the world: "small changes" can have huge implications. It is important to consider all aspects of the change, including the behavioral changes implied for your employees. This level of impact to a business should be driven by goals. Only then can sufficient analysis of the holistic change impact be executed properly.

Reengineering often means some degree of change to one or more sub-goals of the business, and in some cases, there may even be changes to the main goal or goals. The goals could need adjustment to reflect a "leaner" business mindset or a desire to make efficiency a more prominent focus within the business. A new main goal of the organization might be operational efficiency. Sometimes the goal adjustments are more subtle, although just as significant. A main goal may involve cost cutting, which might be accomplished by operational areas setting sub-goals of finding explicit efficiency gains.

Look at your current state goals and consider whether there is anything that focuses on efficiency, and if so, what is there. Start with the main goals: Is there an explicit need for efficiency expressed there? If not, should there be such an expression at that level? Talk to the business executives and make an informed decision. If you adjust your main goals to include a more explicit need for efficiency, you will then need to examine all sub-goals, sub-sub-goals, and so on to see what the resulting impacts will be. Even where the main goals are not updated, a departmental imperative around efficiency could mean an impact to related sub-goals. If you are in a situation in which you have no documented current state Goals view, and you are only updating the goals of a single department, you need not create an entire current state model; simply create the goals for the department. Either way, you must ensure you update your goals to reflect the efficiency focus the business desires and get the updates agreed to by the management team.

Another situation you may find yourself in is one where all the goals in your Goals view already sufficiently reflect the business focus on efficiency, yet the business still desires an increase in efficiency. What you've just discovered is a misalignment between the Goals view and the business. This may have occurred because your model was not fully aligned in the first place. Or it may have occurred because, even though your model was fully aligned, the business either never fully adopted the model or it originally did adopt the model but drifted away from it over time. The misalignment may have happened for all of the above reasons. You need to figure out which reason has driven your business out of alignment in order to confirm the correct restorative actions.

The Goals view then should be where you start on any efficiency-driven reengineering work. When the goals are correctly adjusted to reflect the increased focus on efficiency, it will be easy to ensure all the other views of the business architecture model comply.

Reengineering Facades

The updates to your Goals view should be the starting point for evaluating any necessary changes to your Facades view. Knowing which goals changed will show you, through traceability, the interactions that need to be reconsidered in terms of the new goal or goals that focus on improving efficiency.

Look at whether the interaction still makes sense from an efficiency perspective: Should the business offer the interaction at all? Sometimes an interaction is so inefficient, it just shouldn't be available. In other cases, the interaction is too valuable to the business, so it can't just be forsaken; you will have to improve it. There will, happily, also be some interactions that are efficient enough as they are; you won't have to modify them at all.

After you identify the interactions that require changes for the sake of efficiency, it will be time to do something about them. You will be creating a possible future state with the changes you document. Start by identifying the inefficiencies with the current interaction. Does it require too many steps to execute? Is it prone to incorrect information or rework? Is it prone to manual interventions? (In other words, a supervisor needs to step in at two different points to set up a loan request, when it might be possible for him intervene only once if things were done more efficiently.) In the cases where you decide the entire interaction should no longer take place, you need to determine whether any part of the interaction will need to occur some other way. What you want to do as you rewrite the interaction documents is to look for redundant capture of information, too many steps just to capture a piece of information, or dealing with information not germane to the interaction. These and related issues are what you need to minimize or even eliminate wherever possible.

While traceability from affected goals should give you an indication of the changes you need to make in the Facades view, it makes sense to do a quick inspection of all your business' interactions to look for inefficiencies. If you find any, now is the time to address them.

Make sure the business executives and your stakeholders all understand the impacts implied by the interaction changes you are proposing.

Reengineering Processes

This is where Business Process Reengineering (BPR) has traditionally focused its time and energy. By this time, you already understand why focusing here without considering goals and facades first is likely to limit your success in making a business more efficient. You can make a process as efficient as possible, but if the process doesn't assist the business in a meaningful way, the business will still be inefficient.

When you use your business architecture model as the basis for increasing business efficiency, you don't get to the work on processes until after you've looked at the higher-level views, so you won't end up with "efficient" processes that do nothing of real value for the business.

Every process in your model exists because it supports one or more interactions. Use this traceability from interactions to processes as a means to identify the processes to reengineer first. If the interaction changed, the underlying process will need to change as well.

As a first step, apply the interaction changes to the processes that support it. After this is done, look for additional opportunities for efficiency. There are formal techniques (such as Six Sigma) to find ways to make process improvements, and you are encouraged to use any formal process engineering techniques you are qualified to apply; however, you do not have to apply formal techniques to do this work. The chief points to consider when looking for process improvements include unnecessary handoffs, redundant steps, or manipulation of information that isn't germane to the process. You should also watch for places where automation would significantly improve processing, or where too much manual intervention is currently required to make the process work. These are all indicators of process inefficiencies that are ripe for improvement. After you find these pain points in the process, create a future state that reflects the efficiencies you want to see enacted to meet the goals of the business.

After looking at the processes that were implicated by improved interactions, take a look at the remaining processes to see if there are efficiencies to be gained there as well. The same principles apply to improving these processes as applied to the processes you approached first. Look for the same sorts of problems and solve them in the same sorts of ways.

The Processes view is where you will typically spend the majority of your time and effort when reengineering your business for efficiency. If you do it in the context of improved goals and interactions, you will put your efforts into greater holistic positive change than if you focused solely on the processes.

Reengineering Communications

Communications and the related flows are another aspect of businesses that are typically ripe for efficiency improvements. Often communications have developed over time in an organic manner within businesses, and getting them under control and into shape will greatly improve efficiency. It is best to look at communication efficiencies only after you determine the necessary changes to the processes, because most communications are tied to processes of the business.

When looking for communications efficiencies, consider whether a communication is really needed. Do you really need a call center rep to write a work order for a technician if you have an automated workflow system? Does the communication need to be touched by as many parties as currently touch them? Does the legal department really need a copy of each user agreement, or does it just need access to the ones where there is a user issue that needs to be resolved legally? These are the sorts of questions that you should be asking as you review your current state communications.

After you identify problem areas in your communications, document the future state of the Communications view. Address all the issues that you identified to increase efficiencies. Ensure that the changes you propose align with the processes you've already proposed.

Reengineering Business Entities

You are very unlikely to be able to find efficiencies in the business entities themselves. Business entities just exist, regardless of the business around them. What may help from an efficiency perspective is to find better relationships between the business entities themselves.

The first way you may need to refine your Business Entities view is to look at where new entities might have been discovered during the work done in the Facades, Processes, and Communications views. The process of finding efficiencies in these other areas may actually uncover new types of information for the business to track and manipulate. These new business entities may even help the business operate more efficiently; the capture of new information may allow better interaction with customers, better monitoring and/or reporting of processes, better understanding of customer needs, and so on. These bits of information will need to be incorporated into your future state Business Entities view. Make sure you capture all the attributes of each entity as well as all the relationships and cardinalities that will matter.

The other way to refine your Business Entities view is to ask yourself if you have relationships that are decreasing efficiency. Are there redundant relationships? Are there relationships that can be implied from other relationships? Are there other ways you could more effectively show these relationships? Make sure that you incorporate all of these findings into your future state model.

Tying It All to a Future State

So, you've now found efficiency increases by evaluating all five views of your business architecture model, and you've created a future state model to reflect all these possible efficiencies. You now need to get the efficiencies in place. This will mean creating a roadmap and a portfolio of projects to do the necessary change work.

This is no different than any other time you've been asked to develop a future state business architecture model in this book. Start, as always, by looking for any foundational projects that need to be done before other changes can be applied. You may also want to look for "low hanging fruit," the kinds of projects that will very quickly get significant efficiency improvements into production, thus improving the return on investment (ROI) for your reengineering initiative.

You will be working on a "live" business, a business that is operating and already has an envisioned future state and a portfolio of projects. How can you tie your reengineering work into all this other change that is already planned? Because the theme of all this change is reengineering to improve efficiency, look for ways you can do the project work as efficiently as possible. Are there any regulatory changes that need to be done that you could team up with and deliver two initiatives in a single project? Are there ways to tie into other projects that are already underway or are about to launch?

Look for ways to provide significant improvements to the business with each change you make. At the same time, try to keep in mind the amount of change you are trying to get the operational staff of the business to absorb. You will be changing the way they work on a day-to-day basis. If they feel they are in a state of constant change, they may revolt in one of many different ways. You want to keep the changes to a bearable level while providing maximum value. Consider talking to a people change management expert when looking at any sustained program of change, but especially when the change is an efficiency initiative, where you will be heavily reliant on people accepting and adopting the future state you envision.

Reengineering and Automation

IT automation has had an increasing impact on the way businesses operate for nearly 50 years. The main driver for adopting automation is to increase efficiency. In the early days, the efficiencies were found by automating data access—customer information or transactions. While that was very useful, larger scale gains can be found by automating whole processes or communication flows. When you look at automation holistically, you can find ways to use it that really make the business as efficient as possible.

Look for the highest value processes and communications, the ones that are executed frequently—these will be prime candidates for automation. Make sure IT architects are involved early in the discussion; they will need to understand the implied changes to the technology of the business and what that will mean to its IT roadmap. Give them information about what you are changing, the business domain (or domains) it belongs to (Marketing, Sales, Call Center, Tech Support, and so on), and what you are attempting to achieve from a business perspective by making the change. The IT architects can then look for ways to maximize the use of existing technologies, find new technologies to leverage for this and future work, and plan the technology changes that will be needed.

Keep in mind that point integrations will seldom provide you with the level of efficiency improvements you are striving for. *Point integrations* are simple IT solutions for a single task or point in the business. These sorts of solutions are seldom efficient enough to provide the business with enough efficiency to justify applying them as part of the reengineering work being discussed in this chapter. You want to make sure that the IT architects understand the level of efficiency improvement you are looking for and have them assist you to find ways to have the technology that supports the business supply the improvements in an automated way.

This does not mean that the only way to find efficiency improvements is through the application of automation; it simply means that typically there are great efficiency improvements to be had in this way. A change to a communication that eliminates needless touch-points without any automation may still provide you with significant improvements. Look for all sorts of improvements, not just automated ones, but ensure you don't overlook the opportunity to leverage IT automation if it can get you the results you desire.

In Your Business

Here are some things to consider when thinking about reengineering and business architecture in your business:

- Are there obvious inefficiencies in your business today?
- Is your business less efficient than your competition seems to be?
- Does senior management want to see efficiency improvements?
- Do you have information about the way your business operates that you can leverage in understanding where inefficiencies may be an issue for your business?

Summary

This chapter has discussed how to use business architecture as a means of finding ways to reengineer your business for increased efficiency. There was discussion of the following:

- Using the business' goals as a starting point for making changes of maximum positive impact on efficiency
- Aligning facades, processes, communications, and business entities to goals
- Using the current state model as a means of understanding current pain points
- Using the future state model as a means of addressing pain points and launching the right projects to implement the change
- Using IT systems as part of the projects that will increase the efficiency of the business

All of these points were made to show how the business architecture model is a vital tool in gaining an understanding of where a business suffers from inefficiencies and how the model can be used to launch the right projects to address the inefficiencies. This will allow the business to reengineer itself as quickly as possible and get on with operating effectively.

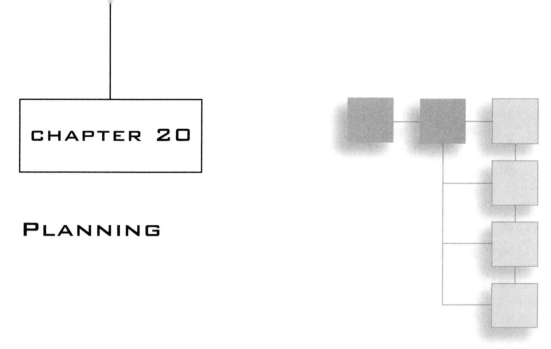

CHAPTER 20

PLANNING

When you plan where you are going, you have a reasonable chance of getting there, but without a plan, your odds aren't as good. You know how to plan within projects, but planning the right portfolio of projects is a tougher prospect. On the surface, many projects that are proposed have merit and would provide benefit to a business. So how do you determine which projects get funded, which get shelved for a later date, and which get discarded outright? What litmus test do you use to evaluate proposed projects?

The business architecture model can provide that litmus test, as it is the decision framework for evaluating what projects should be undertaken. There are two aspects to this: the business architecture model will indicate the work that needs to be done to fill the gaps between the current state and the envisioned future state of the business, and the business architecture model can be used to see whether "bright idea" project proposals would actually move the business closer to its envisioned future state. The business architecture model, then, is an important planning tool for a business to use during regular planning cycles and on an ad hoc basis when bright ideas to change the business are identified.

Planning Business Architecture Work

As previously identified, planning work is an important business behavior. When it comes to the types of changes that business architecture gaps identify, planning is very important. The business needs to know how to budget to make the change happen. The business needs to plan the people change aspect, what will it take to get people adjusted and working in the new way, what the total people change across the proposed portfolio of work is, and how the total change can be accommodated.

The business will typically have a planning cycle, and the business architecture work should be a significant part of the planning cycle. The business architecture needs to be flexible enough, though, to do "out-of-cycle" replanning work when the business environment changes. Having the business architecture model as a framework will be useful for both these planning exercises.

Planning Cycles and Business Architecture

The business planning cycle revolves around setting the budget for the coming fiscal year. As a business architect, you should play a significant part in that budgetary planning. A formal review of the Goals view, both current state and future state, is part of the beginning of the planning cycle. A fresh discussion of the goals will help the executives see very clearly where they have aimed the business with their goals, and you can use this opportunity to confirm the business' direction. If need be, this is also an opportune time to adjust the goals for the upcoming year and for the longer-term future.

If goals change as a result of the initial planning review, you will have to apply the implied changes across the other views of the business architecture model right away. You may do a quick pass of this exercise first, just enough to understand how it's impacting your gaps between the current state and future state models. This quick pass might involve things such as identifying interactions that are impacted, but not documenting the impact; identifying the impacts to processes, but not updating the processes; identifying impacted communications, but not documenting them; and understanding the impacts to the business entities, but not adjusting the model. The actual updates to the model will come later, either as a separate business architecture modeling exercise or as part of project work.

Updating the gap is the next thing to worry about. You have to understand the gap between current state and the future state to calculate the work that will need to be done to shift the business in the direction of the envisioned future state. The best way to sort out the work to be done is to look at the interactions of the facades that need to change (including those that are net new). Put them into logical groupings that provide a meaningful change for the business. A logical grouping might be to arrange all the related changes to interactions that would allow the sale of a new product, better tracking of utilization of a service, or the like. The point is to work with the business leaders to understand what a logical grouping would need to include, and then package it as a potential project. What you may discover, in some cases, is that a single change to an interaction may actually facilitate more than one useful change to the business; it could be bundled into more than one project. This is okay; you will simply place it in one of the projects, mark that one as foundational, and place an assumption in the other project or projects that would utilize that change stating that it is already going to be implemented by the first project.

So, with all the logical groupings of change, the potential projects, and your entire documented future state, it is time to plan the actual work that will be done to change the business. Each one of the projects will need an estimate of time and money amount, along with a list of assumptions that helped you determine the estimated numbers. The money estimate will help create the budget for the year; the time estimate will help determine when projects can be started relative to each other. You also need prioritization of all the projects before you can define a schedule. You need to know which projects are foundational, which will provide greatest value to the business, and which are the riskiest to undertake. Priority will be determined by a combination of these factors.

You identify the foundational projects by determining that they need to occur ahead of other projects that will build on them. Foundational projects tend to provide base functionality, the core of the interaction or process that the business needs. Foundational projects, then, are those that typically introduce something net new to the business.

You identify the high business value projects by discussing the projects with the business people to understand what they value most in change. Ask them to tell you what they need most. Use the Goals view diagram(s) as a means of facilitating this discussion, because the Goals view should help them identify the projects that will most help them achieve their goals. If they identify projects as high priority that do not in any observable way move the business toward its stated goals, you need to go back to the executives to talk about whether the goals are correct. As a result of the executive conversation, you may either need to adjust the goals, adjust the project priorities, or both. If a change to the goals occurs, you'll have to quickly cycle through all the impact analysis again just to make sure you understand the implications of the change.

You will find the riskiest projects that involve technology by having a discussion with the IT architects. When it comes to projects that only change the business without impacting the underlying technology (a *business-only* project), you will determine the riskiest ones by talking to the business subject matter experts (SMEs) that represent the areas impacted by the proposed change. Contrary to popular belief, you do not want to put off risky work until later in the hope that it will magically go away. The reality is that the risky stuff doesn't go away, it festers and breeds and just becomes riskier over time. If you address the risky work first, you will either overcome it, thereby allowing you to move on to the straightforward work, or you will find the risk is insurmountable and will have to rethink your approach to dealing with the risk. The important point is that if you deal with the risk early, you will have a better chance to overcome it, whereas if you ignore the risk, you will never overcome it and you will never be able to make profound changes to your business.

Combine the thinking about what is foundational with what is highest business value and what is riskiest to put together a prioritized list of projects. Use whatever weighting value you feel is valid for mixing the three categories of priority, but make sure that whatever weighting scheme you use, it doesn't result in projects being executed before the foundational projects that will support them.

Now you can get back into the annual planning discussion, and figure out which project from your list of candidate projects can actually be executed in the coming fiscal year. You need to use a combination of priority, cost, and time estimations to get through this planning work. Create a *project dependency chart* to show priority and foundational dependencies. Use the time (duration) estimates to create the chart, and then overlay it with cost estimates. This will give you a graphic representation of the work needed to get to the business' envisioned future state, which you can use to discuss with the business executives what will actually be executed within the coming fiscal year. Consider the example portfolio of projects in Table 20.1.

Table 20.1 Portfolio of Projects

Name	Desc.	Priority	Foundational?	$	Time
Project A	New product	7 (of 10)	No	$250k	3 months
Project B	New CRM	9	Yes	$3000k	15 months
Project C	Update order management	6	No	$500k	9 months
Project D	Add timesheet tracking for staff	7	No	$100k	4 months
Project E	Retire product	3	No	$150k	2 months
Project F	New call recording system for call center	6	Yes	$800k	6 months

In Table 20.1, there are two foundational projects, B and F, that must occur before other projects. The resulting question is this: can Projects B and F both be executed in parallel, or must one of them be completed before the other one? You will have to sort this out with the business and the IT folks; they will be able to tell you what will have to come first. (This is all about understanding if there are dependencies of one project on another, aside from the foundational concept, like the fact that the first project has all the key resources that the second project will need, and so on.) For this example, let's assume the two projects can be executed in parallel. The result of these conversations will be a chart of the portfolio, which can be used to discuss what will be executed during the coming fiscal year (see Figure 20.1).

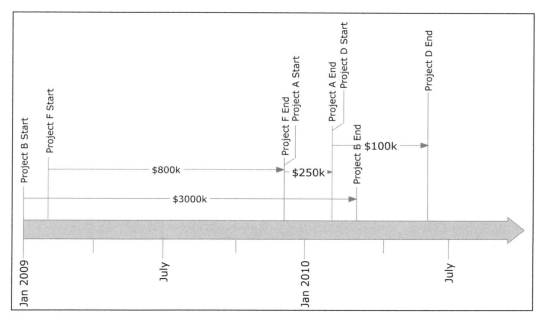

Figure 20.1
Example project portfolio planning chart.

Projects C and E have been omitted in order to simplify the chart. This chart gives you the opportunity to talk about parallelism, capacity, budget, and the capacity for the business to absorb change. From a budget perspective, the chart says that the business will need to spend 12/15 of $3000k, as well as $800k and 2/3 of $250k, for a total of $3367k this fiscal year. There was an assumption made that the business could introduce a new product in parallel with the tail end of introducing the new Customer Relationship Management (CRM). There was another assumption made that the business could absorb the combined change of introducing a new CRM, a new product, and a new call recording system. If any of these assumptions cannot be supported, you will have to adjust the chart to reflect the adjusted assumptions. After this is done, you have a proposed portfolio of work and all the information the business needs to include that work in its annual plan.

Note how the foundational projects are recorded on one side of the timeline, while the remaining projects are all shown on the other side of the timeline. This helps you easily remember and convey to others which work absolutely needs to be done first, and which projects are dependent on them.

Ad Hoc Change and Planning

Not all project work comes neatly in time for annual planning. Bright ideas for change can occur at any time, whenever inspiration strikes. Sometimes the bright idea is a result of an industry trend, an attack by competition, or by an opportunity that the business wants or needs to take advantage of. You cannot plan for the actual ad hoc changes that need to take place, but you can plan for the inevitability of ad hoc changes being proposed.

When the bright idea for change is brought up, the first thing to do is evaluate it against the goals of the business. Does it align or not? If not, does that mean the goals need to be adjusted, or does it mean that the bright idea isn't appropriate for the business, regardless of how bright it might appear on the surface. If the goals need to be adjusted, do so, and then follow along with the impacts to the remaining views of the business architecture model. This will give you the chance to estimate the work it will take to implement the bright idea. After the estimate is done, you can look at the priority of the bright idea project relative to the rest of the portfolio and figure out where it will fit into your portfolio project planning chart.

While it is reasonable to expect that ad hoc requests for change will occur, you need to ensure that it is not the only behavior of the business. The business will need to exercise some discipline regarding when it is appropriate to raise good ideas and have them evaluated for implementation purposes. This will help you avoid the situation where you spend the majority of your time replanning your portfolio of projects.

Planning Business Change Using Business Architecture

The business architecture model provides a great deal of information about the change that is needed by the business, which in turn can be used to plan what change should be executed and when it should be executed.

Planning involves looking at the gap you need to fill, determining what work will be required to fill that gap, dealing with environmental change, and dealing with unforeseen need for change. All of this is needed in order to close the gap.

The Gap

The gap is the difference between the current state of the business and the envisioned future state of the business. The gap represents the work that will need to be done to move the business from where it is to where it needs to be in the future. There will be a gap at all levels of the business architecture model: the Goals view, the Facades view, the Processes view, the Communications view, and the Business Entities view.

You will find that the gap in the Goals view is different in interpretation than the other view gaps because when you consider gaps in goals, the means of filling the gaps is unique. The gaps in goals are filled by building a future state in the remaining views of the business architecture model. A gap between the current state goals of a department and its future state goals might mean that new interactions or processes are needed, new communications might fill the gap, or new business entities might be required. When it comes to the other views, though, the filling of gaps will result in project work.

Gaps in the Facades view can be found by doing a comparison between the current state and future state interactions on a facade-by-facade basis. Use the goals that have changed to indicate what interactions might need to change. The gap could be a completely new interaction or a change to an existing interaction (a new alternate flow, a change to part of an existing flow, and so on). These changes need to be understood and documented so that the implications can be developed. The implications will be used to group the needed changes together into proposed projects.

Gaps in processes will also be in the form of new processes or changes to the flows of existing processes. On occasion, there may even be a need/desire to retire a process that no longer adds value to the business. Use the changed interactions as a means of finding the processes that likely need to change (that have gaps). The processes that have gaps will be part of the work that needs to be planned.

Communications will also need to be inspected for gaps, implying changes that would have to be undertaken. Use the changing interactions and processes to indicate which communications might also have gaps. Identify the gaps and understand the implications. The implications will be used as part of the planning work that is done.

Business entities will also have gaps. These gaps are typically found by a combination of inspecting the current state and future state business entity models, and understanding the changes to business entities implied by the work being done in the interactions, processes, and communications. The implementation of a new business entity is a bit different than a new process or communication, though. Implementation of a new business entity typically involves changing many recording systems to now capture the new information that the business entity represents. These systems may be technology based, or may simply be procedural (e.g., index cards, work orders, and so on). The changes to business entities will not result in direct project work, but will typically influence the scope of project work that needs to be done because of changes in the other views.

The Portfolio of Work

Portfolio: *a selection of work collected over a period of time and used for measuring performance.* (From Merriam-Webster Online: www.merriam-webster.com/dictionary/portfolio.)

In business architecture terms, the *portfolio of projects* is a set of projects that the business is working on and will measure its success against. If you have more than two projects planned, you have a portfolio of sorts; the trick is to manage the portfolio effectively so that you can control the outcome. How do you plan your projects effectively to achieve the desired outcome? You first need to define the right projects, and then you must organize them in a way that will lead to the greatest likelihood of successful change for the business.

So how do you define projects? The business is likely quite used to telling you what it wants as a project, so why change? Often the business will define a solution involving how it wants the underlying technology to change and then call it a project. The problem with this is that the solution often doesn't align well with the goals of the business and is built on somebody's mental model of the way a technology solution works. This doesn't often take into account the real need of the business and the problem or opportunity being solved for—which leads to low quality deliverables. Instead, you should try to create projects that are born from the changes the business needs to undergo in order to achieve its goals.

Consider a single goal that needs to be achieved and look at all the facades, processes, communications, and business entities that will have to change to support that goal. This group of changes could potentially be a single project: evaluate it and see whether it will deliver some sort of meaningful overall change to the business. Would it be useful to the business to release all this change together? Would it be too much change to release at one time? If it is a meaningful change and not too much change for the business, then you have a project that could be added to the portfolio. If it isn't enough work to be a meaningful change to the business, look for related goals that also need to be supported and see if, in aggregate, the work for two related goals will make up a meaningful change to the business. Keep doing this until you have aggregated enough projects to represent a meaningful change for the business, at which time you've identified a project and you can add it to your portfolio. If the work to support a single goal is more change than the business can sustain at one go, consider breaking the work down into a program of related projects; the program and its projects would all become part of the portfolio.

You need to sort through all these projects to understand any overlaps and sort out how you are going to handle them. If two projects need to change the same process, how will you handle that conflict? You need to consider the impact of one project on another and plan things in such a way as to minimize any negative impacts and build on any positive impacts.

You also need to make sure you plan to execute foundational projects before any of the projects that will build upon them. The project list and project portfolio planning chart will help you put the portfolio of project work into the right order and ensure the business can fund the work and absorb the change.

Adjusting to Business Climate Change

Business climate is the environment that the business operates in. This includes any information about the customer base, the competition, the suppliers, and the regulatory bodies that control the industry of your business. A change to any aspect of your business climate might imply a need for you to change your business.

If there is a change to the business climate, the business will have to evaluate the potential impacts and determine how to change to respond to it. Consider that regulatory changes often must be implemented by a mandated date. These sort of changes will have to be addressed in time to meet the regulatory date, which may mean suddenly giving the regulatory change a very high priority relative to the other projects in the portfolio. So what is the best way to judge the impacts? The business architecture model current state gives you a picture of the way the business operates; this is the basis for comparison.

Start by looking at the Facades view to understand which facades are affected by the change to the business climate. When you know which facade(s) is affected, take a look at the interactions to see which ones might need to be updated to comply with the change. When you know which interactions are impacted, you can do a similar analysis on the processes, communications, and business entities that support the interaction. Look for the changes that will have to be made to these views to support the change in the business climate. You will be working from the current state of the business architecture model, but keep in mind the future state; it might already have some of the necessary changes captured as part of the envisioned future state.

After you identify the changes needed to support the business climate change, you need to parcel the change into one or more projects. Typically, business climate change doesn't involve a change to the actual goals of the business, so you can't start there with your project planning; you need to start with the Facades view. Because the business will want to respond to business climate change as quickly as possible, you may, as a starting point, look at all the related change as a single project. After you consider the estimated cost and timelines, as well as the people change that the business will have to absorb, you can decide whether a single project is a good idea or not.

Now it is just a matter of bringing the business climate change project or projects into the project portfolio. Because business climate change needs to be addressed quickly, this work will be given a high priority. You need to determine if there is any foundational project work that this change is going to rely on, and if so, how the foundational work can be accomplished as quickly as possible so that you can get on with applying this other change on top of it. You will likely have to put off the other planned projects of the project portfolio until this business climate change work is completed. This is just as well, because you will need to reevaluate all the other planned work to see whether it makes sense to execute in this new business climate. Perhaps some of that work is no longer going to help your business reach its goals.

A reevaluation of the remainder of the project portfolio means looking at the interaction changes that would be made with the projects. This reevaluation will consist of looking at each interaction to see whether the change to the interaction makes sense in light of the new business climate. After you sort out the interactions that still need to change in the future, you can look at the processes, communications, and business entities that also need to change. Again, look for impacts the new business climate would have on these other views.

The future state business architecture model will need to be updated to include the changes necessary to address the business climate change, and also to remove any changes that no longer make sense given the new business climate.

Unforeseen Need for Change

There are times when a business needs to change immediately without any significant planning. Sometimes this happens as a result of business climate change, as discussed above, and other times the need is based on less obvious pressures/drivers. Sometimes it's something like a bright idea from someone within the business, or sometimes it's a perceived need to deal with a structural issue of the business.

The assumption here has been that the unforeseen change is one that the business does want to undertake once it has been identified. If this assumption isn't valid, the first thing that should be done when the unforeseen change is identified is to evaluate it. You can do this by looking at the envisioned future state and look at how it will be impacted by the unforeseen change. If the business is willing to accept the impacts implied by adjusting the plan and the project portfolio, then undertake to apply the unforeseen change. If the business is not willing to accept the impacts to the envisioned future state, then either reject the unforeseen change or modify it until it is acceptable.

When a need for change has been identified, it needs to be scheduled immediately. This means examining the impact of the change on the business architecture model to see what's going to have to change. After this is understood, you can determine whether the change can be made in a single project or if more than one round of change will be required.

Consider whether the unforeseen change project(s) will need any foundational work, and if so, how that foundational work can be completed as soon as possible. Work quickly to get the business to fund the unforeseen change project(s) and get them underway as part of the project portfolio.

You now need to understand the impact that this unforeseen change has had on the envisioned future state model. You may now have redundant planned work, planned work that contradicts the unforeseen change, or new gaps between the current state and the new future state. Because the unforeseen change may include change to any/all of the views, you will have to inspect each one to understand the impacts. Start with the Goals view, then look at the facades, and after that look at the processes, communications, and business entities. Adjust the future state accordingly.

In Your Business

Here are some things to consider when thinking about planning business architecture and project work:

- Does your business currently have a project portfolio?
- When unplanned projects are proposed, how does your business evaluate and prioritize them relative to the other projects it has undertaken or plans to undertake?
- Does your business have to deal with projects mandated by regulatory bodies?

Summary

This chapter has been about planning the work of business architecture, as well as the portfolio of project work, to reach the desired future state. The planning of the business architecture work considered was as follows:

- Fitting in with standard planning cycles of the business
- How to deal with out-of-cycle planning changes in the business architecture
- How the business architecture model facilitates many business planning activities and can be leveraged as a planning tool

The planning of the project portfolio of work considered the following:

- Leveraging the business architecture model future state to determine the needed projects
- Using the business architecture model to understand the impact of unplanned project work on the portfolio
- Understanding what happens to planned work in the portfolio when unplanned project work takes priority

All of this helps the business executives see how valuable a planning tool the business architecture model is and how well it helps the business get the right work done at the right time.

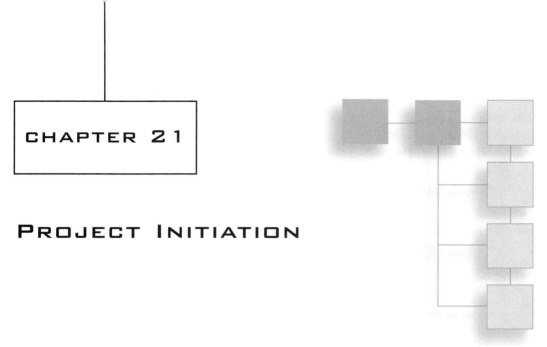

CHAPTER 21

PROJECT INITIATION

All the work of creating a business architecture model is done to help you find out how you need to move your business to better position it for future success. In order to actually move the business, though, you need to execute one or more projects. How do you figure out which projects to execute and which ones should never be done? Once again, the business architecture model provides you with the guidance to make wise choices about the project work to do. (See Chapter 20 for a discussion about planning the portfolio of projects.) The business architecture model also provides content that is useful within projects, and projects can and should provide content back to the model to ensure that it stays current.

Initiating the Right Projects

What is a *right project*? Why should the business be concerned with only initiating projects that are right? The business we're talking about, in many cases, has been running for awhile and has already launched projects, so what's different now?

A right project is one that will advance the business toward its envisioned future state, a project that will move the business closer to achieving its goals than it was before the project was initiated. By extension, any project that doesn't advance a business toward its goals would be a *wrong project*. There is also a *neutral project*, which neither advances the business directly, nor moves it farther away from its goals. Wrong projects should be avoided at all costs, and neutral projects should only be undertaken after serious consideration. How, then, do you determine which projects are right, which are wrong, and which are neutral? The business architecture model is the tool you use to evaluate project proposals to classify them.

Many right projects will be identified during the gap analysis between the current state and the envisioned future state of the business architecture model. These projects will be defined based on logical groupings of change and added to the project portfolio. No neutral or wrong projects will have been added during the gap analysis work because every bit of change identified during the analysis will move the business closer to its envisioned future state, which by definition moves the business closer to its goals.

The real concern over ensuring that the right projects are initiated comes up when projects are proposed that were not part of the roadmap and project portfolio from the business architecture model. Employees of the business will always generate bright ideas, and those bright ideas should be considered. The business has probably done this in the past, but in many cases, it has not had a decision framework as useful as the business architecture model, so projects were initiated that never should have been.

So how do you effectively evaluate project proposals or bright ideas against the business architecture framework? As always, you start by looking at the Goals view. Look at the goals the business wants to achieve in the future and compare them against the proposal. To do this, you need to take a quick pass to understand what interactions, processes, and communications the proposal will create or change. You do not need to document the details of the changes, just document that the changes exist and list a brief description of what they will entail. After you have this information, take a look at how the changes will affect the goals. Will the changes move the business closer to achieving its goals? If the proposal will move the business closer to its goals, then it is a right project and should definitely be considered for the project portfolio. If the proposal moves the business away from its goals, then it is a wrong project and definitely should not be undertaken. If the proposal doesn't move the business closer or farther away from its goals, then it is a neutral project and should be examined more closely before it is undertaken.

Neutral projects need special consideration. They were proposed for a reason, and because they don't harm the business, there may be value in initiating these sorts of projects under the right circumstances. What might those right circumstances be? These may be things like adding revenue or fixing problems that the business has without explicitly advancing the business toward its goals. You and the business executives will need to evaluate these sorts of projects on a case-by-case basis to ensure that they have enough of a positive return on investment (ROI) to justify their execution.

Tying Business Architecture Content to the Project

You've now identified the right projects, and you've added them to the roadmap and the project portfolio. Now it's time to execute one of these projects. In the past, most businesses started their projects pretty much at ground zero, with no existing content to feed into the project itself. If there was any content at all, it was typically in the form of the project proposal, which realistically provided little actual content to leverage once the project was underway.

One of the biggest gaps in many projects was a definition of how the business needed to change. This was often ignored as both the subject matter experts and the IT experts looked straight to the changes the systems needed to undergo to satisfy a perceived (but never well-articulated) need. This often led to gaps in the solution, or even a well-executed solution to the wrong problem. As business architects, you want to avoid that sort of behavior. You want to make sure that the projects are focused on real business needs and that any changes to the business and its underlying systems actually align effectively to satisfy that real need. The business architecture model gives you the content you need to fully understand the change to the business that needs to occur (interaction, process, and so on) for the project to be successful. When this is understood, you can move on to worrying about what, if any, system changes need to take place.

Goals View to Project Content

The Goals view provides direction for a project, a set of guiding principles that the project should strive to uphold. The project is framed on a set of logically grouped changes to the business. The changes can all be traced back to one or more goals of the business that will be advanced if the project is successfully executed.

When you know which goal or goals will be advanced, you can create project objectives based on the goals(s). Objectives are the goals of the project that align with the goals of the business. The objectives are measurable; they should be part of the metrics used to determine whether the project was successful. Objectives are an unambiguous statement of something the project should achieve. Most projects shouldn't have more than about a dozen objectives to meet; beyond that, the project is probably too big to be manageable as a single set of changes.

Facades View to Project Content

The Facades view represents the change the business needs to undergo relative to inter-actions with the world outside. This can be perceived as the set of functional changes to the business. These, then, are functional business requirements in the truest sense.

The project will identify a logical grouping of interactions that need to change. When you have fully documented the business use cases that represent these interactions, you will have the *functional business requirements* of the project. Depending on how thoroughly you've documented the business use cases during the business architecture modeling work, you may have no further documentation work to do at this time.

The project will then have to sort out how to realize these functional business requirements, whether via IT solutions, via procedural changes, or some combination of both. This is done through a process of analysis of the functional business requirements and the business processes (which will be discussed in the next section). The analysis would include stepping through each requirement (or a logical grouping of requirements) and asking if technology could/should be used to help implement them. Would technology be a real value to the business for the requirement? Would it simply be adding technology for the sake of adding technology? Would it possibly hinder being able to execute related work in the business? (In other words, technology might help the account open process, but it might encourage setting up accounts for people who aren't yet confirmed customers because it is so easy to do, and staff are measured on how many accounts they set up in a given period.) The same sort of analysis should be done with processes, looking at each step or set of steps to see if they should be automated.

There is another type of analysis to be done with the functional business requirements as well: to derive appropriate *non-functional business requirements*. These are the requirements of the business as a whole (not specific to any single IT system) that are not functional in nature but that need to be incorporated into the solution. Business non-functional requirements might include the hours of operation of the head office or of the retail stores of the business, or the peak volume of customers a cashier has to handle in a day.

Processes View to Project Content

Business process changes are often a big part of the change that a business needs to undertake as part of the project. You have a logical grouping of changes to processes identified as part of the definition of your project that came from the envisioned future state of your business architecture model, where the need for the change to processes was identified.

Depending on how thoroughly you modeled the envisioned future state Processes view as part of the business architecture work, you may not have to do anything else with the processes model at this point, or you may need to flesh it out further to ensure it is sufficiently detailed to actually realize the changes it represents. Make sure that you are highlighting the aspects of the processes that are actually changing as a result of your project work so that those aspects can readily be identified in the context of the entire process.

After the processes for the project are fully documented and the parts that are changing are highlighted, it is time to analyze the processes to determine how to realize them. This means working in concert with IT architects to parcel out which pieces of the process should be fully automated, which should be partially automated, which should be manual steps with some automation assistance, and which should just be manual steps. This analysis should be done in concert with the analysis of the interactions to get as complete a picture of the intent of the process as possible.

Look at each step of the interaction and the related steps of the process. On a step-by-step basis, consider the degree of automation that should be applied. After this, consider adjacent steps to see if it would make more sense to join them together into a single automation. What you are trying to do at this point is identify use cases (sometimes referred to as *system use cases*), essentially the functional interactions with the IT system or systems that will support the business interaction and business process. This is the first step in identifying all the *interactive functional requirements* of the IT system(s) that will be part of the solution to the business' need for change. Of course, this won't be all the system requirements; you will still need to document the use cases (not to be confused with business use cases that were used to document facade interactions; see Chapter 4 for more information), as well as other functional system requirements. There are also all the non-functional system requirements that will have to be documented and realized, as well. (How to document system requirements is beyond the scope of the book, however, so it is left to the reader to seek more information.) The steps that have any procedural aspect will also have business requirements to update procedure manuals, create training, and put quality checks in place, and so on, to ensure that the entire process gets delivered with the project.

Communications View to Project Content

The communication changes packaged into the project represent the gaps in communication that will need to be addressed as part of the project. In some cases, the business architecture model will identify a change to an existing communication that needs to be enacted; in other cases, it will be the addition of an entirely new communication or the removal of an old communication that is no longer needed.

Each of these identified communications in need of change will be documented as business requirements. You want to understand if there will be any communication documents (reports, work orders, customer letters, contracts, and so on) that will need to be generated as part of the communication flow. If so, create appropriate requirements at the business and IT system level, including any mock-ups of the way the communication documents need to look. Don't forget to consider any requirements related to the management of the state of the communications flow, if that is important in your business.

Business Entities View to Project Content

Business entities that change as part of a project are identified as part of the interactions, processes, and communications that will use them. This means all the business entities that need to change, including new ones, modified ones, and ones that need to be removed, have all been implicated in the work you've already done. All that remains to do now is to create requirements to implement the business entities in some way (typically through IT systems). The manipulation of the business entities is handled through the interactions and processes, and the presentation is handled through the interactions, processes, and communications, so all that remains is to deal with requirements for storage of the business entities.

The storage requirements will be in two parts. The first part is a *logical data model* that explains what entities will be maintained on which systems. This model is very similar to the Business Entities view model, but it goes into certain details that you wouldn't have bothered with as part of the business architecture model. The logical data model will do things like resolve technology implementation issues related to the business entities (which are beyond the scope of this book). The second part of the requirements related to business entities will be around the non-functional aspects of capacity, retention, and access. You will need to document how much storage space you need to allocate to the business entities (either for the paper records, or more likely, for the electronic records). You will need to determine how long you will need to store instances of the business entities (readily to hand, offline, on backup, and so on). You will need to ensure that only the people you intend to see the business entity actually can see it, whether this is online, in print, or as part of a database.

Tying Project Content Back to the Business Architecture Model

You've learned how to launch a project based on guidance from the business architecture model, and you've seen how content from the same model can also help as content within the project that gets initiated. In an ideal world, the project will execute perfectly based on the inputs the business architecture model provided; and business architects will never need to worry about the project again, except to check the project off as complete in the portfolio when the time comes. But the reality is that projects do not always execute as planned and expected. Sometimes the estimates were too aggressive and the project team couldn't meet the budget and/or timelines. This might be addressed by reducing the scope of what gets delivered. It might be addressed by changing some of what gets delivered to simplify it and get it into production faster. Sometimes there is a need to change the scope and/or deliverables of the project. These changes may be (and hopefully were) evaluated against the business architecture model, but sometimes the project may forget to engage the business architect, and so the change goes through without evaluating the impact to the model. Projects don't always deliver what was envisioned at the time the business architecture model defined the initial scope of change for the project.

Does this really matter from a business architecture perspective? Yes. You need to keep the business architecture model current, or *evergreen*, to be able to continue to use it without having to reaffirm the documented current state every time you use it. The current state of the model will be out of sync with the reality of the business if the changes to the scope of deliverables of the project are not reflected in the model. This will make your current state model less accurate and therefore less valuable. Even if the project scope doesn't change at all, and the project delivers exactly what was envisioned, it is important to update the business architecture model upon completion of the project to reflect the changed current state of the business. Looking at the five views of the model and considering how they need to be updated to reflect the new current state will accomplish this.

Feeding the Goals View

As you've learned, the goals don't directly feed into a project; they instead provide guiding principles to the projects that will be undertaken to change the business. The expectation is similar, then, for the project when it comes to updating the Goals view of the business architecture model to reflect the project completion. The only consideration would be when checking to see whether there are changes to the scope of deliverables of the project: Are there any changes to which goals are being supported by the project? Are the goals still being fully supported or only partially supported? Are different goals being supported as a result of the change to the scope?

When the project is complete, the business architect will need to show which goals are now part of the current state. This means that if the goals that are being supported are different than what was originally envisioned by the project, the model will have to reflect the reality of what got delivered and not just what was envisioned.

Feeding the Facades View

You need to update the current state of the Facades view to reflect what was actually delivered as part of the project. This will come in two related forms. The first update is to indicate which interactions are now parts of the current state. Sometimes that will mean showing a new interaction is now there, sometimes it will mean showing that an interaction is actually a different version than was previously part of the future state, and sometimes it will mean removing an interaction from the current state model because the interaction is no longer offered as a result of the project work that was executed. This set of updates to the model should come in the form of simply moving interactions from the future state to the current state.

The second form of update comes from creating more documentation related to the interaction than the model provided at the beginning of the project. This might be in the form of documenting alternate flows that were not part of the original interaction business use-case document (see Appendix A for suggested content of a business use-case document), creating an activity diagram that illustrates the business use case when there wasn't one before, or adjusting the business use case and related diagrams because of a change request that the project undertook but wasn't already considered by the business architect. This set of changes needs to be applied to the current state of the model, and it can only come from the content of the project. Hopefully the project actually updated the business use case and the related illustrations as part of the work they did. If they didn't, you will have to reverse engineer the work they did at the project level to incorporate it into the current state of your model. You will have to figure out what the interactions actually look like based on what they delivered. You will have to create activity diagrams, where you feel it necessary, to illustrate what the business use case is describing textually.

It is really important to ensure that both types of changes be incorporated into the current state model in order to keep it useful to the business.

Feeding the Processes View

The current state Processes view model is very important to the business for a number of reasons. It is used as part of the business architecture model to do what-if analysis and evaluate new bright ideas raised by employees of the business. The business will also use the processes as the basis for training and procedure manuals. If the Processes view model gets out of sync with reality, it will not be useful for all these purposes.

As with the interactions, the processes will be updated in two primary ways. First, the processes that the project delivered as part of its work will be migrated from the future state model to the current state model. Always make sure that you move what actually was executed, and not just what was specified as part of the original project scope.

Second, update process content in the future state model with what was documented during the project. This might include any further elaboration of processes that were developed as part of the project work. This would also include any changes that were incurred as a result of scope changes undertaken by the project. Ensure that all these types of changes are captured and added to the current state documentation for the Processes view. In this way, you will ensure that the Processes view can be used in all the ways you and the business would like to be able to.

Feeding the Communications View

When the project is complete, it will have implemented any communication flows that you specified, except as modified by any scope changes the project might have incurred. These enacted communications need to be reflected in the current state model if it is to be successfully used as an analysis tool for future changes to the business.

First, move appropriate communications from the future state model to the current state. These will be the communications that were enacted as part of the project, whether added, modified, or deleted. Second, consider any scope changes the project undertook to see how they might have affected communication flows. Add these modifications to the current state model, as well. Make sure you take into account all changes to the project scope as part of your understanding of the communications flows.

Feeding the Business Entities View

The Business Entities view also needs to be updated to reflect the work a project has accomplished. This typically is as simple as moving the appropriate business entities to the current state from the future state. After the business entities have been migrated to the current state model, ensure that all the appropriate relationships also are updated. This will mean copying all the appropriate relationships from one model to the other. There will rarely be any issue of business entities only being partially implemented as the result of a project scope change; the business entity will either be implemented or not—there is no half-measure.

In Your Business

Here are some things to consider when thinking about projects and their relationship to the business architecture model:

- Does your business always execute the right projects?
- Does your business have content regarding how it operates that it can leverage as input to project artifacts?
- Does your business ensure that projects update documentation about how the business is organized and operates?

Summary

This chapter is about relating the work done in business architecture modeling and the work done in projects. There was a discussion of the following:

- Right projects, wrong projects, and neutral projects
- How to ensure that your business is expending its efforts on the right projects
- How content from all five views of the business architecture model feed into project artifacts
- How project artifacts feed back into the five views of the business architecture model
- The need to keep the business architecture model evergreen and what that means from a project artifact perspective

This chapter, more than any other in the book, was about how you use the business architecture model to actually get project work done that will move the business in the ways you want/need it to evolve. Remember to keep showing the value of the business architecture model to the business executives, keep applying the business architecture model to the planning and execution of projects, and keep the model evergreen. You will find that if you do these things, business architecture can be a very useful tool in making your business a success.

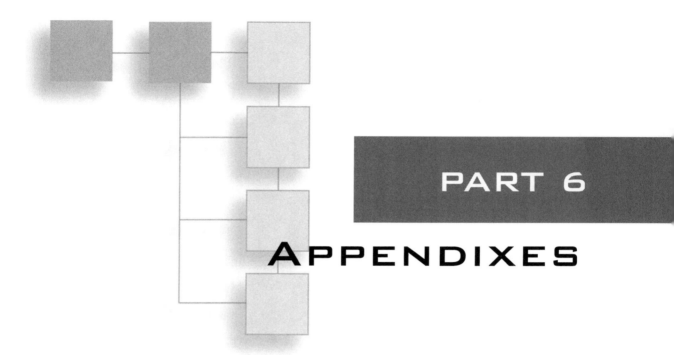

PART 6

APPENDIXES

This section supplies you with some practical tools that you can use to apply the business architecture framework to your business environment. The information here is a starting point, something you can use as is or tweak as necessary for your specific environment.

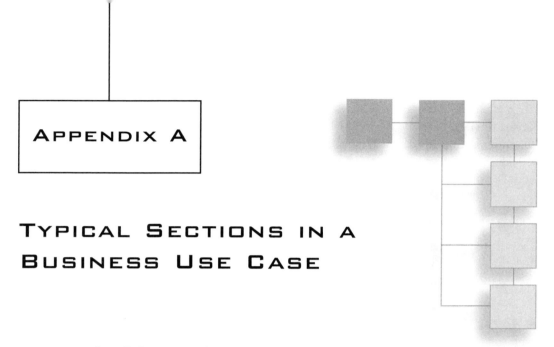

Typical Sections in a Business Use Case

A typical, well-documented business use case will contain the following sections (at a minimum). Remember that each interaction in a facade consists of the symbol on a diagram (with communication to actors and dependencies on other business use cases) and the business use-case document that describes the way the interaction steps will be executed.

Name

The name of the business use case should seem self-evident. The only complexity is that any use case should be named in a specific format: verb-object (e.g., Apply for Mortgage, or Pay Phone Bill). This means the name should say what is being done and what it is being done to. The name should also reflect of the goal of the actor.

Brief Description

The brief description is typically no more than one or two sentences (never more than a paragraph or two) that provides basic information about the purpose of the business use case.

Pre- and Post-Conditions

These are, respectively, the state the business must be in prior to triggering the business use case and the state the business must be in after the execution of the business use case. (Refer to Chapter 4 for more information.)

Trigger

This is the event, detectable by the business, that starts the interaction: "detectable by the business" is a means of ensuring that the trigger is something the business knows about. A customer thinking about purchasing a GIC from a bank isn't a trigger for the Purchase a GIC business use case, but Ask a Bank Teller About Purchasing a GIC certainly could be.

Primary Flow

This is the way the interaction between the actor and the business will occur when things flow the way the business wants them to in order to get the actor to its goal. The interaction should look like the script for a conversation. (Refer to Chapter 4 for more information.)

Alternate Flow(s)

The set of alternate flows represents all the ways in which the interaction can deviate from the steps laid out in the primary flow (whether or not the alternate flow gets the actor to the goal of the business use case). Each alternate flow represents one of these instances and describes how the rest of the interaction flows in this alternate flow's particular case after it branches off from another flow (typically the primary flow, but sometimes it can flow off another alternate flow).

Diagrams

There are two types of diagrams that are useful in documenting a use case. The first is a use-case diagram (see Chapter 4 for information about the UML business use-case diagram), which focuses on the business use case being documented along with all the actors and other business use cases related to it. It is often referred to as a *local view* business use-case diagram. The second type of diagram to include in the document is an activity diagram (see Chapter 6 for more on the UML activity diagram) that just shows the steps of the flows (primary and alternates). This will help communicate the contents of the flows and help you catch errors in the text.

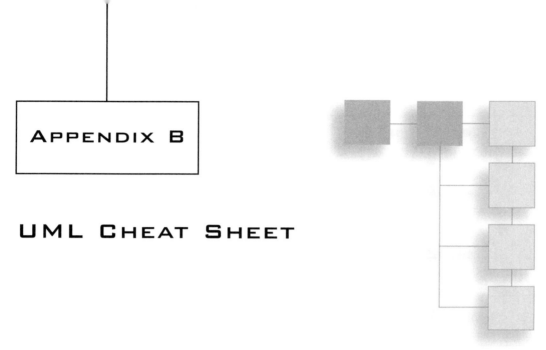

APPENDIX B

UML CHEAT SHEET

This appendix provides you with the UML symbols and their definitions. It is not a comprehensive list, but rather a concise set of the symbols you will be most likely to use when doing business architecture modeling. There will be symbols from the main types of diagrams discussed in the various views, as well as some additional symbols that you can use to communicate more in-depth information about your models. (See www.uml.org for more information on UML and the symbols.)

The symbols are organized into subsets related to the diagram type to which they belong. In some cases, there will be two symbols related to the same definition: one being the basic icon with a <<stereotype>> tag to denote its specialization, and one with the specialized icon that graphically depicts the specialization. *Stereotype specialization* means that the more generic, basic UML symbol has been given a more specific meaning, typically used to help readers understand that the symbol has a more unique meaning. As an example from Chapter 4, UML provides a basic use-case symbol to denote an interaction with a "system," while a stereotyped business use case specifically denotes an interaction with a business.

Business Activity Diagram Symbols

The business activity diagram is a specialization of the UML activity diagram, where primary elements are stereotyped as <<business activities>>. The diagrams in Table B.1 focus on business-level activities.

Table B.1 Business Activity Diagram Symbols

Symbol	Name	Description
<<business activity>> (Activity) (Activity)	Business activity	The step or task element. This is the basic unit, which when strung together with others of its kind, creates a flow or process. Note that this symbol can either be shown as a basic activity with the stereotype explicitly written above it, or as a specialized icon.
●	Start	This is the point at which the flow or process begins. It can be thought of as the initial, or triggering, event. There can only be one start per diagram.
◉	End	This is where a flow or process terminates. There must be at least one end per diagram, but there can be as many as are needed to reflect all the ways that a flow or process may terminate.
◇	Decision	This is where a flow or process may split into one of many possible alternate outcomes based on a decision. There must be at least two possible flows out of a decision, although there can be as many as are needed to accurately reflect the decision being made. No question is written explicitly with the decision. See also the [Guard Condition] in this table.
⟶	Transition	This arrow symbol shows the flow between activities in an activity diagram. When a transition flows out of a decision, it must have a [Guard Condition].
▬▬▬▬	Synchronization bar	Also known as a fork or join bar, this symbol shows where activities can either start in parallel or end in parallel. If there is one transition into the bar, there must be at least two transitions out, each of which must occur; if there is more than one transition coming in, each of which must happen, then there can only be one transition out. Note that these bars can be either vertical or horizontal on a diagram.
[Guard Condition]	Guard condition	Not so much a symbol, this is really an elaboration that is applied to transitions, especially those flowing out of a decision. Each of these types of transitions should have a condition statement attached to it to indicate to the reader when this transition path would be followed. Replace the words "Guard Condition" inside the square brackets with an actual statement of the condition under which you would allow flow on this transition (e.g., [customer credit score > 500]).

Business Entity Diagram Symbols

The business entity diagram is based on the UML class diagram, where the primary elements are stereotypes as << business entities>>. The diagrams in Table B.2 focus on the business-level entities.

Table B.2 Business Entity Diagram Symbols

Symbol	Name	Description
<<business entity>> Class Name attributes operations() (circle with line) Business Entity	Business entity	This is the basic unit of "thing" that the business needs to know about, a unit of logical information. Note that the business entity can be shown as a UML class with the <<business entity>> stereotype written above it, or it can be the graphically specialized symbol. When using the generic class symbol, the operations section would be left empty and may even be omitted.
0..n 1	Relationship (with cardinality)	The basic line between two business entity symbols, without any arrowhead attached, indicates that there is some sort of informational relationship between the entities in question. Cardinality, a number or numeric range (sometimes an indefinite range) shown above and near the ends of the line, denotes a constraint on the number of instances of one type of entity that can be related to an instance of the other entity.
———▷	Generalization relationship	A specific type of relationship to describe the case where the more general case of a type of entity is pointed to by a more specialized type of the same entity. For example, Neurosurgeon is a specialized type of the more generic entity Doctor.
———◇	Aggregation relationship	A specific type of relationship where the entity being pointed to by the diamond-shaped arrowhead is built up from the entities pointing to it. For example, Book is an aggregation of Chapters, among other things (such as Sections, Tables of Contents, Indices, Appendices, and so on).

Business Use-Case Diagram Symbols

The business use-case diagram is based on the UML use-case diagram, where the primary elements are stereotypes, such as <<business use case>>. The diagrams in Table B.3 focus on interactions with the business as a whole.

Table B.3 Business Use-Case Diagram Symbols

Symbol	Name	Description
<<business use case>>	Business use case	This symbol represents an interaction between the business and some entity outside the business. Note that it can be shown as a basic use-case symbol with the <<business use case>> stereotype written above or as the specialized icon.
<<business actor>>	Business actor	This is the entity outside the business that interacts with it to achieve a goal. Note that this can be shown as a basic actor symbol with the <<business actor>> stereotype over top or as the specialized graphic icon.
	Business worker	The business worker does not have an equivalent generic worker symbol; it only exists at the business level. It is used to depict a human, internal to the business, whose participation in the interaction is sufficiently valuable to be made explicit on the business use-case diagram.
	Communicates	The Communicates arrow is used to show which actors communicate with which use cases. When the arrow flows from an actor to a use case, it means that the actor is the primary actor for that use case. When the arrow flows from the use case to the actor, it means that the actor plays a supporting role in that interaction.
<<include>>	Include dependency	This type of dependency, stereotyped with the <<include>> tag above the dashed arrow, is used to show that the steps within one use case are executed as part of executing another use case. This means that the base use case points to the use case it "includes."

Communication Diagram Symbols

Table B.4 shows the symbols for the UML communication diagram; there is no stereotyping needed to illustrate the concept of communication at the business level.

Table B.4 Communication Diagram Symbols

Symbol	Name	Description
Thing	Communication node	This is the thing or entity that plays a part in a communication. The same node may participate multiple times during the course of an entire communication.
(arrow)	Communication flow	This arrow denotes that communication flows from the communication node doing the pointing to the communication being pointed at. Communication flows are usually numbered and may be accompanied by a short phrase explaining the nature of the communication.

State Diagram Symbols

Table B.5 shows the symbols for the UML state diagram. There is no stereotyping needed to illustrate the concept of a state machine for artifacts at the business level. Note that the UML state diagram shares many common elements with the UML activity diagram. In early versions of UML, they were actually treated as a single diagram type.

Table B.5 State Diagram Symbols

Symbol	Name	Description
State	State	This symbol denotes a state that an entity can be in (e.g., an Account can be Open, Suspended, or Closed, which are three states of Account).
●	Start	Start is a pseudo-state that represents the point in time before the entity being modeled exists. There can only be one Start per state diagram.
◉	End	End is a pseudo-state that describes the point in time after the entity no longer exists. There can be as many Ends on a state diagram as are needed to reflect all the ways in which an entity can cease to exist.
⟶	Transition	The mechanism by which the entity can flow from one state to another (e.g., an active account becomes suspended when fraud is suspected on it). A transition can be from one state to another, or from a state to itself.
[Guard Condition]	Guard condition	Not so much a symbol, this is really an elaboration that is applied to transitions. Each of the transitions should have a condition statement attached to it to indicate to the reader when this transition path would be followed. Replace the words "Guard Condition" inside the brackets with an actual statement of the condition under which you would allow flow on this transition (e.g., [fraud suspected]).

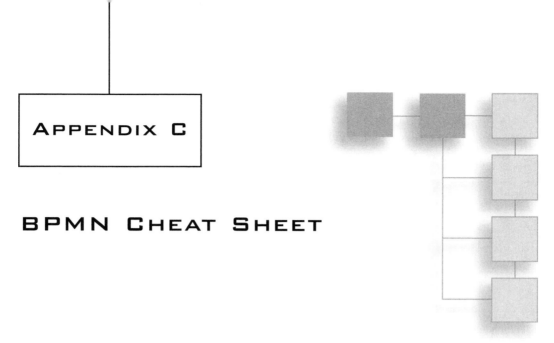

APPENDIX C

BPMN CHEAT SHEET

The tables presented in this appendix represent the Business Process Modeling Notation (BPMN) symbols you will commonly use the most. This is not meant to be a comprehensive set of all possible symbols, nor is it meant to be a tutorial on process modeling with BPMN. (Please visit www.bpmn.org for more details on the language and symbols.)

BPMN can be broken into sets of related symbols. There are collections of the following:

- Events are things that influence the process.
- Activities, gateways, and objects are things that are done or manipulated.
- Flow connectors are things that link the steps of the process together.

Events

Events can be used to start processes or end processes, and they can also show up in interim points in the process (see Table C.1).

Table C.1 BPMN Event Symbols and Definitions

Start	Inter	End	Name	Description
◯			Start	This is the event that kicks off a process.
◉	◉	◉	Message	Messages can be used to start or end a process and can also be used as a communication mechanism during a process.
◉	◉		Rule	Rules are used to start or control processes.
◉	◉		Timer	A timer symbol indicates that time is the trigger for the start of a process or a means of holding a part of a process.
◉	◉	◉	Link	Links connect parts of processes to other parts. They can be used to minimize flow connectors crossing each other or linking between processes.
		◉	Terminate	The terminate symbol indicates that all activities in the process should be immediately terminated.

Activities, Gateways, and Objects

Activities are the steps of the flow (see Table C.2). Activities can, when needed, be modified by events (see symbols). Gateways control flow when a decision has to be made, or where parallel activity is possible. Objects allow you to show where information (application forms, contracts, and so on) is manipulated during the course of a process.

Table C.2 BPMN Activity, Gateway, and Object Symbols

Symbol	Name	Description
	Task	The basic unit of work that occurs in a process.
	Task	A unit with an intermediate event associated. (Any intermediate event may be used.)
	Task	A unit with an End event associated. (Any End event may be used.)
	Sub-process	A collection of activities and other symbols collected into a flow.
	Exclusive Or gateway	Only one of any number of possible flows out of the gateway may be taken during any instance of the process.
	And gateway	All flows out of the gateway will be taken in parallel.
	Object	A thing manipulated through the process.
	Group	A way to collect like objects.

Flow Connectors

There are two distinct flows possible within BPMN (see Table C.3):

- The flow of activities
- The flow of objects relative to the activities

Table C.3 BPMN Flow Symbols

Symbol	Name	Description
──────────▶	Activity flow	Links activities to indicate how the process flows from step to step.
○┈┈┈┈┈▷	Object flows	Indicate where an object is associated specifically with an activity within a process. Object flows can be used to indicate the creation, modification, or destruction of an object.

INDEX

models
architecture, 4-6
business architecture models. *See* business architecture models
defined, 5
party models, 71
physical data models, 72-73
systems architecture model, 6-7

N

non-functional business requirements (Facades view), 218
notes (business use-case diagrams), 35-37
noun challenge processes, 65, 84

O

object flow (processes), 59-60, 237-238
Object Management Group (OMG), 110
object model diagrams. *See* UML
objects (BPMN), 236-238
Omega Enterprises case study (communication), 48-50
OMG (Object Management Group), 110
Open Group Architecture Framework. *See* TOGAF
operational projects, 10
organizational charts (Goals view), 24

P

packages (business use-case diagrams), 35-39
parallel processes (BPMN), 57-58
party models (entities), 71
personal goals, 21
physical data models (entities), 72-73
planning
being acquired, 188-190
business architecture models
cycle, 106-107
top-down approach, 92-93
overview, 203
projects
changing, 208, 211-212
climate, 211-212
cycles, 204-208
environment, 211-212
gaps, 208-209

overview, 203-204
portfolios, 209-210
planning cycle, 106-107
PMOs (project management offices), 17
point integrations (reengineering efficiency), 200
POLDAT (Process, Organization, Location, Data, Applications, Technology)
Business Entities view, 131
Communications view, 131
Facades view, 130-131
Goals view, 130
overview, 129-130
Processes view, 131
pools (BPMN), 55, 59
portfolios
bottom-up approach, 87-88
business architecture models, 9-10
defined, 209
planning projects, 209-210
PMOs, 17
price-driven businesses
communication, 158-159
entities, 159-160
facades, 156-157
goals, 156
overview, 155
processes, 157-158
Process, Organization, Location, Data, Applications, Technology. *See* POLDAT
processes (Processes view)
bottom-up approach, 79, 84
BPMN, 54-55
activity flow, 237-238
actors, 57
communication, 59-60
current state, 61-62
future state, 61-62
milestone states, 62
object flow, 59-60, 237-238
parallel processes, 57-58
pools, 55, 59
structure, 60-61
sub-processes, 58
swimlanes, 55, 59
time triggers, 55
timing, 57-58
UML comparison, 59